W. George

Cotton Goods Guide for Buyer and Seller

W. George

Cotton Goods Guide for Buyer and Seller

ISBN/EAN: 9783744670388

Printed in Europe, USA, Canada, Australia, Japan

Cover: Foto ©ninafisch / pixelio.de

More available books at **www.hansebooks.com**

COTTON GOODS GUIDE

— FOR —

BUYER AND SELLER.

(ILLUSTRATED.)

A POCKET MANUAL

EMBODYING THE MOST ESSENTIAL, PRACTICAL AND USE-
FUL HINTS, SUGGESTIONS, POINTS, FACTS, FIGURES,
ETC., RELATIVE TO THE MANUFACTURE, PUR-
CHASE AND SALE OF PLAIN, DYED AND
PRINTED COTTONS;

Together

WITH A SYNOPSIS OF THE ORIGIN, CHRONOLOGY, PRO-
DUCTION, KIND, CHARACTER, QUALITY, WEIGHTS,
MEASURES, COUNTS, ETC., OF THE LEADING COT-
TON MANUFACTURES OF THE WORLD;

Also

A CONCISE HISTORY OF THE RAW MATERIAL, ITS
CHARACTER, VARIETIES, QUALITIES, CULTIVATION,
PRODUCTION, CONSUMPTION, ETC.

PREMIUM BOOK

FOR SUBSCRIBERS TO THE DRY GOODS CHRONICLE ONLY.
CAN BE OBTAINED IN NO OTHER WAY.

1890.

DRY GOODS CHRONICLE PRESS.
143 CHAMBERS STREET AND 335 BROADWAY,
NEW YORK.

Entered according to Act of Congress, in the year 1889, by the
DRY GOODS CHRONICLE PUBLISHING COMPANY, in the Office of
the Librarian of Congress, at Washington, D. C.

All Rights and Privileges Reserved.

CONTENTS.

A

	PAGE
Acid Colors in Calico Printing	93
Acres on which Cotton Crop of the World is Produced	46
Acreage of Cotton in the ten Cotton Growing States, 1879 to 1889.	144
Additional Points on Calico Printing	96
Adulterated or Loaded British Cottons	88
African Cotton	129
Ageing Process in Calico Printing	97
"Allen" Cotton	132
Alhambra Quilts	38
Alizarins in Calico Printing	101
American Cotton	127
American Print Cloths	92
American Cotton Plant—Illustration and Description	122
American Ginghams	37
American Cambrics	39
Analysis of the Widths, Weights, Counts, etc., of Domestic Cottons	170, 171, 172
Ancient Spinning Wheel of Hindostan	36
Aniline Blacks and Blues in Calico Printing	100
Aniline Colors in Calico Printing	93
Annual Crops, Exports and Home Consumption of American Cotton Since 1841	152
Anthracene Colors in Calico Printing	100
Appleton Company in 1835	72
Austro-Hungarian Exports of Cotton Yarns and Tissues	78
Austrian Cotton Industries	124
Azo Colors in Calico Printing	94
Average Length of American Cotton	132
Average Weight of American Cotton Bales	146
Average Selling Price of Ordinary Plain Cotton Cloth in England from 1814 to 1833	80

B

Back Starching Printed Cottons	104
Badly Covered Cotton Cloth	33
Bahia Cotton	128
Bed Ticking (Made in the United States in 1809)	75
Beginning of American Cotton Manufactures	17
Belgian Cotton Industries	124
Bengal Cotton	129
"Bender" Cotton	132
Benzol Colors in Calico Printing	100
Berbice Cotton	128
Beverly Cotton Company	17
Biaz (Cotton Cloth)	74
Bleached Canton Flannels (American) Widths, Weights and Picks	201
Bleached Sheetings and Shirtings (American)—Widths, Weights and Picks	185 to 195
Bleaching Printing Cloth	91
Block Calico Printing	105
Blue Mottle (British Cotton Cloth)	120
Bokharian Biaz (Cotton Cloth)	74
Bourbon Cotton	129
Bourette (Cotton Cloth)	37
Bottom, or Swamp Cotton	132
Bowing Cotton	31
"Bull-hide" (British Cotton Cloth)	37
Burnley "Lumps" (British Cotton Cloth)	119
Bundling Cotton Yarn	54
Bundling (Cotton Yarn) Press	54
Bunting (Cotton)—Widths, Weights and Picks	199
Burnley Printers (British Cotton Cloth)	119
Butternut (Cotton Cloth)	23
Buying Cotton for Future Delivery	42

CONTENTS.

Brazilian Cotton Industry 126
Brilliants (British Cotton Cloth) 74
British Calicoes and Muslins Printed in 1796 and 1800 115
British Cottons—Widths, Lengths, Reeds, Picks and Weights... 203
British Exports of Cotton Yarns and Tissues 78
British Exports Sewing Thread 86
British Muslins in 1793 151
British Shirtings 118
Brocades 32
Broken Picks in Cotton Cloth 33
Brown Sheetings and Shirtings (American)—Widths, Weights
  and Counts .... 173 to 184
Brown Cotton Flannels (American) Widths, Weights and
  Picks 200, 201

C

Calico Finishing Machine 111
Calico in the Form of Sateen 110
Calico Printing (Additional Points) 96
Calico Printing Machine—Illustration and Description 95
Calender Machine—Illustrated 102
Calendering Printed Cottons 104
Cambrics (American) 39
Cambrics (British) 120
Cambrics (American) - Widths, Weights and Picks 199
Camlets (American)—Widths, Weights and Picks 199
Canadian Cotton Goods Industry 126
Capacity of our Cotton Bagging Mills 124
Capital, Earnings and Dividends of some New England Cotton
  Mills 142
Caraccas Cotton 128
Carding, Roving and Drawing Cotton 53
Carthagena Cotton 128
Cayenne Cotton 128
Census Report of United States Cotton Factories in 1810 18
Chambrays 74
Character of Bed ticking, Stripes, Checks, Ginghams, Shirtings
  and Counterpanes Made in United States in 1809 75
Characteristics of Some Cotton Textures 130
Character of Cotton Goods Trade of New York, Boston and
  Philadelphia Forty Years Ago 47
Checks (American)—Widths, Weights and Picks 199
Checks (British) 120
Checks (Made in United States in 1809) 75
Cheviots (American)—Widths, Weights and Picks 198
Chronology of American Cotton Manufactures 165
Chronology of Raw Cotton, Cotton Yarn, Cotton Goods, etc., of
  the World .... 204 to 208
Classification of Leading American Cottons 60
Classification of Cotton in New York 138
Classification of Cotton Cloth 34
Cleaning and Opening Cotton 21
Cleaning Cotton by Hand 72
Cloth Looking or Examining 33
Cloth Selvages 107
Coal Tar Colors in Calico Printing 94
Colors (Definition of Tones, Scales and Hues) 103
Colors—Fastness of 164
Cockley Cotton Cloth 33
Comparative Cost of Compressing and Stowing Cotton in United
  States 141
Comparative Expenses of Cotton Manufacturing in 1860 and
  1880 in United States 60
Comparative Filaments in a Pound of Cotton 124
Comparative Strength of Mule Twist 52
Comparative Values of Different Kinds of Cotton 143
Comparative Wages of American and English Cotton Operatives 60
Common Cotton Fabrics of the World Compared 55
Common Jenny and Stock Card 18

CONTENTS.

Consolidation of British Customs in 1787....	114
Consumption of Cotton in Southern Mills.................... ..	142
Consumption of Cotton Goods Throughout the World..........	46
Consumption of Twine in United States..................... ..	46
Cops (Cotton Yarns)...	50
Cost of Cotton in Lowell and Lancashire.......................	136
Cost of Cotton Spindles in United States......................	133
Cost of Heavy Cottons in United States	38
Cost of Operating Northern and Southern Mills..........	48
Cost and Selling Prices of Various Kinds of Cottons in United States for a Series of Years.. . ... 62 to	70
Cost of Raising Cotton per Pound.............................	133
Cost of Shipping Cotton at Various United States Ports......134,	135
Cost of Weaving Print Cloths in England and America	92
Cost of "Woven Wind" Muslins........	152
Cotton Beating with Sticks and Rattan Frames............... ..	26
Cotton Bunting—Widths, Weights and Picks...................	199
Cotton Centre of the United States............................	140
Cotton (Classification in New York)...........................·	138
Cotton (Cleaned by Hand).....	72
Cotton Cloth (Classification of)...............................	34
Cotton Cloth (Cockley)..	33
Cotton Cloth (Looking or Examining)............................	33
Cotton (Comparative Expenses of) Manufacturing in United States in 1860 and 1880.	60
Cotton (Cost of Spindles in United States)	133
Cotton (Cost of Shipping at Various United States Ports... 134,	135
Cotton (Cost of in Lowell and Lancaster)	136
Cotton (Cost of Raising per Pound)	133
Cotton (Consumption of in Southern Mills)......	142
Cotton Consumed in Manufacturing in United States in 1805....	159
Cotton Cords (British)	37
Cotton Consumed in Manufacturing...........	110
Cotton Consumed in England in 1787...........................	112
Cotton Crops of Egypt....	86
Cotton (Different Staples of).................	149
Cotton Export Sacks (United States)...........................	59
Cotton Fabrics (Common) of the World Compared.............	55
Cotton Factories in 1810.............	18
Cotton Factories in Providence, R. I., in 1809.................	18
Cotton Factories (American) in 1791, 1805, 1812 and 1817........	159
Cotton Factory—Illustration and Description......	87
Cotton Flannels (American)—Widths, Weights and Picks... 200,	201
Cotton Gin—Illustration and Description.. 40,	41
Cotton Goods (Consumption of Throughout the World).........	46
Cotton Goods Credits in United States in 1818.............	101
Cotton Goods, Domestic (Sold in Philadelphia in 1804-1806).....	31
Cotton Goods Industry (Displacement of Labor by Machinery in United States	55
Cotton Goods Trade of United States Forty Years Ago....... ...·	47
Cotton Industry of the World in 1888	110
Cotton Loom—Illustration and Description.....................	23
Cotton Looms of United States in 1887........................	147
Cotton Looms of Other Countries in 1888.....................	147
Cotton Manufacturing in Providence, R. I., in 1809.....	75
Cotton Mills (Old and New)	78
Cotton Mills, Rhode Island, Massachusetts and Connecticut, in 1815.............	18
Cotton Manufacturing in Lowell. Mass., in 1835...............	72
Cotton Manufactures of United States in 1880....... 154,	155
Cotton Manufactures of Augusta, Ga....................... ...	34
Cotton Manufacturing in the North and South Compared.......	160
Cotton Manufacturing Districts of England 116,	117
Cotton Manufactures of Philadelphia in 1782...................	161
Cotton (Opening and Cleaning).................................	21
Cotton Operatives (Daily Wages of American, 1827)............	75
Cotton (Our Long Staple).	139
Cotton Picking in United States	135
Cotton Plant in Bloom—Illustration and Description..........	143

CONTENTS.

Cotton Power Loom—Illustration and Description 81, 82
Cotton Power Looms of Great Britain in 1833................ 113
Cottons Printed at Lowell, Mass., in 1827. 75
Cotton Production of the World Prior to 1880. 139
Cotton Spindles in United States in 1807................... 18
Cotton Spinning in Rhode Island in 1788 17
Cotton Spindles in the United States in 1889............... 158
Cotton Spindles of Other Countries in 1889................. 158
Cotton Skips and Cops (Cotton Yarns)....................... 50
Cotton Stowing and Compressing in United States 41
Cotton Supply of the World in 1889-90...................... 141
Cotton Terry Cloth 39
Cotton Thread of American Origin........................... 161
Cotton Twine and Shoe Thread............................... 48
Cotton Warp Yarn 50
Cotton Yarn Calculations................................... 51
Cotton Yarns (Duties in Foreign Countries)................. 76
Cottonades (Decline in Demand for)......................... 42
Cottonades—Widths, Weights and Picks 201
Cottons (Classification of Leading American)............... 60
Cottons (Cost and Selling Prices of Various Kinds in United
 States for a Series of Years)................... 62 to 70
Cottons (Diversification of American)...................... 56
Counterpanes 34
Counterpanes (Made in United States in 1809)............... 75
Corduroy 37
Cretonnes 121
Cumana Cotton.. 128
Curtain Damask 32
Customs, British (Consolidation of in 1787) 114
Cylinder Printing on Cotton Cloth.......................... 105
Cypress Cotton... 129

D

Daily Wages of American Cotton Operatives in 1827.......... 75
Damask... 32
Decline in the Demand for Cottonades....................... 42
Definition of Tones, Scales and Hues of Colors............. 108
Demarara Cotton 128
Denims (American)—Widths, Weights and Picks................ 202
Derries (British).. 37
Design of Fabric... 27
Dhooties (British)... 118
Diapers (British).. 37
Differences in Textile Fibres.............................. 88
Difference Between Mule and Throstle Twist................. 52
Difference Between Cylinder and Block Printing on Cotton
 Cloth.. 105
Difference between Twill Cloth and Plain Cloth 29
Different Staples of Cotton................................ 149
Dimity (British)... 32
Discharging Process in Calico Printing..................... 98
Displacement of Labor in the Cotton Goods Industry of
 United States by Machinery........................... 55
Diversification of Kind, Style and Quality of American Cottons. 56
Domestic Cotton Goods Sold in Philadelphia in 1804-6....... 31
Domestics (British).. 121
Doriah Stripes (British)................................... 121
Dunging Process in Calico Printing......................... 97
Duties on Cotton Yarns in Foreign Countries................ 76
Duties on English Cottons in 1700, 1712, 1714, 1720, 1736, 1774,
 1784, 1785, 1787 to 1831..................... 113, 114
Duties on Foreign Cottons Imported into United States Reduced
 from 55 to 23 per cent. in 1883..................... 74
Duty of Cloth Looker....................................... 33
Drawing Cotton... 53
Drawing Frame.. 22
Draw-Loom.. 160

CONTENTS.

Dressing Machine.. 24
Drawing and Slubbing.. 22
Drills (British) 120
Drill Sacks (American).. 59
Drills (American)—Widths, Weights and Picks.............. 191
Dyewood Extract Colors in Dyeing and Printing Cotton Cloth.. 94

E

Early Restrictions on Calico Printing in England............ 113
Early British Cotton Industries 112
Early History of Calico Printing.............................. 89
East India Cotton... 129
Effect of Heat on Cotton Fabrics............................. 110
Egyptian Cotton.. 129
Electricity in Printing Cottons............................... 109
Embroidery Cloth (British).................................... 120
Engraved Copper Cylinder and Blocks in Calico Printing...... 105
Engraving Copper Rollers for Printing Calico................ 106
English Cotton Blankets and Flannels......................... 47
English Print Cloths 92
English Cotton Goods of Standard Make in 1800, 1830 and 1846.. 74
English Cotton Yarn Standard.................................. 51
English Ginghams 37
English and Scotch Cotton Power Looms in 1820 and 1829..... 112
Establishment of Cotton Goods Commission Houses in New York.. 47
Estimated Number of Working Spindles in United States, 1880-1889 153
Estimated Number Cotton Spindles in Europe, 1888-89........ 153
Ethics of Cotton Buying in United States..................... 135
European Exports of Cotton Yarns and Cotton Tissues......... 78
Exports of American Cottons in 1887 and 1888................ 148
Exports of British Cottons to United States from 1831 to 1846.... 147
Exports of Cottons from England from 1701 to 1800........... 112
Exportation and Consumption of British Calicoes in 1814, 1820 and 1830.. 115
Extract Styles in Calico Printing 98

F

Fabrics Produced from Different Varieties of Cotton......... 61
Fancy Jacquard Cloths (British)............................... 121
Fastness of Colors.. 164
Faults in Cotton Cloth... 33
Fibres of Cotton Magnified...............................156, 157
Fibres (Difference in Textile) 88
Figured Borders (British Cotton Cloth)........................ 34
Figured Canvas (British Cotton Cloth)......................... 32
Figured Checks (British Cotton Cloth)......................... 34
Figured Gauze (British Cotton Cloth).......................... 32
Finishing Printed Cottons................................103, 104
First Cotton Goods Made in England............................ 105
First Mechanical Invention Employed in Spinning Cotton...... 36
Fixing Process in Calico Printing............................. 97
Fixing Colors on Cotton Cloth 96
Flannels, Cotton (American)—Widths, Weights and Picks...200, 201
Floats in Cotton Cloth... 33
Furniture Damask... 32
Fustians (British).. 37
Friction Calender for Calendering Cottons.................... 104
Freight and Insurance on Cotton 141
French Cotton Manufactures 123
French Cotton Yarn Standard................................... 51
French Exports of Cotton Yarns and Tissues.................. 78
French Nainsooks 39
From Raw Cotton to Cotton Cloth............................... 20
Future Delivery (Buying Cotton for).......................... 42

CONTENTS.

G

Gauze-Leno (British)	74
General Method of Planting Cotton	146
Genoa Cotton Cloth (British)	37
German Cotton Manufacturing Interests	123
German Exports of Cotton Yarns and Tissues	78
Ginning Cotton	20
Ginghams (American)—Widths, Weights and Picks	198
Ginghams (British)	120
Ginghams (Made in United States in 1809)	75
Giron Cotton	128
Glossop Printers (British Cotton Cloth)	119
Grecian Quilts (British)	38

H

Hamilton Company in 1835	72
Hand-Loom—Illustration and Description	49
Hair-Cord Muslin (British)	120
Highest and Lowest Prices for Middling Upland Cotton in New York and Liverpool, 1882 to 1890	138
Hindoo Bowing Cotton—Illustration and Description	31
Hindoo Churka—Illustration and Description	26
Hindoo Cotton Cloths (British)	119
Hindoo Cotton Foot Roller—Illustration and Description	19
Hindoo Cotton Loom—Illustration and Description	45
Hindoo Cotton Weaver at his Loom—Illustration and Description	45
Hindoo or East Indian Cottons	74
Hindoo Woman Spinning Cotton—Illustration and Description	36
Hooking or Plaiting Machine	33
Holland Cotton Industries	124
Homespun Cotton Cloth	23
Honey Comb Quilts	38
How Cotton Rollers for Printing Calico are Engraved	106
How Cotton Yarns are Measured	161
Horse Power for Propelling Cotton Machinery	57
How Indigo Prints are Made	90
How to Distinguish Cotton from Flax	124
How Spool Cotton is Made	44
Hues of Colors in Dyeing and Printing on Cotton Cloth	108
"Hungarians" (British Cotton Cloth)	37

I

Italian Cotton Industries	124
Import Duties (United States) on Bleached Cottons	58
Imported Cambric	39
Import Duties (United States) on Cotton Galloons, Gimps, etc.	59
Import Duties (United States) on Cotton Thread, Yarn, Warps	163
Import Duties (United States) on Unbleached Cottons	58
Import Duties (United States) on Strictly Cotton Goods	58
Index to Selling Agents of Domestic Cottons	166, 167, 168, 169
Influence of Light on Dyed Colors	108
Interweaving of Warp and Weft Threads in Cotton Cloth	30
Introduction	13, 14
Invention of Cotton Thread	43
Iron Steam Blacks in Calico Printing	100

J

Jaconets (British)	120
Jacquard Cotton Cloth	32
Jacquard Loom	164
Javanese Cotton Cloths (British)	119
Jeanette (British Cotton Cloth)	37
Jean Stripes (British Cotton Cloth)	37
Jute Export—Sacks (American)	59

K

Kinds and Qualities of Raw Cotton Produced Throughout the World	127

CONTENTS.

L

La Guayra Cotton	128
Largest Cotton Mill in the World	163
Lawrence Company in 1835	72
Liming Print Cloth	91
Loaded British Cottons	88
Location of the Cotton Goods Trade of Great Britain	86
Logwood Extract in Calico Printing	101
Loose Reeds in Weaving Cotton Cloth	33
Long Cloths (British)	119
Loss of Length in Twisting Cotton Yarn	75
Loss of Weight in Bleaching Cotton	86
Lowell Company in 1835	72

M

Madapollams (British Cottons)	119
Madapollam Percale (American)	39
Madder Styles in Calico Printing	99
Madras Cotton	129
Manufacture of Cotton Counterpanes and Quilts	38
Manufacture of Cotton Cords, Fustians, etc.	37
Manufactured Cottons Consumed by the World	151
Maranham Cotton	128
Marseilles and Toilet Quilts	38
McCarthy Cotton Gin	20
Merrimack Company in 1835	72
Metric System of Length	159
Mexicans (British Cotton Cloths)	119
Mill Brands of British Cottons	46
Mills in United States Making Brown, Bleached and Colored Cottons	56
Mineral Colors in Calico Printing	93
Moleskins (British Cotton Cloths)	37
Mordants in Calico Printing	94
Movement of Cotton Production in United States Southward and Westward	140
Mule-Jenny	57
Mule Yarn	57
Mulls (British Cottons)	120
Muslins (British) in 1793	151

N

Nainsooks, Cambrics and Percales for Underwear	39
Nankeen Cloth	42
Nankeens—Widths, Weights and Picks	199
Naphthaline Colors in Calico Printing	100
Naturally and Artificially Dyed Nankeen Cloth	42
Natural Organic Colors in Calico Printing and Dyeing	94
Needle Saw Cotton Gin	20
New Orleans Cotton	127
Norwegian and Swedish Cotton Industries	124
No Sheetings, Shirtings, Ginghams, etc., Made in United States Before 1790	106
Numbers in Threads	43

O

Old and New Cotton Gins	140
Old and New Cotton Mills	78
Old Time Spinning Wheel—Illustration and Description	35
One Pound of Cotton Yarn Reaching 1,000 Miles	59
Only Two Ways of Producing a Heavy Cotton Fabric	51
Our Cotton Goods Trade Forty Years Ago	47
Our Long-Stapled Cotton	139
Ornamental Weaving of Cotton Cloth	25
Original Gingham	37
Original Spinning Frame	22
Origin of the Manufacture of Thread	43
Osnaburg Sacks (American)	59
Oxidation Colors in Calico Dyeing and Printing	94

CONTENTS.

P

Padding Styles in Calico Printing	98
Passing Warp Over and Under the Weft in Weaving Cotton Cloth	30
Percentage of Different Lengths in the Staple of Cotton	136
Percentage of Sizing in English, French and American Cottons	55
Perched Quiltings (British)	38
Perforations Between Warp and Weft Threads in Cotton Cloth	28
Perforations in Plain Cotton Cloth—Illustration	28
Pernambuco Cotton	127
Philadelphia "Blue Goods" (Colored Cottons)	47
Philadelphia Cotton Manufactures in 1782	161
Picks of Standard American Sheetings and Shirtings	145
Pick or Thread Counting Machine—Description and Illustration	170, 171, 172
Picks per Minute in Weaving Cotton Cloth	55
Pigments Used in Dyeing and Printing Cotton Cloth	93
Pira or Cop (Cotton Yarn Spinning)	36
Plain Cotton Cloth	27
Plain and Ornamental Weaving of Cotton Cloth	25
Plain Weaving of Cotton Cloth	25
Price (Average Selling) of Plain Cotton Cloth in England from 1814 to 1833	80
Price of American Cotton Goods in 1789-91	79
Price of American Bleached Cottons in 1827	75
Price of British Printed Cotton Cloth Exported to United States from 1827 to 1832	80
Price of British Cottons Exported to United States and Other Countries in 1833	79
Price of Cotton Lands in United States	133
Price of Domestic Ginghams in 1818	101
Prices of Domestic Cottons in 1859, 1860, 1887 and 1889	83, 84, 85
Price of Hudson (N. Y.) Calicoes in 1836	26
Price of Middlings Cotton in United States in 1859, 1860, 1887 and 1889	138
Price of Prints in United States in 1827	75
Price of Standard Printing Cloths in United States During the War	133
Principal Colors, etc., Used in Dyeing and Printing Cotton Cloth	93, 94
Print Cloth (Cost of Weaving in England and America)	92
Printed Colors and Dyed Colors Used on Cottons	97
Printers (British Cotton Cloths)	119
Principal Machinery Used in Cotton Spinning	21
Processes Cotton Cloth in the Gray Undergoes Before it Becomes Printed Calico	90
Product of Almy & Brown, of Providence, R. I., in 1789-90	18
Product of Printed Cottons in New England in 1824 and 1860	89
Production and Exportation of British Cotton Goods	150
Production per Week of Print Cloths at Fall River and Lowell	92
Production of Cotton Goods in England from 1793 to 1833	162
Production of Cotton Goods in Philadelphia in 1788	162
Profits of Cotton Manufacturing in United States	150
Progress in Cotton Spinning and Weaving	107

Q

Qualities of Cotton Used in Making Different Kinds of Cottons	61
Qualities of Raw Cotton Produced Throughout the World	127

R

Raw Cotton to Cloth	20
Raw Cotton Consumed by the World	145
Red Woods Used in Dyeing and Printing Cotton Cloth	99
"Reeler" Cotton	132
Reedy Cotton Cloth	33
Regular and Fancy Brands of American Cottons	56
Relative Cost of Cotton in New England and Old England	60
Report of Committee on Manufactures to Congress in 1815	13

CONTENTS.

Requirements of a Cotton Factory ... 73
Resist Process in Calico Printing ... 98
Rio Cotton ... 128
Rope—Hints on Selecting ... 163
Roving Cotton ... 53
Russian Cotton Industry ... 125

S

Salonica Cotton ... 129
Sateens (American) ... 34
Sateens (Calico in the Form of) ... 110
Sateens (American)—Widths, Weights and Picks ... 202
Satin Checks (British) ... 74
Scales of Colors Used in Dyeing and Printing Cotton Cloth ... 108
Singeing Print Cloth ... 91
Six-Cord Spool Cotton ... 43
Sizing or Dressing Cotton Cloth ... 54
Sea Island Cotton of Georgia—Illustration and Description ... 131
Seersuckers (British) ... 37
Selecting Rope – Hints on ... 163
Selling Prices of Cotton in England in 1780 ... 115
Selling Prices of American Cottons and Prints in 1827 ... 75
Scouring or Boiling Print Cloth ... 91
Sheetings (British) ... 120
Sheetings, Brown (American)—Widths, Weights and Counts. 173 to 184
Sheetings, Bleached (American)—Widths, Weights and Counts ... 185 to 195
Shirting Cloth (British)—Widths, Weights and Picks ... 202
Shirtings, Brown (American)—Widths, Weights and Counts. 173 to 184
Shirtings, Bleached (American)—Widths, Weights and Counts ... 185 to 195
Shirtings (British) ... 178
Shirtings (Made in United States in 1809) ... 75
Skips (Cotton Yarns) ... 50
Skirtings (American)—Widths, Weights and Picks ... 199
Slasher and Sizing Machine—Illustration ... 76
Slater, Mrs. Samuel ... 43
Slater, Samuel—Portrait and Biographical Sketch ... 2
Sliver of Cotton ... 53
Slubbing Frame ... 22
Snick in Cotton Yarn ... 50
South American Cotton ... 127
Spanish Cotton Industries ... 124
Spinning Cotton ... 22
Spinning Cotton on the Hand-Wheel ... 35
Spinning Wheel (Old Time) ... 35
Stamping Print Cloth ... 91
Standard Makes of British Cottons ... 121
Standard American Grain Sacks and Bags ... 59
Statistics of Special Cotton Mills in United States in 1880 ... 153
Starching Printed Cottons ... 103
Steam Mineral Colors in Calico Printing ... 94
Steam Styles of Prints ... 107
Stretching Printed Cottons ... 104
Stripes and Checks ... 34
Suitings—Widths, Weights and Picks ... 199
Suffolk Company in 1835 ... 72
Surat Cotton ... 129
Surinam Cotton ... 128
Smyrna Cotton ... 129
Swiss Cotton Industry ... 126
Syrian Cotton Industries ... 125

T

Taffechelas (British Cottons) ... 120
Tan Jibs (British Cottons) ... 74, 120
Tanty or Hindoo Weaver ... 45
Tape Checks (British Cottons) ... 121
Tariff Revision (United States) on Foreign Cottons in 1883 ... 74

CONTENTS.

Tarletan Muslin (British) ... 120
Tashkend Biaz (Cotton Cloth) ... 74
Technical Classification of Cotton ... 132
T-Cloths (British Cottons) ... 119
Tendel or Buyak (Cotton Cloth) ... 74
Tenuity of Cotton Fibres ... 124
Tenison of Cotton Fibres ... 54
Terry Towelling ... 39
Thickening or Sizing Materials Used in Dyeing and Printing Cotton Cloth ... 94
Thicksets (British Cottons) ... 37
Thread (Cotton)—United States Import Duties ... 163
Three-Cord Spool Cotton ... 43
Three Operations in Dyeing Cotton Cloth ... 115
Throstle—Illustration and Description ... 61
Throstle and Mule-Jenny ... 23
Throstle Yarn ... 57
Tickings (American)—Widths, Weights and Picks ... 196, 197
Tones of Colors ... 108
Topical Process in Calico Printing ... 98
Turkey Red Goods ... 101
Turkey Reds (British) ... 119
Turkish Towelling ... 39
Tremont Company in 1835 ... 72
Twilled Cotton Cloth ... 29
Twill of Very Common Order ... 29
Twine (Consumption of in United States) ... 46
Twist (Difference Between Mule and Throstle) ... 52
Twist in Thread of English Muslin ... 54
Twist in Thread of Dacca Muslin ... 54
Twist in Thread of French Muslin ... 54
Twist of Weft and Warp in Cotton Cloths ... 29
Two Kinds of Cotton Goods Printers ... 92

U

Umbrella Ginghams ... 37
Upland Cotton ... 127

V

Value of American Cotton Crop in 1889 ... 27
Value of English Cotton Manufactures in 1767 and 1787 ... 112
Varieties of British Cotton Cloth ... 118 to 121
Varieties of American Cotton ... 130
Velveteens (British Cottons) ... 34
Victoria Lawns ... 120

W

Wages of American and English Cotton Operatives ... 60
Warping and Dressing Cotton Yarns ... 24
Warping Frame—Illustration ... 71
Waste Plains (British Cottons) ... 120
Water Frame Cotton Spinning) ... 22
Water Twist (Cotton Yarn) ... 22
Warp and Weft Threads (Cotton)—Illustration ... 27
Weaving Plain and Twilled Cotton Cloth ... 27
West India Cotton ... 128, 129
West Indian Cotton Plant—Illustration and Description ... 137
Where 25 Per Cent. of our Brown Cottons are Made ... 34
Whitney Cotton Gin ... 20
Widths, Lengths, Reeds, Picks and Weights of British Cottons. 203
Winding Machine (Cotton Winding)—Illustration ... 67
Woven or Warp Pile Cotton Cloth ... 34
Wrapping Cotton Yarn ... 51
"Woven Wind' Muslins (Cost of) ... 152

Y

Yarns (Cotton)—How they are Measured ... 161

Z

Zephyrs (Cotton) ... 37, 120

INTRODUCTION.

THE DRY GOODS CHRONICLE, appreciating the want, on part of the general trade, of more specific and practical information relative to the cotton goods which they handle, buy and sell, has prepared this book for their behoof and benefit.

In its preparation (which has extended over many months) great care, exactitude and research have been used in the writing, collecting, collating, compiling and arranging of matter specially interesting and useful to the buyers and sellers of plain, dyed and printed cottons, as well as to the grower, the factor and the manufacturer of raw cotton.

Aside from the varied research indicated, and the consultation of manufacturing and other textile authorities bearing directly upon the subjects treated—skilled experts have been employed in the examination, the measuring, the weighing, and the computation of the weft and warp threads which obtain to the square inch respectively in the various domestic makes of brown, bleached and colored cottons, ginghams, prints, etc.

For these purposes mechanical appliances of the most accurate description—specially made to order at home and abroad—have been employed, viz.: weighing scales, counting-glasses, width and length measures, automatic and graduated pick or thread enumerating machines, such as are now used by the most progressive of the modern cotton factories of Europe and America.

The work has also been freely illustrated with cuts of the principal machinery employed in cotton manufacturing—showing the various processes which raw cotton undergoes before it becomes yarn, thread or woven cloth.

The most reliable authorities in each instance have been referred to, and facts, figures, and other data of trustworthy character have been drawn from nearly every available source—embodying much matter which heretofore has not appeared in print—and all arranged in such a compact, ready-reference form as to make the book an invaluable pocket-companion, not only for the cotton goods manufacturer and dealer, but also for the grower and the factor of the raw material.

It is the work of the "DRY GOODS CHRONICLE," and its counterpart can be found in no publication in any language or country under the sun. It is issued as the "*Premium Book*" for *Subscribers* to the "DRY GOODS CHRONICLE," and can be obtained only through that means, as it is not for sale, nor will it be placed on sale.

The "pocket" form in which it appears was selected and adopted with especial reference to the convenience of the men for whom it is intended to be a guide—its size and shape making it readily transportable in the coat-pocket, without bulkiness.

As a great deal of the information contained in it has been drawn from almost every accessible source under circumstances making it impossible to give due credit in all instances—suffice it, that we extend herewith a general tender of thanks for all such indebtedness.

THE DRY GOODS CHRONICLE.

NEW YORK, Jan. 1, 1890.

Beginning of American Cotton Manufacture.

In a petition to the Senate and House of Representatives of Massachusetts, presented June 2, 1790, only three years after the Beverly Cotton Company had commenced operations, the owners stated that their expenditure had already amounted to "nearly £4,000, whilst the value of their remaining stock was not equal to £2,000, and a further very considerable advance was absolutely necessary to obtain that degree of perfection in the manufactures which alone could insure success.' This petition and other collateral facts, sufficiently prove that cotton spinning in this country, further than the hand-card and one-thread wheel, was carried through its first struggles by the Beverly Company, in Massachusetts. And from this State the manufacture was carried to Rhode Island, though it must be acknowledged that both States were indebted to foreign immigrants for instruction and assistance in spinning and weaving, as well as in preparing the cotton.

Cotton spinning commenced in Rhode Island in 1788, in which year Daniel Anthony, Andrew Dexter and Lewis Peck, all of Providence, entered into an agreement to make what was then called "home-spun cloth." The idea at first was to make jeans of linen warp spun by hand; but hearing that Mr. Ore, of Bridgewater, and the Beverly Company, of Massachusetts, had imported some models of drafts of machinery from England, they sent thither and obtained drawings of them, according to which they constructed machinery of their own. The first they made was a carding machine, which was something similar to those now in use for carding wool, the cotton being taken off the machine in rolls and afterward being roped by hand. The next was a spinning frame, something similar to the water frame, or rather the common jenny, but a very imperfect machine.

It consisted of eight heads of four spindles each, being thirty-two spindles in all, and was wrought by means of a crank turned by hand. Such were the rude machines used for spinning cotton previous to 1790, and the wonder is not that the manufacturers failed in their undertakings, but rather that they were able to persevere. And we can now perceive that from these small beginnings the present brightened prospects received their foundation.

COMMON JENNY AND STOCK CARD.

Previous to 1790 the common jenny and stock card had been in operation in various parts of the United States, and mixed goods of cotton and linen were woven principally by Scotch and Irish weavers. Mr. Moses Brown, of Providence, R. I., had several jennies employed in 1789, and some weavers at work on linen warps. The jennies were used for making weft, and operated by hand in the cellars of dwelling houses. During 1790 Almy and Brown, of Providence, R. I., manufactured 326 pieces, containing 7,823 yards of various kinds of goods. There were also several other companies and individuals in different parts of the Union who manufactured goods from linen warps and cotton weft.

In 1807 it was estimated that the whole number of cotton spindles in operation in the United States aggregated 4,000. In 1809 there were seventeen cotton mills in operation within the town and vicinity of Providence, R. I., working 14,296 spindles.

Tench Coxe, in his report of the census of 1810, gives the number of cotton factories as follows:

Massachusetts	54	Pennsylvania	64
Vermont	1	Delaware	3
Rhode Island	28	Maryland	11
Connecticut	14	Ohio	2
New York	26	Kentucky	15
New Jersey	4	Tennessee	4

None in any other State.

In 1815 the following number of cotton mills and spindles in Rhode Island, Massachusetts and Connecticut were enumerated in a memorial to Congress:

	Cotton Mills.	Spindles.
Rhode Island	99	68,142
Massachusetts	52	39,468
Connecticut	14	11,700
Total	165	119,310

A report of the Committee on Manufactures to Congress in 1815 also gives the following particulars of the cotton manufacture of the United States at that date:

Capital	$40,000,000
Males employed of age of 17 and upwards	10,000
Boys under 17	24,000
Women and female children	66,000
Wages of 100,000, averaging $1.50 per week	$15,000,000
Cotton manufactured, 90,000 bales	lbs. 27,000,000
Number of yards	81,000,000
Cost, averaging 30 cents per yard	$24,300,000

Hindoo Cotton Foot Roller.

The following is the explanation of the above cut: A, a smooth stone; B, a stool; C, an iron; DD, wooden soles; E, the seed; F, the cotton.

In ancient times the natives of India literally separated the cotton from the seed with their feet, and then cleaned it with their hands. This practice still obtains in the Southern Mahratta country. The cotton is placed on a flat stone. A woman sits on a stool before it. Her only implement is an iron roller, but wooden soles are fastened to each of her feet. This iron roller she places on the cotton, and then rolls it backwards and forwards with her feet, until the cotton is fairly separated from the seed, and the seed is rolled out in front, while the cotton comes out under the stone in a continuous web. The woman picks this cotton with her hands—picking away all the dirt, pieces of leaf, stray seeds, smashed seeds, and other objectionable trash.

FROM RAW COTTON TO CLOTH.

The lobes in every boll of cotton contain seeds resembling unground coffee which, when removed, leave only about one-third of the quantity gathered from the plant in clean cotton; or, in other words, according to the best authorities on the subject, two-thirds of the cotton grown and picked consist of seed, and one-third of the raw material fit to be used by the manufacturers.

The most primitive machine for removing the seeds from the fibre is the *Churka*, used in the East Indies. It consists of two rollers, made of hard wood, fixed in a rude frame, through which the cotton is drawn and the seeds forced out in the process. The operation is said to be tedious and laborious, and the quantity of cotton that can thus be cleaned by any one machine is exceedingly small. The fibre, however, is not injured, except in some slight degree by the curl which it receives in passing through the *Churka*.

GINING.

The invention of the saw gin by Eli Whitney in 1792, inaugurated an entirely new system of separating the seed from the fibre or wool. This gin and those made upon a similar principle consist of a "series of saws revolving between the interstices of an iron bed upon which the cotton is placed, the fibre being drawn through the slits in the bed, leaving the seeds behind." Of late years the saw gin has been variously improved, but still it is stated by many manufacturers that the fibre is somewhat injured by this mode of ginning, especially long-stapled cottons. However, more work can be performed by the saw gin than probably any other machine used for a similar purpose made. Its use is very general throughout the cotton-growing belt of the South.

Other inventions for removing the seed from the wool have latterly been perfected, such as the "needle saw, consisting of steel wire set in block tin, leaving the bottom of the teeth round and smooth," which, it is said, prevents the fibre from being "cut and nepped;" and a machine called the "McCarthy gin," which is of very simple construction. By the means of the latter "the cotton is drawn by a leather roller between a metal plate called the *doctor*, fixed tangential to the roller, and a blade called the *beater*, moving up and down in a plane immediately behind and parallel to the fixed plate. While the cotton is drawn through by the roller the seeds are forced out by the action of the movable blade." This machine has undergone several improvements and is considered the most successful competitor of the saw gin yet produced. Other new inventions of similar design and character might be adverted to, but their application and use are rather exceptional than otherwise.

CLEANING AND OPENING.

The next process which follows in regular order is spinning. The principal machinery in use for this purpose comprises the opener, scutcher and lap machine, carding engine, drawing frame, slubbing frame, intermediate frame, moving frame, throstle, self-acting mule, hand-mule, doubling frame or mule doublers or twiners.

The raw cotton is cleaned and opened out in the first two of these machines, and in the lap machine into flat folds; in the carding machine it is still further cleaned and the fibres straightened; in the drawing frame the fibres are laid parrallel; the process of twisting is commenced and carried on in the slubbing and intermediate frames, and in the throstle and mule it is converted into yarn.

The raw cotton, which is received in bales, has first of all to be opened and thoroughly mixed, in order to lessen the irregularity which might arise from a difference of quality. This process is performed by spreading out the contents of various bales in layers one above another; and to insure that a portion of each layer shall be in the opening machine, vertical slices are taken from the stack of cotton or mixing, and placed in position to feed the opener. This machine is used to break up any hard lumps that there may be, and to remove any dirt which the cotton may contain. Different machines are employed for the purpose which bear various designations, and their action carries the cotton, first placed on a feeder, forward by a combination of rollers, and before delivery by these rollers, it is struck several times by revolving blades or teeth which serve to loosen the fibres, at the same time disengaging the dirt and permitting it to fall through grids, which allow the impurities to pass, but retain the fibre. The draught caused by a fan carries the cotton forward to cages, whence it is delivered to the lap machine. The scutching and lapping machine is designed to effect a further separation of the fibres of the cotton, and to remove such refuse material as may still remain. The cotton is left by the opener in fleecy state, but by means of the scutcher, to which the lap machine is attached, is formed into a roll or "lap," preparatory to the operation of carding.

CARDING.

The carding engine comprises a large or main cylinder, covered with cards, a smaller cylinder, called the *doffer*, and a still smaller one, called the *taker-in*. The last named is the first to operate upon cotton, which it receives from a pair of feed rollers, and which, after striking out the heavier part of the dirt, it delivers to the main cylinder. This main cylinder is furnished with small ones, called rollers, also covered with cards, revolving in an opposite direction to that of the large cylinder, and with different velocities, by means of which the cotton is carded and put on the second cylinder called the *doffer*. The fleece of cotton is taken from the doffer by a vibrating *cam* and is then called the *sliver*, which passes through a trumpet-mouthed aperture with the fibers straightened, and is coiled in the doffing tins or cans in readiness for the drawing frames.

The process of elongation or attenuation are carried on through the drawing, slubbing, intermediate and finishing roving frames. The drawing frame comes into operation after carding, and is a machine for straightening and laying parallel the fibres of cotton. In it the process of doubling is commenced, and the cotton is drawn out by doubling and drawing out the slivers repeatedly through successive pair of rollers with which the drawing frame is furnished, the low or bottom rows being fluted and the upper or top roller covered with flannel or cloth and leather neatly cemented together and weighted down to the under rollers, so as to be driven by friction from the lines of the under rollers.

DRAWING AND SLUBBING.

The next operation which follows drawing is that of *slubbing*, where the sliver has a certain amount of twist imparted to it, and is wound on a bobbin. The slubbing frame (quoting the same manufacturing authority) is a machine which draws out the end, or sliver, from the last head of the drawing frame by means of three pairs of rollers, and this is twisted as it emerges from the front line of rollers by means of vertical spindles and flyers, which at the same time wind the ends upon bobbins in successive layers.

The slubbing frame answers three purposes: it draws out the cotton, twists it and winds it upon a bobbin, the first being done by the rollers, the second by the spindles, and the third by the flyers and pressers. The intermediate frame follows the slubbing frame, which it resembles in construction, though it has a larger number of spindles and generally smaller-sized bobbins. Instead of having cans put up at the back it has "creels" in which the slubibng bobbins are put, so as to be drawn off through the rollers of the frame and doubled two into one. In spinning low numbers of yarns this frame is sometimes entirely omitted, and the slubbing frame bobbins put directly into the "creels" of the roving frame. The latter resembles in principle the slubbing and intermediate frames, and is the last required before the operations of spinning, strictly so-called, commence.

It has a greater number of spindles than either of the two preceding frames, which are set closer together, and its bobbins are also shorter and smaller than the intermediate frame. The degree of elongation completed by the roving frame is technically described by the number of hanks per pound, each hank consisting of 840 yards, and the thread of a certain thickness is called so many hanks roving. In the spinning of fine numbers or counts the "jack frame" is used for a second roving, making a 30 or 40-hank roving from the bobbins of the first roving frame.

SPINNING.

In the spinning operations proper there are two kinds of frames, or machines, in general use—throstles and mules. The throstle, an extension and modification of the original spinning frame, first called "water frame," is employed in the spinning of yarn for warps, and the yarn so spun is still known by the name of "water twist."

This frame consists of a "creel containing the bobbins for the roving frame in the centre, having on each side a set of three rows of rollers, through which the roving is passed or drawn out to the required fineness. The bottom rollers are iron fluted, and the top ones are covered with leather, the speed being so adjusted that the front rollers move faster than those behind them. Below the rollers on each side is a row of spindles filled with bobbins, and on the top of the spindles flyers are screwed, around which the thread passed and is twisted by the spindles revolving at a great velocity, while it is lapped upon the bobbin by the flyers."

THROSTLE AND MULE-JENNY.

The ring and traveler spinning frame is also more or less extensively used in this country, and has, instead of a flyer on the top of the spindle, a small steel traveler working in a ring, placed in a rail called the ring rail, passing over the bobbin, and moves up and down the whole length of the bobbin. The twist is given by the revolutions of the spindle, and the winding of the thread on the bobbin (fixed to the spindle and carried round with it) is effected by the friction of the traveler in its revolutions round the ring.

The mule or mule-jenny differs from the throstle in having the spindles placed in a carriage moving backwards and forwards. "The twist is put in as the carriage recedes or is drawn out, and the winding of the yarn upon the cap is performed by a separate motion as the mule or carriage moves up, the principle of drawing being the same in both throstle and mule.'. The yarn spun upon the throstle has the fibre closer twisted than that spun upon the mule, and is more esteemed for certain purposes, especially for making thread, than the latter.

Throstle yarn is stronger and more even than mule yarn, and better adapted for warps, but the range of throstles is limited, and the counts seldom exceed 40s, though throstles are made capable of spinning yarn up to 80s or even 100s. The reason is that the fine thread has not strength to stand the 'drag' required to wind the yarn on the bobbin. The mule, on the other hand, will spin both twist and weft as high as No. 100s or more, while still finer numbers can be spun by hand-mules. Mule yarn is softer and more wooly in texture than throstle yarn, which arises from the vibration of the thread as the carriage is drawn out from the rollers." Yarn when spun, besides being woven into cloth, is also doubled and used for a variety of purposes.

THE LOOM.

The loom is the machine on which weaving is performed. The simplest form of which is the hand-loom, which is not now used in this country in weaving cotton fabrics unless in some few families in the Southern States, where "homespun," "butternut" cloth, etc., are still produced in the household. But even the production of these by the hand-loom is now very rare. The power-loom has greatly facilitated and cheapened the production of cotton fabrics so that it has entirely replaced the former.

Weaving is always preceded by warping, the object of which is so to arrange all the longitudinal threads which are intended to form the chain or warp of the web, as to form, when spread out, a plane of parallel threads. In forming the warp a sufficient number of bobbins, filled with yarn, must be taken to furnish the number of threads of the required length of the piece of fine cloth, would be unhandy to operate with. The warp is usually divided into six or eight parts, and as many bobbins are used to form one of the strands as there are threads in such a part. These strands are then united on the reel and form the complete web. The spools of thread are mouted horizontally upon a square frame and revolve upon wire skewers, so that the yarn may pass off them as freely as possible.

WARPING AND DRESSING.

There are two distinct forms of warping machines, one of which, the reeling machine, is used chiefly in the formation of chain for the hand-loom. This reel is of a vertical shape, from 5 to 9 feet in diameter, 7 feet high, and is moved by hand. The strands of thread are wound upon this reel in a screw line, and the winding is repeated six times, or oftener, or, in fact, until the required number of threads for the chain is laid upon it. The threads are run singly through the steel plate, called a heck, which forms the lease of the warp and serves for the weaver to put his lease rods in.

In weaving formerly done on the power-loom the dressing of the warp was a serious obstacle, and required a frequent stoppage of the loom and unwinding of the beam.

The difficulty was overcome by the dressing machine, which led to the invention of the warping machine. On the latter the warp is wound directly upon a beam; six or eight or even a greater number of these are mounted upon the dressing machine, and, on being unwound, form the warp. These machines are very simple and ingenious. Such a warp mill, with its numerous threads and spools, would require much attention, and would work but slowly if the motion of the machine was not checked by a very simple contrivance in case one of the threads break.

This object is attained by the drop wires; a hook made of iron wire is hung upon each thread, or rather, thread passes through it; this hook has a long stem which moves in the frame of the machine, and as soon as the thread breaks it drops down and arrests the motion of an iron rod, which then leads the strap upon the loose pulley.

The dressing machine on which the warp-beams are placed and are unwound slowly until their contents are united upon a single beam. "During its transit to a single beam the yarn passes over brushes, which move backwards and forwards, from which it receive a dressing, and is again dried before it reaches the main warp-beam. This drying is done by a current of heated air, which is forced upon the warp by a revolving fan, and in passing through the moist threads of the warp it dries them and makes the warp fit for winding and weaving.

PLAIN AND ORNAMENTAL WEAVING.

It is almost next to impossible to accurately describe the power-loom without the aid of diagrams as it is such a complicated machine. According to the best manufacturing authorities on this subject, power-looms are now in operation in this country and Europe at the rate of 140 revolutions per minute, and on plain goods 160 revolutions per minute, and some looms will make 200 and even 250 revolutions per minute. According to this statement, as "common sheetings and shirtings require about seventy to eighty picks or threads to the inch, the loom would make at least 200 picks per minute or about five yards per hour, but coarse goods can of course be woven much faster. There are, in fact, looms in operation which work six treadles and as many shuttles with perfect ease and security, and of course weave much faster."

The weaver of cotton goods, in all cases, makes it his first business to adapt those parts of his loom which move the warp and which is technically called the draught, drawing or readying-in.

In every kind of weaving, whether direct or cross-weaving, the whole difference of the pattern is produced either by the order of succession in which the warp is introduced into heddles, or by the order of succession in which the heddles are moved. When the heddles have been thus far adjusted, it is the weaver's next business to connect the leaves, or heddles, with the levers or treadles, by which they are moved in such a manner as to form the desired plan. When this operation is performed correctly there is no further difficulty in obtaining the pattern wanted in the goods; the only thing necessary is to move the treadles in the order in which they have been placed.

The method of operation in ornamental weaving is first, to draw the pattern upon paper, which has previously been laid out into small rectangular spaces, each line or space representing one thread of the warp as well as of the filling. The pattern thus drawn represents in its enlarged size the figure as it will appear in the cloth when reduced to the size of the number of threads contained in it. The paper pattern thus forms a double scale, by which, to judge of the effect and to determine with great precision the readying-in, and all the subsequent operations. If great strength and thickness of the cloth are wanted, two different modes of weaving are resorted to, one of which makes double cloth, or weaves two webs and joins them together in one operation, and the other consists chiefly in laying three or more threads upon the face of the cloth. with such intervals between as the pattern requires, instead of crossing each thread as is done in ordinary plain weaving.

Plain weaving is done by the power-loom more perfectly than it can be done on the hand-loom, and the former can be so adjusted as to weave the heaviest goods to advantage; any number of shuttles—at least as many as six—may be used with ease, and damask figured goods, such as table cloths, etc., may be produced in great perfection, with the assistance of the Jacquard machine.

The Hindoo Churka.

This simple implement is only one step in advance of the cotton foot roller. It consists of two rollers set in a wooden frame, with a small interval between them. These are turned with an ordinary handle, the motion of one being communicated to the other by a sort of endless screw. The cotton is passed between these rollers, and the staple is thus separated from the seed; but the cotton is turned out in a matted state, with the fibres all lying confused in different directions, so as to give a great deal of trouble to European carders. Moreover, the cotton is mixed up with all the dirty bits of leaf and seed already indicated. The natives, however, can completely clean it by the laborious process of hard picking, and they appear to resort to this process for home consumption; but for exportation they seem to content themselves with beating it with sticks on rattan frames.

Price of Hudson Calicoes in 1836.

In 1836 the calicoes made by the Hudson Print Works at Stockport, N. Y. were sold for 18c. per yard. These works were established in 1826; employed 42 block printers and 5 printing machines—2 printing four colors at once, and 3 three colors each.

Weaving Plain and Twilled Cotton Cloth.

We are indebted to Thomas R. Ashenhurst, Head Master of the Textile Department of the Technical College of Bradford, England, for the following general plan of plain and twilled cotton cloths:

PLAIN COTTON CLOTH.

The illustration given immediately below (Fig. 1) represents the general plan of what is known as plain cloth. It will be seen by examining it that there are two sets of threads, which cross each other at right angles, and which interweave alternately.

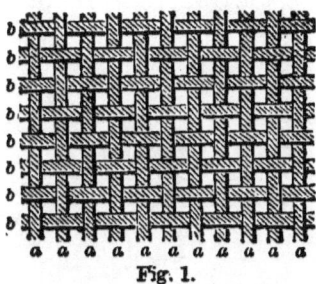

Fig. 1.

WARP AND WEFT THREADS.

The threads marked a, or the longitudinal threads, or those running in the direction of the length of the piece, are termed the *warp* threads, and the transverse threads, b, are termed the *weft* threads. In all woven fabrics we have these two sets of threads to deal with, and the relation which one bears to the other, as well as the order of interweaving for the purpose of forming patterns, constitute *the design of the fabric*.

In the plain cloth plan in figure 1 it will be seen that although there is produced a very firm texture by the manner in which the two sets of threads interweave, yet there cannot possibly be produced a very close texture. Certainly the fabric will be strong, each thread supporting the other to the utmost, yet it cannot be made sufficiently compact to produce a heavy fabric. By the very manner in which the threads intersect each other, they are prevented from lying perfectly close together; consequently, the fabric must be, in a greater or less degree, perforated.

PERFORATIONS IN PLAIN COTTON CLOTH.

The perforations in a plain cotton cloth will vary greatly under certain conditions. For instance, the thicker the threads from which the fabric is made, the larger will be the perforations, and the thinner the threads the smaller the perforations. Of course, in such cases the perforations will bear exactly the same ratio to the diameter of the thread if the relation of the warp to weft be the same, but cloth made from fine yarns will possess the useful properties in a much greater degree in proportion to its weight than that made from thick threads.

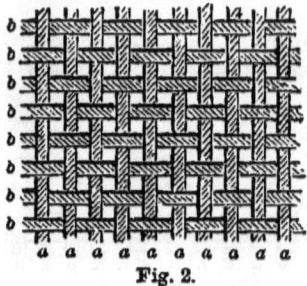

Fig. 2.

PERFORATIONS BETWEEN WARP AND WEFT THREADS.

If we desire to produce a cotton fabric of close texture—one which will have the perforations reduced to the smallest possible dimensions—we must use a yarn in which the fibres of which it is composed are laid as loosely together as possible. We can then, in the mechanical operation of weaving, bring these threads closely together, and the looseness of the fibres will permit of their spreading out and so of reducing the interstices to the lowest point.

On the other hand, if the threads are twisted very hard—that is, if the threads are made solid and compact—they will resist compression in the operation of weaving, and, the fibre being held firmly together in the thread, there is nothing left to spread out and cover the interstices; consequently we shall have an open fabric, but the fibres being firmly interlocked in the thread, we shall have a fabric which will bear more strain, and will offer also more resistance to friction than in the other case.

TWIST OF WEFT AND WARP.

Another matter which materially affects the closeness of texture in a plain cotton cloth is the direction of the twist of the weft in relation to that of the warp. On reference to figure 1 it will be seen that the two sets of thread, when placed together in the fabric, have the twist running in the same direction; that being so, the fibres—or, if one may so term them, the strands—of the two sets of threads will become embedded into each other, and so make a close and compact fabric. If, on the other hand, the twist of the weft be contrary to that of the warp when the two are placed together, as shown in the figure 2, the threads cannot become so intimately connected, and, consequently, the fabric cannot be so close and free from perforation.

Twilled Cotton Cloth.

The class of fabrics which comes nearest to plain cloth is that known as twills or twilled fabrics; and in their production we may have two objects in view—first, increase of bulk or bulkiness of fabric; and second, ornamentation.

Fig. 3.

TWILL OF VERY COMMON ORDER.

The first and chief difference between twill cloth and plain cloth is that on the latter the warp and weft interweave alternately, whereas in twilled fabrics they interweave at such intervals as may be required for the formation of the pattern. Again, what is termed the complete pattern in plain cloth is represented by two ends of warp and two picks of weft, while in twilled cloth a greater number of ends and picks are required to complete the pattern; or, in other words, in all plain cloths every alternate end is a repetition; the same holds of the picks, but in twilled cloths the repetition will occur at longer intervals.

Figure 3 shows the plan of a twill of a very common order, and one regularly in use in fabrics made from cotton as well as from all other kinds of materials.

PASSING OF WARP OVER AND UNDER THE WEFT.

In figure 3 it will be seen that each warp thread passes alternately over and under two weft threads or picks, and in like manner each weft thread passes alternately under and over two warp threads. But each end does not pass under and over the same two picks, nor does each pick pass under or over the same two ends, nor are they alternate in their action, as are the ends and picks of plain cloth; but they change in regular consecutive order; that is, if the first end passes over numbers one and two picks, the second end passes over numbers two and three picks, and so on, each end advancing one pick before it rises to the surface, or passes to the back, and each pick advancing one end in the same manner. This order of changing of the ends and picks will have the effect of producing a distinct pattern upon the fabric, a species of cord running in a diagonal direction across it.

But another matter of much more importance than the mere pattern is the fact that the order of working permits us to introduce more material into the fabric, and so make it more bulky and closer in construction. The reason for this is to be found in the simple fact that the weft and warp interweaving only at intervals of two ends or picks permit the two threads, both warp and weft, to lie closely together, and consequently to allow of a greater number per inch to be introduced into the fabric than can be done in plain cloths.

True, as previously shown, we may make plain cloths in which the warp threads lie close together, and others in which the weft threads lie perfectly close together; but in the one case the weft threads are a considerable distance apart, and on the other the warp threads are a considerable distance apart, whereas in the twill cloth the weft and warp both lie equally close together, so that we obtain the requisite closeness of texture in both directions, and a corresponding one in the bulk of the fabric. Along with the closeness of texture, and increased weight or bulk, we also obtain another advantage over the plain cloth, viz.: that by the order of interweaving the warp bends round the weft, and the weft round the warp in an equal degree, exactly as in the first order of plain cloth.

Hindoo Bowing Cotton.

The Hindoo bow for cleaning cotton is made of bamboo, and is fastened by strings to the wall of the room, at about five feet from the floor. To the middle of this bow a cord is tied, to which a second bow is attached of a larger size, strung with thick cat-gut. This second bow hangs about two feet above the ground. The man sits down, lays hold of it with the left hand, and holds a strong ebony club in his right. Thus equipped, he strikes the string of the bow with his club, so as to make it toss a flock of the cotton, spread upon the floor round about him, up into the air with great violence, and thus discharges its impurities.

Domestic Cotton Goods Sold in Philadelphia from 1804 to 1806.

The amount of domestic cotton goods sold in Philadelphia, the produce of New England, from 1804 to 1806, inclusive, is given in the following statement:

	1804.	1805.	1806.
Cotton Yarn	$2,388	$3,805	$6,185
Cotton Woven Goods	1,526	1,581	2,185
Total	$3,914	$5,386	$8,370

Total of sales for the three years, $17,670.

Jacquard Cotton Cloth.

Regular cloths vary from small patterns on twenty ends and twenty picks to others with 2,000 ends and picks in a round, while for exceptional cases these limits are far exceeded, according to textile authority.

"A feature of many Jacquard cloths is a figure more or less fanciful on a ground which may be plain, twill, satin or oatmeal weave. Spots and brilliants are examples of this style.

"Damasks are extensively made. The true damask weave consists of a design of large extent, woven, we will suppose, with weft predominating in the figure, which may be bound by satin or twill weave. The ground is also in similar weave, but with warp predominating. Thus the cloth is firmly bound at all parts of the surface, and is reversible.

"The damasks woven in cotton do not always fulfill these conditions, but are sufficiently similar to warrant their being classified together. Frequently they are made in light goods of about sixty ends and picks per inch for export to China and other countries, or heavier both in yarn and pick, with a finér reed, for the home grade. These goods are of great variety of pattern, and are generally finished before use, or, as in the case of furniture and curtain damasks, dyed.

"Dimity is a cloth of smaller pretentions with regard to figure, which is arranged in stripe form. The cloth is firmly bound and the figure somewhat raised, which gives it an embossed effect.

"Brocades are Jacquard cloths of fine yarns, the pattern arranged in weft spot on plain ground, or narrow stripes of spotted figures, which, when well finished, have a charming effect. The brocade is not limited to the longitudinal stripe or figure, but may be arranged as a brocade check, while the ground cloth in either case may be of plain weave. A good effect is also produced by arranging this style in diamond figures by introducing honeycomb diagonally.

"Figured canvas gives a pleasing effect when dyed. The figure is woven in plain cloth, and the work between the figures shows the ends cramped together alternately with open spaces, so as to give an open effect, on which the figures show to advantage.

"Figured gauze cloths are woven by the Jacquard."

Cloth-Looking, or Examining.

In England the pieces are brought into the warehouse of the mill by the weavers, and are hooked in folds of one yard. This operation is performed on the hooking or plaiting machine. In some concerns the looking is done on this machine. Probably the cost is lessened, and the outlooker sees the whole of the piece (not missing one side of the "flue," as it not infrequently happens in the counter-looking), but the fact that the smaller faults are not all seen renders the advantages questionable, unless the cloth is afterwards counter-looked.

The cloth-looker's duty is to examine each piece of cloth, reporting any fault to the person responsible, and throwing out as seconds the pieces which are not up to the quality

Faults in Cotton Cloth.

Bare, badly-covered cloth is caused by the back rest of the loom being too low, the shed too large, late treading and picking, too much weight or uneven sheds. Cockly cloth looks raw, and has raised lumps on the face, caused by too little weight. Cracks are sometimes weavers' faults, in not letting back after weft breaking, take up motion working unequally, or through some parts not being screwed up tightly. Uneven cloth is generally attributable to the weft, although anything tending to unequal release of the warp from the beam, such as weights touching the floor, damp ropes or loose pivots, cause it.

Reedy cloth is caused when a few dents of the reed are bent out of position.

Bad sides are either slattered, caused by unsatisfactory bottoming, or are frayed or raw from lack of sufficient side ends. Occasionally a bad picker catches the weft and causes a peculiar ridgy selvage.

Floats are the result of obstruction in the shed generally, broken twist keeping down the warp threads and preventing their interweaving with the weft.

Mashes are on a larger scale. If the shuttle is entrapped without the reed flying out, in loose reed looms, or the protector acting in fast reeds, the twist is generally broken out for several inches in the width.

Broken picks are caused by several layers of weft coming off the cop into one shed.

Classification of Cotton Cloth.

Woven fabrics of any material may be divided into four main classes, says Prof. Brooks: "Plain, figured, gauze, and woven pile cloths; laces formed on an entirely different structure being disregarded.

"Plains show no figure of any nature on the face of the cloth, have every end and pick interwoven alternately, while the warp forms a right angle with the weft. Apparent figures, ribs and stripes may be made by using fine and coarse weft or alternate counts of warp. Stripes or checks of color may be introduced, but if the weave be unaltered the cloth is still classed as plain.

"Figured is a very comprehensive group, consisting of the twills, sateens, velveteens, figured borders, figured checks, damasks, brocades, dimity, weft pile, counterpanes, fustians, cords, etc., and almost all fancy cloths, except gauze and warp pile.

"Gauze has a peculiar structure, pure gauze differing from plain cloth in the ends, weaving at an angle more acute than a right angle. Leno is one kind of gauze.

"Woven or warp pile cloth has a nap woven on the face, and cut whilst in the loom—a class of cloth not frequently met with in cotton, but generally in the silk and carpet trades."

Where 25 Per Cent. of our Brown Cottons are Made.

A reliable authority states that 25 per cent. of the brown cotton goods manufactured in the United States are made in Georgia, within a radius of ten miles of Augusta, where there are thirteen plants or mills operating 179,236 spindles, 5,883 looms, and furnishing employment to 4,320 hands, to whom is paid in salaries annually $991,039.96. The amount of capital employed in these mills is $8,755,000; 75,224 bales of cotton are consumed annually, and the value of their combined production is $5,444,823.

During the year 1888 the number of spindles was increased by 17,840 and 476 looms, and these, together with other improvements, caused a further investment of capital to the extent of $286,500.

Old Time Spinning Wheel.

Two kinds of household spinning wheels are said to have been used from time immemorial. The first is commonly called in this country the "big wheel," from the magnitude of its rim, or the "wool wheel," from its being employed in spinning sheep's wool. It was well adapted to spin cotton, from the analagous form of its filaments, which it did in two independent operations. At first the spongy cylinder turned off from the hand card was drawn out and slightly twisted into a porous cord, called a roving; at the second, this cord was stretched and twisted into a fine cohesive thread; in either case the spinster, having fixed round the spindle the extremity of the carding or roving, seized it a few inches from the end with the finger and thumb of the left hand, and, while she turned round the wheel with the right, so as to make the spindle revolve, she progressively extended the cotton cord by drawing her hand from near the spindle to the position in which it is placed as represented in the above cut.

She now completed the torsion of the cotton by turning the wheel till the thread had acquired the desired degree of twist, and then, by a slow counter rotation of the wheel and proper giving-in of the left hand, she wound up the thread upon the spindle into a conical shape, called pira or cop. This is the ancient spinning implement of Hindostan. The first mechanical invention regularly employed in England was constructed upon this principle; several spindles—at first eight, afterwards eighty—being made to whirl by one fly-wheel, while a movable frame, representing so many fingers and thumbs as there were threads, alternately receded from the spindles during the extension of the thread, and approached to them in its winding on.

Hindoo Woman Spinning Cotton Yarn.

The above illustration represents a Hindoo woman spinning cotton yarn on the primitive spinning wheel of India. In that country women of all castes prepare the cotton thread for the weaver, spinning the thread on a piece of wire, or a very thin rod of polished iron, with a ball of clay at one end; this they turn round with the left hand, and supply the cotton with the right; the thread is then wound upon a stick or pole, and sold to the merchants or weavers; for the coarser thread the women make use of a wheel very similar to that used by our grandmothers.

Manufacture of Cotton Cords, Fustians, etc.

Cotton cords, moleskins, corduroy, fustians, bullhides, thicksets, made in England, are all pile fabrics of a heavy character. The pile is all in the weft, floating upon a ground cloth. Different makes of each fabric are woven and named frequently according to the style of the ground or backing weave, e. .g. tabby back means plain, Genoa is a 4-end twill, Jeanette is a 3-end twill, double Genoa, double Jeanette. The cords show a broad wale or stripe running lengthwise of the piece, consisting of weft floating over the warp and ground cloth, and in such a manner that when slit along the centre of each stripe the divided threads stand up to form a cord. The weft of the next wale being cut similarly, a stripe of pile fabrics is now formed, having its centre above the groove which divided each stripe of uncut yarn.

A rounded effect is given to these cords by having the threads forming the centre of greater lengths than the sides of the cord, they having had a longer float in the weaving. This cloth is dyed and finished, being sold as corduroy.

The Original Gingham.

Gingham was originally introduced with its present name from India, and in the early days was more or less largely imported into Europe. At first the India ginghams consisted of cotton cloths, with two or more colors arranged as a small checkered pattern. Now a great variety are formed of this material, and in the case of umbrella ginghams, the whole piece is woven with yarn of one color. In England ginghams are known by the following names: Plain, common light grounds; plain, common dark grounds; Earlston ginghams, power loom seersuckers and checks, colored diapers, crossover stripe, derries, Hungarians, jean stripes and umbrella ginghams. American ginghams include staples, fancy staples, fancies, cords, crinkle seersuckers, novelties, light and dark dress styles, zephyrs, indigoes, bourettes, and also the particular names or brands of the different makes, such as Amoskeag, Abbotsford, Arlington, Bates, Johnson, Lancaster, Manchester, Park Mills, Plunkett, Renfrew, Slatersvllle, Westbrook, White Manufacturing Co., Whittenton, York, etc.

Manufacture of Cotton Counterpanes and Quilts.

The Jacquard loom is largely used in the counterpane and quilt industry. Marseilles and toilet quilts, with which may be associated the well known toilet cloths, on the double-cloth principle, present a good face of plain weave in fine yarns, being embossed, as it were, in the cloth by additional warp threads. This backing weft sometimes floats outside the cloth, sometimes is bound inside just below the plain face, and at other parts the whole of the yarn is firmly united. Where the backing is brought inside, the top cloth is raised up, while at those places where all the ends are woven together a depression is caused. Large embossed figures may thus be shown on the cloth, although it appears to have an unbroken surface. A coarser quality is made where both face and back wefts are coarse and from the same cop.

Perched quiltings are in this style, but the figures are small, diamond-shaped and irregular. The honeycomb quilt, as its name implies, is a cloth with the figures on its surface formed by raised ridges, both warp and weft way. This is generally woven in bleached knitting cottons two or threefold, and as with this weave others may be combined and stripes of colored worsted inserted, great scope is given to the designer. A Grecian quilt is woven in bleached knitting cottons, and yet the coarse threads give a smooth, glossy surface in consequence of the weave being on the damask principle— *i. e.*, the figure may be formed in a weft satin while the ground is a warp satin. The Alhambra quilts are figured in various designs and woven with vari-colored yarns.

Cost of Heavy Cottons.

A writer of some experience says the expense of the Eastern cotton mills for coarse goods, such as common heavy sheetings, may be estimated as follows:

	Cents.
Middling cottons, delivered	13.40
Waste	1.48
Labor	3.80
General Expenses	2.08
Total	20.86

2.80 yards cloth to one pound of cotton would equal 7.45 cents per yard.

Nainsooks, Cambrics and Percales for Underwear.

Many American women now use French nainsooks, linen cambric and percales for underwear. There is less of imported cambric used than formerly, owing to the superiority of our own domestic cambrics. The Wamsutta, Lonsdale, and especially the Berkeley mills all make cambrics which rival the best imported goods, and are sold at less than one-half. Madapolam is a heavy quality of percale which sells at about twenty-five cents per yard, retail, and is especially recommended as durable goods for underwear. Nearly all stores now keep Hamburgs worked on madapolams, for use on garments made of this material. These embroidered bands are finished without dressing, and are far superior to all Hamburgs, even French Hamburg, which has been considered the best of all. Unfortunately, they are sold only in four and a-half yard lengths, in all widths—a length which does not always cut to advantage.

Cotton Terry Cloth.

A pile fabric of cotton which has attracted great attention during the last few years is the Turkish or Terry towel. This is woven with two beams, one for the loop pile, and the other carrying the ground warp, which is always kept tight. After two picks have been inserted and tightly beaten up, the reed is allowed to fly loose by a peculiar arrangement, and both warps being kept tight, two picks are put in without beating up. Then the reed is fastened, the loop warp slackened, and on the next pick being beaten up, the two previous ones are also driven home, and with them the loop warp, which stood between the fell and the two neglected picks, thus forms loops on both sides of the cloth.

This weave is not confined to the making of fabrics with an unbroken pile surface, but is adopted in stripes for bath towels and wraps, in check and even figures for quilts, combined with color in other effects, and also woven alternately in some special cloth with entirely different patterns. The headings, also for the towels, are of a firmer weave and afford great scope for ornamentation.

The Cotton Gin.

Dr. Ure gives the following description of the cotton gin:

"The principal parts of the saw-gin are two cylinders of different diameters (see F H, Figs. 1 and 2) mounted in a strong wooden frame (A), which are turned by means of a pulley and belt, acting upon the axis of a fly wheel attached to the end of the shaft opposite to that seen in the section of figure 1. Its endless band turns a large pulley upon the end (D) of the saw cylinder (F) and a smaller pulley on the end (E) of the brush cylinder (H, Fig. 2), so as to make the latter revolve with greater rapidity. Upon the wooden cylinder (F), ten inches in diameter, are mounted three-quarters of an inch apart, fifty, sixty, or even eighty circular saws, edged as at 1, figure 1, of one foot diameter, which fit very exactly into grooves cut one inch deep into the cylinder.

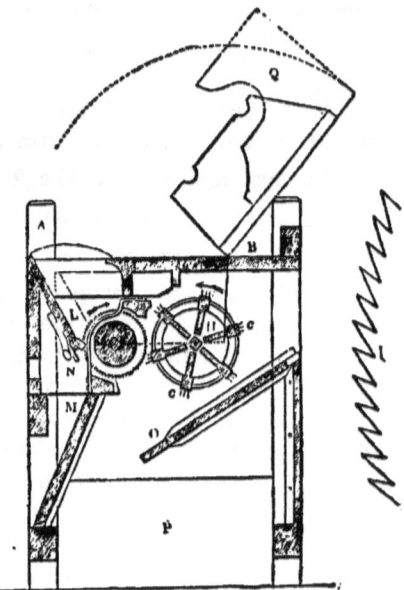

FIG. 1.—SECTION OF WHITNEY'S SAW-GIN.

"Each saw consists of two segments of a circle, and is preferably made of hammered sheet iron. Opposite to the interstices of the saws are flat bars of iron, which form a parallel grid of such a curvature that the shoulder of the slanting saw tooth passes first and then the point."

"The hollow cylinder, H, is mounted with the brushes c, c, c, the tips of whose bristles touch the saw-teeth, as at d, d, fig. 2, and thus sweep off the adhering cotton. The cylinder H revolves in an opposite direction to the cylinder F, as is indicated by the arrows in fig. 1.

"The seed cotton, as picked from the pods, is thrown into the hopper, L, fig. 1; the disc-saws, I, in turning round encounter the cotton filaments resting against the grid, catch them with their sharp teeth, and drag them inwards and upwards, while the stripped seeds, too large to pass between the bars, fall through the bottom, N, of the hopper, upon the inclined board, M. The size of the aperture, N, is regulated at pleasure by an adjusting screw to suit the size of the particular species of seeds. The saw-teeth, filled with cotton, after returning through the grid, meet the brushes c, c, c, of the cylinder H, and deliver it up to them."

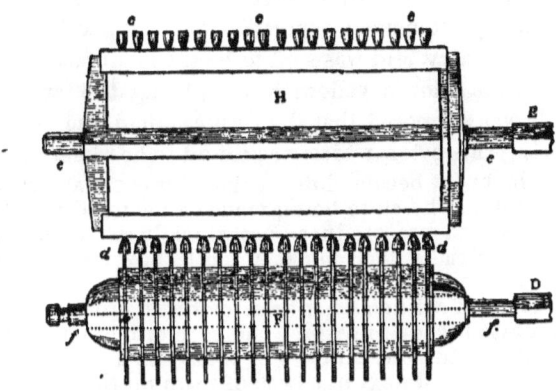

FIG. 2.—PLAN OF SAW BRUSH AND CYLINDER OF WHITNEY SAW-GIN.

"The cotton is thereafter whisked down upon the sloping table, O, and thence falls into the receptacle, P. A cover, Q, fig. 1, encloses both the cylinders and the hopper; this cover is turned up round its hinges (as shown in fig. 1) in order to introduce the charge of seed cotton into the machine, and is then let down before setting the wheels in gear with the driving power. The axes, e, e, f, f, of these cylinders (fig. 2) are well fitted into their plummer box-bearings, so as to prevent any lateral swagging, which would greatly injure their operation. The raised position of the cover is obvious in fig. 1, the hinges being placed at B."

Decline in the Demand for Cottonades.

The reason why cottonades have lost their former popularity, according to a manufacturer's authority, is found in the very great improvement in the manufacture of woolen goods, and the constantly declining prices at which they are sold. The improvement in woolen manufactures was succeeded by the production of stylish cotton cassimeres by the cottonade mills, many of which to-day do not make a piece of the old fabric except in small quantities for special orders. Several of the once prominent cottonade makers are even scarcely remembered. The decline in the demand for cottonades is one of the many things to be noted in the period covered, but as a specialty for men's clothing the decrease in the production of this article has been wonderful.

Naturally and Artificially Colored Nankeen Cloth.

Cotton cloth of the kind called "nankeen," or naked, was formerly extensively exported from China to Europe and this country, and was said to be the manufacture of Nanking, the color, a yellowish buff, being the favorite one. It was supposed that the Chinese held the secret for dyeing this color, which was found to be remarkably endurable, but it became known that it was not an artificial color at all, the cloth being made of a colored variety of cotton, which was produced occasionally in China and India. Artificially dyed nankeen cloths now form a considerable export from England to China.

The color of artificial nankeen cloth is produced by an elaborate process, in which the yarn or cloth is first dipped in a saturated solution of alum, then in a bath of lime water, and next in a bath of nitro-muriate of tin. Another, but less permanent, nankeen dye is produced by boiling annatto in a strong solution of pearl ashes and diluting with water to the required tint.

Buying Cotton for Future Delivery.

Cotton bought for future delivery is purchased on the basis of the price for middling cotton, that is, the terms of the sale apply to middling cotton, but the seller has the option of delivering higher or lower grade cotton when the time agreed upon arrives, adding or subtracting from the basis of the contract, the current difference in price between middling and the grade he delivers. The purchaser does not necessarily buy middling cotton, but a certain number of bales of cotton on a basis of such a price for middling.

Origin of the Manufacture of Thread.

The use of the spinning wheel, which is an improved method of twisting the thread, was introduced into England in the time of Henry VIII., from India, where it had long been in use. The modern application of machinery to spinning thread began in England in 1767 by James Hargreaves' invention of the spinning jenny. This was improved upon by Richard Arkwright, and in 1779 by Samuel Crompton, of Bolton, England. The latter completed a machine which combined the jenny of Hargreaves and the roller of Arkwright, which was called a *mule jenny*, or now more generally known as the *mule*. In this country spinning has been a very important industry from a very early date. At first it was necessarily a domestic industry, and the spinning wheel was an indispensable utensil in every household. The first sewing thread ever made of cotton was produced at Pawtucket, R. I., in 1794. Prior to this time flax had been the material used in this manufacture. The idea of using cotton is said to have been suggested by Mrs. Samuel Slater, the wife of the pioneer of the cotton industry of this country. With the introduction of machine-made thread the development has been very rapid.

Numbers of Thread.

When 840 yards of yarn weigh 7,000 grains, a pound of cotton, the yarn is No. 1. If 1,680 yards weigh a pound it will be No. 2 yarn. For No. 50 yarn it would take fifty multiplied by 840 yards to weigh a pound. This is the whole of the yarn measurement. The early manufactured thread was three-cord, and thread took its number from the number of the yarn from which it was made. No. 60 yarn made No. 60-thread, though, in point of fact, the actual calibre of No. 60 thread would equal No. 20 yarn, being three 60 strands.

When the sewing machine came into the market as the great consumer, six-cord cotton had to be made as a smoother product. As thread numbers were already established, they were not altered for the new article, and No 60 six-cord and No. 60 three-cord are identical in size as well as in number. To effect this the six-cord has to be made of yarn twice as fine as that demanded by the three-cord. The No. 60 six-cord would be six strands of No. 120 yarn. The three-cord spool cotton is the same number as the yarn it is made of. Six-cord spool cotton is made of yarn that is double its number.

How Spool Cotton is Made.

Few people ever stop to think of the twistings and turnings and the various processes that cotton fibre goes through after it is taken from the pod before it is wound upon a spool and ready for the housewife's needle. The Sea Island cotton is used for thread on account of the length of the fibre. The first thing that is done with the cotton is to subject it to the "picker" process, by which the cotton from several bales is mixed to secure uniformity. During the picker process much waste, in the form of dust, dirt and short fibres, is separated from the good fibres by the picker. Next the picked cotton is wound on a machine, in sheets or laps, into a roll.

The next process is the carding, by which the sheets of cotton are combed or run out into long parallel fibres. The cotton is next seen drawn through a trumpet-shaped opening, which condenses it into a single thread or sliver. Then eight such slivers are run together into one, six of the strands thus produced are drawn into one, and again six of the strands from the last drawing are combined into one.

Then comes the slubbing or fast "roving" process, which consists of widening the strand and bobbin. Two strands are twisted and again wound on a bobbin. After a number of other twistings and windings, during which the strand is gradually reduced in size until it begins to assume a thread-like appearance, two strands of this fine "roving" are run together and twisted, under considerable tension, on a bobbin that makes 7,000 revolutions a minute. Two of the cords thus produced are then wound together on a spool, and then twisted from that spool to another, and then three threads of two cords each are twisted together, forming six-cord thread. One who has followed the process sees the cotton gradually transformed from a wide band or sheet of loose cotton to a thread that will pass through the eye of a needle.

The six-cord thread is at last taken from bobbin and reeled into a skein, in which form it is bleached or dyed. Then it is wound back from the skein upon a big spool, from which it is supplied to little white birch spools, upon which it is wound in regular courses, and is then ready for the market. The machine that regulates the last winding measures the number of yards wound on each spool. The spools are made of various sizes, to hold from 200 to 12,000 yards of thread. The labels that decorate the ends of the spools when they are sold are last put on. They are cut and pasted on by machinery with great rapidity.

Hindoo Cotton Weaver at his Loom.

The Hindoo loom consists of two bamboo rollers—one for the warp and another for the woven cloth—and a pair of heddles for parting the warp in the decussation of the woof. The shuttle performs the double office of shuttle and lay for driving home the parallel yarns.

The *Tanty* (weaver) carries this rude apparatus to any tree which may afford a comfortable shade. There he digs a hole large enough to receive his legs and the lower part of the gear or treadles; he then stretches his warp by fastening his two bamboo rollers at a proper distance from each other with pins into the turf; the treadles he fastens to some convenient branch of the tree overhead; he inserts his great toes into two loops under the gear to serve him for treadles; he finally sheds the warp, draws the weft, and afterwards strikes it up close to the weft with his long shuttle, which thus performs the office of a bobbin.

Consumption of Cotton Goods.

The world, it is estimated, uses probably about 12,000,000 bales of cotton of 480 pounds, commercial weight, annually. The yearly consumption of cotton goods in the United States is stated to average about fifteen pounds per capita, and of the entire world over three and under four pounds per capita. The portion of the world's cotton product, worked on modern machinery, does not exceed 7,000 000 bales. Of the whole force of labor engaged in specific cotton manufactures in this country—numbering in 1880, 172,000—about 160,000 were employed in making woven goods and yarns for our home consumption. It is also calculated that it would take 16,000,000 persons to make the same number of yarns by hand that these 172,000 turned out through the use of improved machinery. Calculating the present average per acre, the cotton of the world could be produced on less than 25,000,000 acres. Our export trade of cotton fabrics takes about seven to eight per cent. of our annual manufactured product.

Consumption of Twine.

Few persons have an idea of the enormous consumption of twine in this country. One of the greatest demands for the article comes from the farmers, who consume 35,000 tons annually upon self-binding harvesters. Allowing five pounds to the mile, this would be equal to a string long enough to go more than six times around the earth. It takes a length of about three feet of twine to tie a bundle of straw. The farmer sits on his machine, drives alone through his grain field, and without any assistance cuts, bundles and ties twelve acres of wheat grain per day.

Mill-Brands of British Cottons.

Few cottons in England are known by the name of the factory which produced them. The yarn is mostly spun in one establishment, woven in another, and finished in a third. In this country the yarns are spun and the goods woven usually in the same factory, and the cloth, whether sold in the gray or bleached, is marketed under the name of the factory in which it is made. This also applies to calicoes.

Our Cotton Goods Trade Forty Years Ago.

About forty years ago the dry goods commission houses were mostly centred in Boston for the sale of domestic cottons mainly, such as brown and bleached shirtings and sheetings, prints, ticking, etc. In Philadelphia they manufactured what was called "blue goods," which included checks, denims, stripes, etc. The general trade of the country were then obliged to make visits to the two markets—Boston and Philadelphia—to obtain their supplies of cottons. They had to go to Boston to buy their brown and bleached sheetings and shirtings and printed goods, mostly calicoes. They returned to New York and bought their imported goods, and then went to Philadelphia on their way home, and bought their lines of checks, denims, stripes, ticks, etc.

It was then suggested, for the convenience of country merchants, that the commission houses doing business in Boston and Philadelphia should send agents or open branches in New York City. At first the Boston merchants, who were the agents of the Eastern mills, opposed the project, and only a few of them could be induced to open small offices in New York.

But it was soon discovered that in the small offices opened in New York a larger business was transacted in the same given time than was done by the parent houses in the East, and so one house after another, and mill after mill, opened agencies in New York for the sale of the goods which they represented or manufactured, and the business soon developed into very extensive proportions.

The prices of nearly all kinds of textiles in those early days were much higher than they are now. No good American calico could be procured for less than $12\frac{1}{2}$ cents a yard, and some of it even at that price was often found to be steam colors instead of being printed with madder.

The best and choicest foreign calicoes brought from 20 to 30 cents a yard, and even higher prices.

English Cotton Blankets and Cotton Flannels.

In England there is a heavy cloth woven from coarse (waste) yarns named cotton blankets and cotton flannels. This fabric passes through a razing machine in which its surface is scratched by pointed steel teeth. It is largely exported.

Cotton and Hemp Twine and Shoe Thread.

It is estimated that there are about $8,000,000 worth of flax and hemp strings made in this country every year, not the big sorts, such as lines, ropes, cables and hawsers, but just such strings as are lumped together under the broad name of twines. And, besides, there are great quantities of cotton strings, and here and there still a few paper ones, though the latter—invented when cotton was high priced during the war, and then quite common—are now seldom seen.

There are eight twine factories in the country: three in the upper part of New York, two in Masachusetts, two in New Jersey, and one (the largest) in New York city. The latter employs 800 hands, and turns out 14,000 pounds per diem of finished twines and shoe thread, ranging in value from 14c. to $1.50 per pound. In addition to these eight, there are scattered through the Eastern States several small establishments, but there is none, large or small, in the West or South.

Cost of Operating Southern and Northern Cotton Mills.

Comparison of the cost of running a weaving room of 500 looms in the South and 500 looms on the same class of goods in Philadelphia, Pa., is given as follows:

Southern Mill: 500 looms; overseer, $18 per week; second hand, $12 per week; 10 fixers, $90; 4 filling boys, $12 per week; 2 sweepers, $8 per week; total, $140. Production of Southern weaving room, 156,250 yards of domestic checks, 42 picks to the inch, weight about 5 yards to the pound; warp and filling about number 15 at 50 yards to the cut give 3,125 cuts at 30c. per cut, $937.50. This is a trifle over 50 yards per day. Some Southern mills will run close up to 60. Running expenses South, $140; weavers' pay South, $937,50; total, $1,077.

Philadelphia Mill: 500 looms; overseer, $18 per week; 7 loom fixers at $15 per week, amounting to $105; filling boys, $12; total, $135; second hands are unknown in Philadelphia mills. Production per week of domestic checks, 500 looms; 42 yards per day, each loom 126,000 yards, divide by 50 yards for each cut, $1,512; running expenses per week, $135; total, $1,647.

Hand Loom.

The following represents the hand loom in its simplest form:

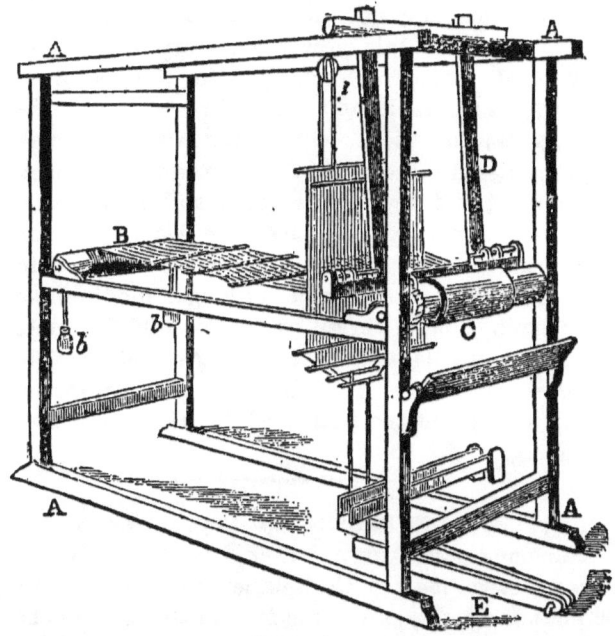

A A is the frame of the loom, and is of no other use than to hold the working parts in their proper position. At each end of the frame two rollers are placed, B C, so that they will readily turn on their axis; and from one to the other the threads of the *warp* are attached, and kept tight by the weights *b b*. The warp threads are wound around the roller B, which is called the *beam* or *yarn-roll*, only as much of each thread being left unwound as will reach the other roller, C, which is the *cloth-beam*, to which the ends are fastened, and upon which the cloth is wound as it is woven. The next step is to divide the warp thread into two equal sets by raising up every alternate one, and inserting between a smooth rod of wood to prevent them entangling or returning to their former position. This separation takes place before the final fixing of the ends of the threads to the cloth-beam, because, previous to that, each thread must be passed through a small loop in a perpendicular thread called the *heald*. The united action of the two healds opens the space between the two sets of warp threads, and this space is called the *shed*, and through it is thrown the *shuttle*, a small boat-like instrument which carries the thread of the *weft*. The *harness* in a loom is that portion of the apparatus by which the warp threads are moved to make the decussation.

Cotton Warp Yarn.

Warp yarn is generally stronger than weft, and the hardness is generally obtained by extra twisting of the thread. Owing to this peculiarity, warp yarn is generally called "twist." For heavy sizing purposes a soft spun twist is advisable, and one made out of the harder and wiry stapled cottons. The spongy and size-absorbent properties are obtained at the expense of the strength of the yarn, and therefore a good sizing twist often winds badly. The color of the warp yarn is not important, and therefore whiter cottons are reserved for weft. Fine twists are spun out of longer and finer cottons, forming a close thread, which is used for better classes of cloth lightly sized. Strength and elasticity are great advantages in twist, and these properties should be obtained and preserved for the last process of weaving.

Cotton Skips and Cops.

In England cotton warp yarn is generally received by the manufacturers from the spinners in skips of 200 to 250 pounds weight, and in the form of a cop. This has a cylindrical formation, coned at each end, the more pointed end, on which the yarn is wound, being called the nose, and the opposite end the cop bottom. The best spinners make the cop about $7\frac{1}{2}$ inches long and $1\frac{3}{8}$ inches in diameter.

In each twist of the yarn preference is given to the most even thread, round and free from motes, knotty places and snarls; the latter is recognized by slack ends at the mule, tortion of the thread taking up the loose yarn in the form of a twisted cop.

A similar effect, called a "snick," is caused by loose ends and inferior traverses at the winding frame, but wherever caused the fault is most annoying to the weaver, and deteriorative to the weft which is intended for printing, as the loops arise after the weft has received the impression of the pattern, showing white specks of an objectionable character. The twisted cop should be of full dimensions, firm and hard, cop free from loose ends, and being clear from apertures at the bottom of the winder's skewer. Any fault in this respect causes an increased percentage of waste most objectionable to manufacturers.

Cotton Yarn Calculations.

The fineness of cotton yarns is indicated by the counts (otherwise numbers or grist). The counts refer to the number of hanks in the pound, avoirdupois. "A cotton hank is always 840 yards, and, therefore, if we speak of 10s, we refer to yarn of which 10 hanks, or 8,400, weigh one pound; or, in referring to 36, of that which 36x840, or 30,240, weigh one pound. This applies to either twist or weft. The cotton yarn measure is: 120 yards equal 1 lea; 7 leas, or 840 yards, equal 1 hank; and the cotton yarn weight is peculiar, being an avoirdupois pound divided into pennyweights and ounces, as in Troy weight: 24 grains equal 1 pennyweight; $437\frac{1}{2}$ grains equal 18 11-48 pennyweights, equal one ounce; 7,000 grains equal 16 ounces, equal 1 pound; 1s are taken as a standard with 840 yards in 7,000 grains, and a higher count means finer yarn; then 840 yards of say 2s would weigh 35,000 grains, or 70s would weigh 100 grains.

"If we measure a hank of yarn and find that it weighs 100 grains, then 7,000 divided by 100 gives the counts. It is convenient in wrapping yarn to measure 840 yards; therefore a lea of yards is taken as the standard length for 1s, and also the proportionate weight equal to 1,000 grains. The wrapping roll is $1\frac{1}{2}$ yards in circumference, and by revolving eighty times we can wind 120 yards from a cop placed in the machine. Suppose this lea of 120 yards weighs 25 grains, then 1,000-25s equal 40s. Should less than a lea be taken, say 60 yards, the 500 grains must be the dividend. Generally the grade to obtain the counts of any yarn, 120 yards are weighed.

"In French, the cotton standard is 1,000 metres in 500 grammes—equivalent to 992.4 yards in 1 pound. Thus 1.18 1s in English would be 1s in French. To transfer cotton measure to any other, take the cotton count and equivalent inversely to the cotton in the hanks."

Only Two Ways of Producing a Heavy Fabric.

A well-known cotton goods manufacturer says that to produce a heavy fabric there are only two ways of doing it—either the use of thick, bulky threads or the use of an increased number of fine ones. "If we use bulky threads our fabric must present an appearance of coarseness, no matter what may be the order of interweaving, and we have no possible means of reducing the coarseness. If we use fine threads it is more than likely that the order of interweaving will prevent the introduction of as many threads as will produce the weight of fabric we desire."

Difference Between Mule and Throstle Twist.

Mule twist is used for weaving muslins and the finest kinds of cotton goods. The essential difference between this and water-twist is, that the mule produces much finer articles than can possibly be made upon throstles, at the same time making a softer thread. As it requires much less power to run the same number of mule spindles than throstles, the manufacturer spins every kind of yarn which he can upon the mule; but it will produce only the softest kinds of thread. It will spin all numbers, from the lowest up to 300 hanks to the pound.

The yarn spun upon the throstle has its fibre closer twisted than that spun upon the mule, and is more esteemed for certain purposes, especially for making thread, than the latter. Throstle yarn is stronger and more even than mule yarn, and better adapted for warps; but the range of throstles is limited, and the counts seldom exceed 40's, though throstles are made capable of spinning yarns up to 80's or 100's. The reason is that the fine thread has not strength to stand the "drag" required to wind the yarn on the bobbin.

The mule, on the other hand, will spin both twist and weft, and as high as No. 100's, or more, while still finer numbers can be spun by hand mules. Mule yarn is softer and more woolly in texture than throstle yarn, which arises from the vibration of the thread as the carriage is drawn out from the rollers.

Comparative Strength of Cotton Mule Twist.

The following table, prepared by an English expert, will give a general idea of the comparative strength of mule twists having for American cotton the standard turns in—*i. e.*, square root of counts multiplied by $3\frac{3}{4}$:

20's American Cotton			....	equal 80	pounds.
30's	"	"	....	" 54	"
40's	"	"	....	" 40	"
40's Egyptian	"	....	" 50	"
50's American	"	....	" 28	"
50's Egyptian	"	....	" 37	"
60's	"	"	....	" 30	"
70's	"	"	....	" 36	"

In yarn diameters of the threads do not vary inversely as the counts, but inversely as a square root of the counts.

Carding, Drawing and Roving.

The accompanying cut gives a more or less graphic illustration of the operations of the carding, drawing and roving of cotton.

The carding engine derives its name from the cards by which its functions are fulfilled. Each fibre of cotton is more or less twisted around those near it, and the object of the carding process is to separate these fibres and to lay them all in parallel directions, because if this were not done the yarn produced would be uneven and knotty.

The sliver or long ribbon of cotton produced from the carding machine has to undergo the process of "drawing," that is, it must be made of an even thickness throughout, and its width diminished. This is effected by the drawing frame. The sliver thus produced is next converted into "roving." This is effected by giving a moderate amount of twist to the cotton to form a yarn of about the thickness of an ordinary lead pencil. The next process is spinning. On the right of the above plate the roving frame is shown, with the carding and drawing machines on the left. The above cut represents machinery in use in some of our older cotton mills, modern fixtures being lighter, more complex and automatic.

Bundling Cotton Yarn.

In order that cotton hanks may be conveniently packed for sending to market, they are squeezed into a *bundling-press*. All hanks are the same length, 840 yards; all are weighed by the same unit of weight, 1 lb.; and the number attached to each kind denotes the number of hanks of that kind which go to a pound. Usually about ten pounds, of whatever number or fineness, are pressed together to form a *bundle* ; and from thirty to forty of these bundles are *pressed* together into a *bale*, which then weighs from 300 to 500 lbs.

Sizing or Dressing Cotton.

Cotton is never woven in its natural state. It always receives a dressing or coating of some kind of liquid size, which is allowed to dry before the weaving begins. The object is to diminish the roughness on the fibrous surface of the yarns, and thereby facilitate the weaving. The yarns from several rollers are unwound and made to pass through a vessel of hot liquid size, and then between rollers, which squeeze the glutinous composition into the very heart of the thread. Thence the yarns pass over *drying cylinders*, made of sheet iron or copper, heated within by steam pipes. This quickly dries the size, and prepares the yarn to be wound upon the *weaver's beam*, a **roller which** receives uniform layers from end to end.

Tenison of Cotton Fibres.

The average length of staple Sea Island cotton is nearly two inches, while that of Surat is but a little over one inch. The tension strength of this cotton is, however, much inferior to that of many other cloths, breaking with 83 grains, while Pernambuco and Surat stand a weight of 140 grains. It is said that the amount of twisting in cotton thread is a very important element in the establishment of its strength, and that the Dacca muslins of India, owe a large part of their superiority in lightness and strength to the lightness of the twist of the delicate film of which they are composed. According to Dr. Watson, the average number of twists in the French muslin is 68; in the English, 56; in the Dacca they amount to 110. Some idea of the lightness of this Dacca muslin may be inferred from the fact that a piece of it, one yard wide and ten yards long, weighs only a little over three ounces.

Displacement of Labor in the Cotton Goods Industry by Machinery.

The cotton goods industry of the United States offers perhaps as striking an illustration as any of the apparent displacement of labor by machinery. With a hand-loom a weaver used to weave from 60 to 80 picks per minute in weaving cotton cloth of good quality, with twenty threads of twist to each one-quarter square inch. A power loom now weaves 180 picks per minute of the same kind of cloth. Even in power machinery, a weaver formerly tended but one loom. Now, one weaver minds all the way from two to ten power looms, according to the grade of goods. The ratio of cost per pound for labor of common cotton cloth for the years 1828 and 1880 was as 6.77 to 3.31, wages for the same dates being as 2.62 to 4.84. The average consumption of cotton, which indicates the standard of life as well as any one item, was per capita of total population for the year 1831, 5.90 pounds, while in 1880, the consumption rose to 13.91 pounds, this being exclusive of exports. In Great Britian in 1833 the consumption, exclusive of exports, was 6.62 pounds per capita, and in 1880, 7.75 pounds. Working time has been decreased on an average 12 per cent.

Common Cotton Fabrics of the World Compared.

The common cotton fabrics of England, Belgium and Germany could now hardly be sold in the United States at any price. French cottons, however, are better. The calicoes produced in the United States for the masses are better, finer in color, and more varied in style than those made in Europe. In this country, the sizing up on the warp, in order to weave it, is made from corn or potato starch, which contributes about 2 1-2 to 5 per cent. of the weight in the gray color. In England, pure sizing is made of wheat flour. One hundred pounds there has been known to be used to one hundred pounds of cotton. Sizing is intended to lose 10 to 12 per cent. of weight on first washing. English cotton fabrics exported or used by the working classes at home are generally loaded with 10 to 40 per cent. clay and other substances.

Mills in United States Making Brown, Bleached and Colored Cottons.

On a more or less close calculation it is estimated that there are about the following number of mills engaged directly and indirectly in the production of brown, bleached and colored cottons, print cloths and prints in the United States:

Mills making brown and bleached cottons........... 125
Mills making brown, bleached and colored cottons.. 150
Mills making colored cottons....................... 250
Mills making print cloths.......................... 70
Mills making prints................................ 15

The above, if added together, would make 610 establishments, but the number is not so large as that, for the reason that many of the same make in varying quantity all the different classes of cottons described, while others are devoted exclusively to specific manufactures, such as brown and bleached sheetings and shirtings, or brown, bleached and colored cottons, or print cloths, or prints, and are necessarily contained within each respective classification. However, the above exhibit shows one thing, that all the various regular and standard tickets, as well as fancy brands of brown, bleached and colored woven cottons made in this country, are produced by these factories, and that the names of the same have been so multiplied in number and variety within the past few years that they now extend well into the thousands in number.

While diversification of kind, quality and style of our domestic cotton fabrics is steadily and rapidly enlarging, it is a question whether they will keep pace in this direction with the increase in the variety of the fancy names given to them. As an illustration: one make of brown, bleached or colored cottons that has a standard reputation will not only be maintained and sold under its own original and regular ticket, but to satisfy the caprices or contingencies of the trade in various parts of the country, will have probably a dozen different fancy names that bear no relation whatever to the original cognomen. This is due to the keen and close competition on the part of both the jobbing and the retail trades, which reduces sometimes the profits of both to such a low ebb, that they cannot afford to carry the goods unless they have some protection or compensation in the way of fancy tickets that are not strictly competitive so far as brand is concerned.

The Mule-Jenny.

The above gives the front and side views of the *mule-jenny*. For the spinning of fine cotton yarns this machine is generally used. The bobbins containing the cotton rovings are placed on a fixed frame; the spindles by which these rovings are to be twisted into yarn are on a movable frame; the movable frame, by traveling four or five feet outward, then an equal distance backward, and so on alternately, stretches and attenuates the threads. The two sets of operations, elongating and spinning, succeed each other with exquisite regularity; 600 or 700 threads, all arranged parallel, being managed by self-regulating mechanism. *Mule-yarn*, as it is technically called, being twisted more softly and carefully than *throstle-yarn*, is suitable for the weft, or cross-threads of coarse goods, and for both warp and weft of fine goods.

Horse Power for Propelling Cotton Spinning Machinery.

Baird gives the following illustration of a horse-power in cotton spinning:

A one horse-power is calculated to drive, at an average speed, 100 throstle spindles, on No. 25 cotton-yarn twist, including the necessary preparation.

A one horse-power will drive 250 mule spindles, with preparation, on No. 25 yarn filling.

A one horse-power will drive 500 mule spindles, with preparation, on No. 60 yarn filling, and for intermediate numbers in proportion.

A one horse-power will drive 12 power-looms, with warping, sizing, etc.

U. S. Import Duties on Strictly Cotton Goods.

According to the tariff act of March 3, 1883, the following are the import duties on strictly cotton goods:

UNBLEACHED COTTONS.

Not over 100 threads to square inch, value not over 8c. per square yard, 2½c. per square yard.

Not over 100 threads to square inch, value over 8c. per square yard, 40 per cent.

Over 100, not over 200, threads to square inch, value not over 8c. per square yard, 3c. per square yard.

Over 100, not over 200, threads to square inch, value over 8c. per square yard, 40 per cent.

Over 200 threads to square inch, value not over 10c. per square yard, 4c. per square yard.

Over 200 threads to square inch, value over 10c. per square yard, 40 per cent.

BLEACHED COTTONS.

Not over 100 threads to square inch, value not over 10c. per square yard, 3½c. per square yard.

Not over 100 threads to square inch, value over 10c. per square yard, 40 per cent.

Over 100, not over 200, threads to square inch, value not over 10c. per square yard, 4c. per square yard.

Over 100, not over 200, threads to square inch, value not over 10c. per square yard, 40 per cent.

Over 200 threads to square inch, value not over 12c. per square yard, 5c. per square yard.

DYED, COLORED, STAINED OR PRINTED COTTONS.

Not over 100 threads to square inch, value not over 13c. per square yard, 4½c. per square yard.

Not over 100 threads to square inch, value not 13c. per square yard, 40 per cent.

Over 100 and not over 200 threads to square inch, value not over 13c. per square yard, 5c. per square yard.

Over 100 and not over 200 threads to square inch, value over 13c. per square yard, 40 per cent.

Over 200 threads to square inch, value not over 15c. per square yard, 6c. per square yard.

Over 200 threads to square inch, value over 15c. per square yard, 40 per cent.

Cotton cloth, the threads of which are incapable of being counted under a glass, or actually separated, not otherwise specified, 35 per cent.

U. S. Import Duty on Cotton Galloons, Gimps, Etc.

Cotton goods, such as galloons, gimps, gloves, goring, unhemmed handkerchiefs (single or in strap), webbing, suspenders or braces, and all goods made of cotton, not otherwise specified, 35 per cent.

Cotton damask embroideries, handkerchiefs (hemmed), insertings, laces, lace window curtains, trimmings, velvet, and cotton hosiery, fashioned, narrowed, or shaped wholly or in part by knitting machines or frames, or knit by hand, 40 per cent.

One Pound of Cotton Yarn Reaching 1,000 Miles.

An English cotton manufacturing concern some years ago produced the finest, that is, the thinnest, cotton yarn ever seen—700s—of which muslin was made. The same firm has produced since, yarn of 2,150, which is much finer than that of the famous Dacca muslin. A pound of the finest Sea Island cotton spun of this fineness would be 1,000 miles in length.

Standard Grain Sacks and Bags.

One hundred and forty pound jute export sacks should be from the best material, double stitched, not using less than an equivalent to 40x49-inch mangled or crape-finished material, weighing not less than 12 ounces per yard, of 40 inches in width, or 16 ounces for the complete bag. If from starched or sized material, the complete bag should not weigh less than 17 ounces.

Two hundred and eighty pound jute export sacks should be from the best material, double stitched, not using less than an equivalent to 50x63-inch mangled or crape-finished material, weighing not less than 15 ounces per yard, of 50 inches in width, or 25 ounces for the complete bag. If from starched or sized material, the complete bag should weigh not less than $26\frac{1}{4}$ ounces.

Seamless jute sacks must be from same heft and quality of material, etc., but require 4 per cent. less material, and may weigh 4 per cent. less.

One hundred and forty pound cotton export sacks should be double stitched, best drill or osnaburg, free from starch or sizing, using of drill not less than an equivalent to 40x47 inches, or if osnaburg not less than $37\frac{1}{2}$x$51\frac{1}{2}$ inches to material, the complete bag weighing not less than $9\frac{1}{4}$ ounces.

Comparative Expenses of Manufacturing in 1860 and 1880

Mr. Edward Atkinson, the well-known statistician, in referring to the comparative expenses of cotton manufacturing in the United States in 1860 and 1880, says:

"While the cost of labor was higher in 1880 than in 1860, it has been reduced in the finest fabric by the greater productive power of the machinery. The fabrics upon which by far the largest part of the spindles and looms of the country are operated may be divided substantially into the following classes:

1. The printing cloth 28 inches wide and 7 yards to the pound. The cost of mill labor in making this fabric, including the salaries, wages or earnings of every one employed, is now less than 1 cent, or half a penny, per yard.

2. The heavy sheeting, 36 inches wide, and the heavy drill, 30 inches wide, each weighing from $2\frac{3}{4}$ to 3 yards to the pound. The cost of mill labor in making these fabrics is about $1\frac{1}{4}$ cents per yard.

3. Shirtings and sheetings, 30 to 36 inches wide, Nos. 20 to 30 yarns, each weighing from 3 to 4 yards to the pound. The cost of mill labor in these goods is from $1\frac{1}{2}$ to 2 cents per yard.

4. The fine sheeting or shirting, from 30 to 40 inches wide, Nos. 30 to 40 yarns, weighing from 3 to 4 yards to the pound. The cost of mill labor in these goods is from $1\frac{1}{2}$ to 3 cents per yard

5. Fabrics of similar kind to the above from 1 to 3 yards wide.

6. Heavy cotton duck, cotton grain bags, cotton hose and other special articles.

7. Blue denims, stripes, tickings, brown denims and duck, and other heavy colored goods, substantial ginghams, cottonades and other fancy woven fabrics of medium and heavy weight.

These seven classes comprise more than 95 per cent. of our cotton fabrics of weight; to these are to be added lawns, woven fabric of light weight for dresses and spool cotton.

In respect of one-half of these fabrics, being those of heavier grade, our proximity to the cotton field, computed at not less than half a cent per pound—often three quarters—enables the New England manufacturer to pay 15 to 20 per cent. higher wages, and yet make the goods, other things being equal, at the same cost as his competitor in Lancashire. On a large portion of other kinds of cotton this advantage in the cost of cotton is from 10 to 15 per cent.

The Throstle.

The above cut represents the front and side views of the throstle. Bobbins full of prepared cotton roving are placed on the top of the machine. Rollers and bobbins and flyers draw out the fibres, elongating and attenuating them, and at the same time twisting them tightly into a compact yarn, well adapted for the warp or long threads of woven goods. In the technical language of a cotton mill, the throstle is used for the hard, coarse yarns up to about No. 40.

Fabrics Produced from Different Varieties of Cotton.

According to a well-known authority who has closely studied the manufacture of cotton in all its various stages, in India, England, the United States and other countries, "the finest qualities of cotton (the Sea Island class) are made into lace and muslin of the most beautiful texture.

"Other qualities—Egyptian, New Orleans and 'Boweds' (Bowed Georgia, etc.)—are made into cambrics and calicoes for printing, as well as into shirtings, sheetings and fustians, and, when mixed with the better kinds of waste, into bed covers and heavy fabrics.

"But East Indian cotton is rarely at present used alone, except for the lowest purposes, because of its general inferiority, and it is generally disposed in adulteration."

Cost and Selling Prices of Various Kinds of American Cottons for a Series of Years.

The following tabular statements of the selling prices of various kinds and classes of cottons, together with the labor cost involved in the production of the same, are from the United States Census reports of 1880. They have been prepared by leading manufacturers, and are actual transcripts from their books.

A leading firm gives the following selling prices of sheetings and bags in 1870, 1875 and 1880:

SHEETINGS AND BAGS.

	40-in Sheeting, per yd. Cents.	77-in Sheeting per yd. Cents.	16 ounce 2-bush Bags, each. Cents.
1870	15	37	31
1875	12	27	26
1880	9	23	20

The cost of labor in producing the same at the three different periods is given in the annexed statement:

	40-in Sheeting, per yd. Cents.	77-in Sheeting, per yd. Cents.	16 ounce 2-bush Bags, each. Cents.
1870	.03 46-100	.06 48-100	.06 7-100
1875	.03 20-100	.05 75-100	.05
1880	.02 10-100	.03 28-100	.03 11-100

As illustrating the percentage of wages to total cost of the production of such goods in the years named, the following showing is presented:

	40-in Sheeting, per cent.	77-in Sheeting, per cent.	16 ounce 2-bu. bags, per cent.
1870	29	24	20
1875	35	31	25
1880	32	25	19

WIDE SHEETING.

The accompanying table from the same firm also gives the selling price, labor cost and percentage of wages to cost per yard for wide sheeting in 1875-80:

	Cents.
Selling price	0.06¼
Labor cost	0.01 21-100
Percentage of wages to cost	0.02 15-100

SHEETINGS, DRILLING AND BATTING.

An Indiana cotton manufacturing company gives the following as the selling prices of their sheetings, drilling and batting for the years named:

	Sheeting, pr yd. Cts.	Drilling, pr yd. Cts.	Batting, pr yd. Cts.
1875	.09	.09½	.10
1880	.07½	.08	.10

GRAIN BAGS.

As regards the selling prices, cost, etc., of bags, a Kentucky bag manufacturer furnishes the following:

	—Selling price.—		— —Labor cost.—	
	Grain sacks, per 100.	Picking sacks per 100.	Grain sacks, per 100.	Picking sacks, per 100.
1870	$33 00	$—	$6 50	$—
1875	25 00	40 00	6 00	9 00
1880	20 00	35 00	5 50	8 00

CHEVIOTS, QUILTS, ETC.

Another concern in Kentucky also gives the following statement of the labor cost of various classes of cottons in 1870, 1875 and 1880:

	Ginghams, per yd.	Crochet quilts, each.	Marseilles quilts, each.	Basket cheviots, per yd.
1860	.17	....	....	....
1865	....	....	....	....
1870	14	$2 00	....	....
1875	10	1 65	$3 60	12½
1880	10	1 12	2 50	10½

SEERSUCKERS, FANCY DUCK, ETC.

A leading cotton factory in Maine sends the annexed statement of the selling prices of ginghams, quilts, cheviots, etc.:

	Ginghams. yard.	Dress goods. yard.	Basket sheeting. yard.	Fancy duck. yard.
1870	04.83	....	...	....
1875	04 03	...	04.83	....
1880	03 86	04.24	03.69	03 22

	Cottons. yard.	Seersuckers. yard.	Cheviot quilts. each.	Marseilles quilts. each.
1870	05 99	07.23	32 45	....
1875	06 02	....	37.07	$1 46.72
1880	04.06	04.43	26.28	1.03.04

SHIRTINGS AND SHEETINGS.

Another leading cotton manufacturing establishment in Maine gives the following synopsis of the selling prices, etc., of the shirtings and sheetings which it produces, covering a number of years:

	Selling price			
	Shirting, per yard.		Sheeting, per yard.	
	36-in.	40-in.	42-in.	48-in.
1870	$0.14	$0.15	—	—
1875	11¾	12	$0.14	$0.15
1880	08	09	13	13

	Labor cost			
	Shirting per yard.		Shirting per yard.	
	36-in.	40-in.	42-in.	48-in.
1870	$02.71	$03.11	—	—
1875	02.28	02.50	$02.71	$03.04
1880	01.69	01.69	01.76	02 03

	Percentage of wages to cost.			
	Shirting		Sheeting	
	36-inch. per cent.	40-inch. per cent.	42-inch. per cent.	48-inch. per cent.
1870	22	22	—	—
1875	26	26	26	26
1880	25	25	25	25

DRILLING, DYED DUCK, ETC.

From a cotton manufacturing concern in Maryland, which has been in existence since 1808, making standard lines of sheetings, twills and ducks, the annexed tabular statement is presented:

	Selling price.			
	Four-yard sheeting pr yd.	Standard sheeting pr yd.	Three-yard drilling pr yd	Dyed duck pr yd.
1830	$0.08	$0.10¾	...	....
1835	...	12	....	....
1840	....	09	....	....
1845	....	06	....	....
1850	....	08	....	....
1855	....	05¾	....	....
1860	....	06	....	....
1865	45	..	....	....

	Cost of labor per yard, cotton cloth weighing 3 yds to lb.	Percentage of wages to cost of cotton cloth.
1830	$0.03.26	28.50
1835	02.58	26 10
1840	02.03	22.75
1845	01.88	27.05
1850	01.73	....
1855	02.09	29 00
1860	02.40	23.48
1865	03.36	25

SELLING PRICES OF PRINT CLOTH FOR A SERIES OF YEARS.

The latter firm also gives the selling price, labor cost, and percentage of wages to cost of a yard of 64x64 print cloths covering the same periods of time, as below:

	Selling price per yard. Cents.	Labor cost per yard. Cents.	Percentage of wages to cost.
1855	05.20	01.45	35
1860	05.13	01.35	30
1865	12.27	01.45	15
1870	09.33	01.96	28
1875	05.36	01.75	31
1880	04.40	01.23	32

The foregoing establishment worked their employees 11 hours per day fom 1850 to 1859, and since that time to 1880, 10¾ hours per day, and paying them cash monthly.

EXTRA 64X64 CLOTHS.

The foregoing is supplemented by the following additional showing from a well-known print cloth factory in the same State, which produces extra 64x64 cloths:

	Selling price, per yard. Cents.	Labor cost, per yard. Cents.	Percentage of wages to cost per cent. Cents.
1870	06.8	01.75	27.5
1875	05.6	01.43	28.5
1880	04.6	01.01	32.5

The manufacturing concern last noted paid their employees cash and worked them only ten hours per day.

COST OF COTTON IN A YARD OF PRINT CLOTH.

From a New Hampshire print cloth manufacturing firm, which was established away back in the forties and which produces 64x64 cloths in grey, using warp No. 30 and filling No. 38, we have the following statement of the cost of the cotton necessary to make a yard of 64x64 print cloth:

A POPULAR BRAND OF TICKING.

Another cotton manufacturing establishment in New Hampshire, making tickings, denims, cotton flannels, shirtings, stripes and ginghams, gives the following exhibit of the labor cost per yard for making one of the most popular brands of ticking produced in this country, for two periods, with twenty-five years intervening:

Per yard.
1855... .02.78
1880... .02.42

This establishment was founded in 1826, and states that the wages of their employees were 25 per cent. lower in 1855 than they paid in 1880, and that by the utilization of improved machinery they were enabled to accomplish the reduction in the labor cost as above in 1880.

SELLING PRICES OF TICKING, ETC.

The same factory also gives the subjoined list of the selling prices, labor cost, etc., per yard of ticking and gingham which it produced in the years named:

	Selling price. Tick'g, p r yd.	Gingh'm. per yd.	Labor cost Tick'g per yd.	Gingh'm. per yd	Percentage of wages to cost of t'k'g, pe cent.
1845	14½	....	03.97	....	28
1850	14½	....	02.38	....	25
1855	14¾	....	02.87	....	25
1860	15½	....	02.41	....	20
1865	77	....	02.65	....	10
1870	31¼	17	04.28	04 44	19
1875	21.15	10.39	04	03 43	22
1880	16	08	02.42	02.95	28

YARNS, TWINES, ETC.

A cotton factory in Missouri, which makes sheetings, yarns, twines, batts and bags, which have large sale in the West and Southwest, furnishes the subjoined list of the selling prices of sheetings, yarns, twines, batts and bags for a series of years:

	Sheet Yd. Cents.	Yarns. Lb. Cents.	Twines. Lb. Cents.	Batts. Lbs. Cents.	Bags. each. Cents.
1860	09	22	19	10@12	20
1865	30	90	..	40@45	65
1870	16	40	35	20@25	30
1875	08	21	20	11@14	21
1880	08½	20	19	09@11	20

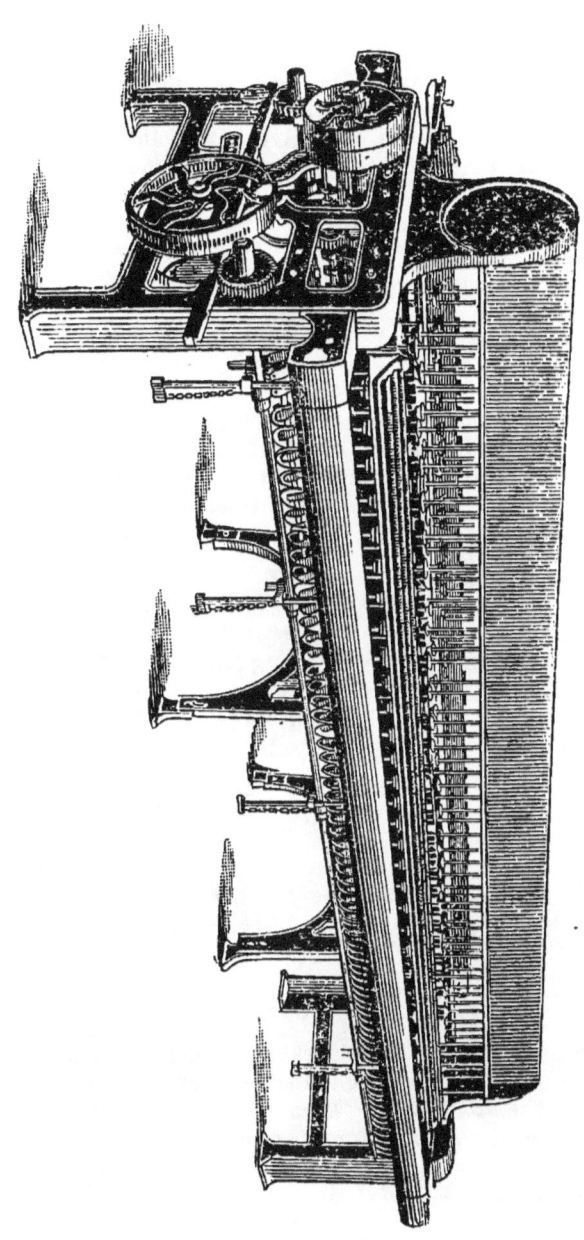

GINGHAMS AND COTTON DRESS GOODS.

A well-known cotton manufacturing concern in Connecticut, which was established in 1824, and which has been in successful operation ever since, says that from "1830 to 1855 all classes of their operatives worked 12 hours per day; from 1855 to 1865 11½ hours, and from 1865 to 1880, 10 to 11 hours per day."

This same concern also gives the following selling prices of ginghams and cotton dress goods for a series of years:

Year.	Ginghams. Pr yd. Cents.	Dress Goods. Pr yd. Cents.	Year.	Ginghams. Pr yd. Cents.	Dress Goods. Pr yd. Cents.
1845	12	....	1865	20	....
1850	12	....	1870	11	....
1855	12	....	1875	09	12½
1860	14	....	1880	10	12½

According to the statement of this concern, "the labor cost for the production of ginghams 1877 was 3.44c per yard, and of cotton dress goods, 3.78c per yard, and wages were 44 per cent. of the total cost of ginghams for that year."

BROWN SHEETING.

A large and well-known cotton mill in the State of Connecticut makes the following transcript of the selling price, labor cost, etc., of brown sheeting, the brand of which is very popular, and largely sold in all markets:

	Selling Price b'wn sheeting per yard Cents.	Labor cost b'wn sheeting per yard Cents.	Percentage of wages to cost of b'wn sheeting.
1864-5	.54	.02 54-100	48
1870	.11	.02 36-100	38
1875	.08	.01 90-100	25
1880	.06	.01 21-100	27

SPOOL COTTON.

Of spool cotton, a celebrated concern in the New England States, which makes several varieties, gives the folllowing range of the selling prices of the same per dozen for a period of years:

	Selling price.
1860	.40 to $1 75
1865	.80 to 1 10
1870	.72 to 80
1875	.55 to 72
1880	.55

WHITE COTTONS.

A cotton factory established in Massachusetts since 1823, which worked its employes twelve hours per day from 1845 to 1859; eleven hours per day from 1859 to 1874, and ten hours per day from 1874 to 1880, making use of the most improved machinery during the periods noted, submits the subjoined statement of the selling prices, etc., of white cottons:

SELLING PRICES AND LABOR COST.

	Selling price		Labor cost	
	per yard.	per lb.	per yard.	per lb.
1845..	....	....	$0.01.517	$0.05.305
1850..	....	....	01.649	06.290
1855..	$0.07.31	$0.25.58	01.583	05.310
1860..	08.55	29.75	01.387	04.330
1865..	25.70	1.12.00	02.562	08.605
1870.	14.30	50.00	02.884	04.615
1875..	11	33.00	02.259	07.008
1880..	09.50	28.30	01.465	04 217

The above concern also states that latterly, through the use of improved machinery, it has not only increased its output and reduced the cost of the same 12 to 15 per cent., but has also diminished the number of its employees 10 to 12 per cent.

PRINTING CLOTHS.

An old and prominent print-cloth and print-manufacturing concern in the same State furnishes the following interesting list of the labor cost per yard of print cloths for every five years intervening between 1850 and 1880:

PRICES.

1850	$.01.74
1855	01.56
1860	01.40
1865	02.65
1870	02 02
1875	01.44
1880	00.87

HOURS OF LABOR.

The hours of labor per day of the employees of this concern, during the time named, were as follows: 1830 to 1845, 12 1-6 hours; 1850 to 1855, 11 54-60 hours; 1855 to 1860, 11 34 60 hours; 1860 to 1870, 11 hours; 1870 to 1880, 10 hours.

COTTON CLOTH.

An establishment in Connecticut submits the following exhibit of the labor cost, etc., of cotton cloth, since 1855:

	Labor cost of cotton cloth per lb. Cents.	Percentage of number yarn used. Cents.	Percentage of wages to cost of cotton cloth
1855	12 22-100	30.00	42.70
1860	09 6-100	25.36	39 20
1865	12 23-100	34.72	15.45
1870	22 2-100	42.83	40.10
1875	13 95-100	35 21	38.70
1880	09 87-100	25.37	36.70

The latter firm also state that the improvements in machinery, in pickers, cards, winders, railway heads, drawing frames, speeders, spinning frames, mules, spoolers, warpers, creels, cylinders, looms, etc., of late years have been very marked and have considerably lessened the general cost of production. The same establishment also says wages have averaged about 25 per cent. of the total cost of production, and divides the latter up as follows:

	Cost, per cent.
Raw material	65
Labor	25
Coloring	10

COTTON WINDOW SHADE CLOTH.

A well-known Delaware cotton manufacturer gives the subjoined selling prices for cotton cloth in the grey, 39 inches wide, counting 52 by 50 picks and weighing 6½ yards to the pound, which is bleached and starched for window makers use:

	Selling price per yd. Cts.
1860	.08
1865	25¼
1870	09 7-16
1875	.06¾
1880	.06½

PLAIDS, DRILLS, ETC.

A cotton factory still further South—in the State of Georgia—submits the following table of selling prices of their sheetings, plaids, etc., for a series of years:

4-4 sheeting per yard. Cents.	Standard plaids. per yard. Cents.	Ball Thread Cents.

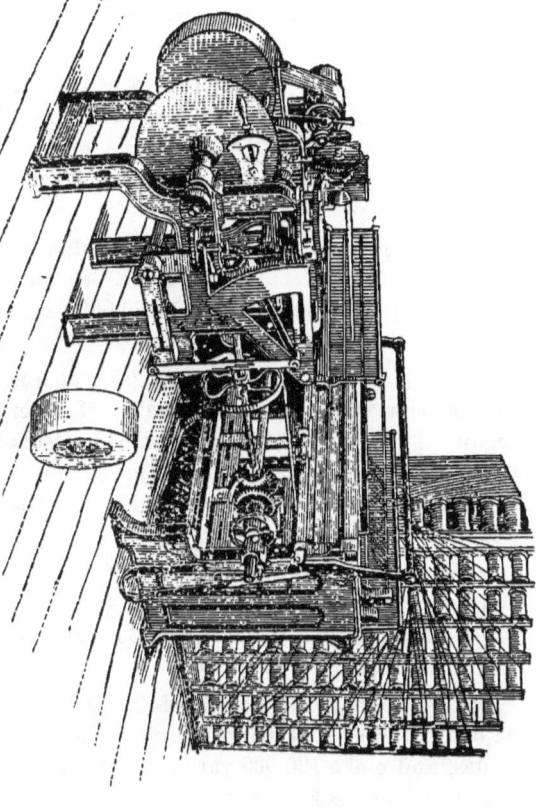

Sectional Warping Machine.

The warping machine is so constructed as to unwind the yarn from the bobbins, and wind it round a large roller, with as much parallelism as possible and an equal degree of tension.

Cotton Manufacturing in Lowell, Mass., in 1835.

The following is taken from a letter dated Lowell, Mass., April 20th, 1835, written by Kirk Boott, the wealthy merchant of Boston, after whom the Boott Cotton Mills are named:

"*The Merrimack Co.*—Capital, $1,500,000; have extensive print works and five cotton mills. They run 34,432 spindles, 1,253 looms, give employment to 1,321 females and 437 males, and make 172,000 yards cloth per week.

"*The Hamilton Co.*—Capital, $900,000; have large printing establishment and three cotton mills. They run about 19,000 spindles, 600 looms, employ about 800 females and 200 males, and make 78,000 yards of prints and drillings per week.

"*The Appleton Co.*—Capital, $500,000; run two mills, between 10,000 and 11,000 spindles, 350 looms, employ 475 females, 70 males, and make 80,000 yards of No. 14 sheetings and shirtings per week.

"*The Lowell Co.*—Capital, $500,000; manufacture cotton, carpets, rugs, negro cloths, etc., of a very superior quality. They run 4,500 or 5,000 spindles in their cotton mills, 140 cotton and 68 carpet looms, employ 330 females, 150 males, and manufacture in the aggregate about 43,000 yards per week.

"*The Suffolk Co.*—Capital, $450,000; run two mills in the manufacture of No. 14 drillings, with 10,240 spindles, 350 looms, give employment to 460 females, 70 males, and make 90,000 yards per week.

"*The Tremont Co.*—Capital, $500,000; run two mills, 11,000 spindles, 400 looms, employ 450 females and 80 males, and make 120,000 yards of No. 14 sheetings and shirtings per week.

"*The Lawrence Co.*—Capital, $1,200,000; went into operation since either of the above. They run at present four cotton mills for the manufacture of sheetings and shirtings, Nos. 14 to 30, 37 to 41 inches wide."

Cleaning Cotton by Hand.

In early times cotton was cleaned from its seeds, etc., by hand, a method, which while it was wholly imperfect, caused also a considerable loss of the fibre.

Equipment of a Modern Cotton Factory.

The following requirements of a modern cotton factory in the way of equipment are given by a British manufacturing authority:

Condensing engine, cylinder 37 inches diameter; stroke of piston, 7 feet; volume of piston space, 53.6 cubic feet; average pressure of steam, 16.73 pounds per square inch; revolutions, 17 per minute; friction of engine and shafting (indicated), 4.75 pounds per square of piston; indicated horse-power, 125; total power = 1; available deducting friction = 717.

(The foregoing has reference to an English mill for driving 22,060 hand mule spindles, with preparation, and 200 looms, with common sizing.)

REMARKS.- Each additional horse-power will drive 305 hand-mule spindles, *with preparation;*
    Or 230 self-acting,
    Or 104 throstle,
    Or 10.5 looms, with common sizing.

Including preparation:
    1 throstle spindle = 3 hand-mule, or 2.25 self-acting, spindles.
    1 self-acting spindle = 1.2 hand-mule spindles.

Exclusive of preparation, taking only the spindle:
    1 throstle spindle = 3.5 hand-mule, or 2.56 self-acting, spindles.
    1 self-acting spindle = 1.375 hand-mule spindles.

The throstles are the common spring, 34 twist, for power-loom weaving; the spindles 4,000 times per minute. The *self-acting* mules are one-half spring, 36's weft, spindles revolving 4,800; the other half spring, 36's twist, spindles revolving 5,200. The hand-mules spring about equal quantities of 36's weft and twist. Weft spindles, 4,700, and twist spindles 5,000 revolutions. Average breadth of looms 37 inches (weaving 37 inch cloth), making 123 picks per minute. All common cottons about 60 reed, Stockport count, and 68 picks to the inch. No power consumed by sizing When the yarn is dressed, instead of sized, one horse-power cannot drive so many looms, as the dressing machine will absorb .17 to .14 of the power.

English Cotton Goods of Standard Make in 1800, 1830, and 1846.

The English cotton goods of all standard makes at the commencement of this century comprised prints, muslins, corduroys, fustians, sheetings, shirtings, twills and ginghams. In 1830 the records give madapolams, tanjibs, domestics, jaconets, gauze leno, figured muslin, splits and velveteens. In 1846 there were chronicled lawns, books, nainsooks, figured counterpanes; and in 1864, brilliante, chambrey, blue mottle, satin checks, in addition to previously mentioned goods, from which list the absence of dhooties, turkey reds, Turkish towels and cloths of later origin will be noted.

Hindoo or East Indian Cottons.

Biaz is a cotton material resembling linen, manufactured in Central Asia to a considerable extent, both for native use and exportation to Russia. There are three sorts of it: the best, or Bokharian; the medium, or Khivan, and an inferior variety manufactured at Tashkend. The Bokharian biaz is brought to the bazars and purchased by dealers for Russia. It is sold in pieces from 12½ to 16¼ yards in length and 10½ inches in breadth. The Tashkend biaz is slightly inferior in quality to the Bokharian. A blue biaz called *tendel*, or *buyak*, dyed with indigo, is also exported from Bokhara, Khiva and Tashkend to Russia.

Tariff Revision on American Cottons in 1883.

The tariff revision of 1883 made a heavy cut in the duties on cottons, the cotton goods schedules being reduced from 55 per cent. on the lower grade of unbleached goods or cloth containing less than 100 threads per square inch, to 23 per cent. on bleached goods exceeding over 200 threads per square inch. On cotton warp yarns or thread the reduction ranged from 16 67-100 to 33 33-100 per cent., according to the value of the yarn.

Selling Prices of American Cottons and Prints in 1827.

"In 1827 Lowell, Mass., had six cotton mills, four stories high, 155 feet by 44, containing 25,000 spindles, and about 150 looms, in which were made in 1826 5,042,408 yards of cotton cloth, weighing 1,045,386 pounds, from 1,176,082 pounds of raw cotton. The numbers of yarn were 22, 26, 30 and 40. There were two mills for twilled and four for plain goods. There were employed 12,000 persons in the mills—nine-tenths of whom were females—20 from 12 to 14 years of age. Daily wages average 50c., the minimum being 37½c. and the maximum $2. About 2,500,000 yards of cottons were annually printed, and the residue sold bleached. The average value of the prints was about 18c., and of the bleached goods 12c. to 13c. per yard."—*Kirk Boott's Letter to Matthew Carey, Oct. 25, 1827.*

Cotton Manufacturing in Providence, R. I., in 1809.

"In 1809 seventeen cotton mills were in operation within the town of Providence and its vicinity, working 14,296 spindles, and using 640,000 pounds of cotton, which yielded 510,000 pounds of yarn. About 1,000 looms were employed in weaving cotton cloth. The cloths manufactured were bed-ticking, stripes and checks, ginghams, shirtings and counterpanes. They were superior to the imported goods of the same kind."
—*Benedict's History of Rhode Island, published in* 1813.

Loss of Length in Twisting Cotton Yarn.

Yarn must always lose a litttle length in twisting, the loss being proportionate to the thickness of the yarn, and the hardness of the twist, and therefore, of course, varying with every count of spinning woolen and worsted yarns. If two bobbins of the same counts are twisted together, the count will, of course, become half of what it was before, just as the weight will be double. Thus, two-folds 40's is equal to single 20's, not allowing for running up of the twist. When different counts are twisted together, to find the count of the combination multiply the numbers by the two counts together and divide the product by the sum of the two added together.

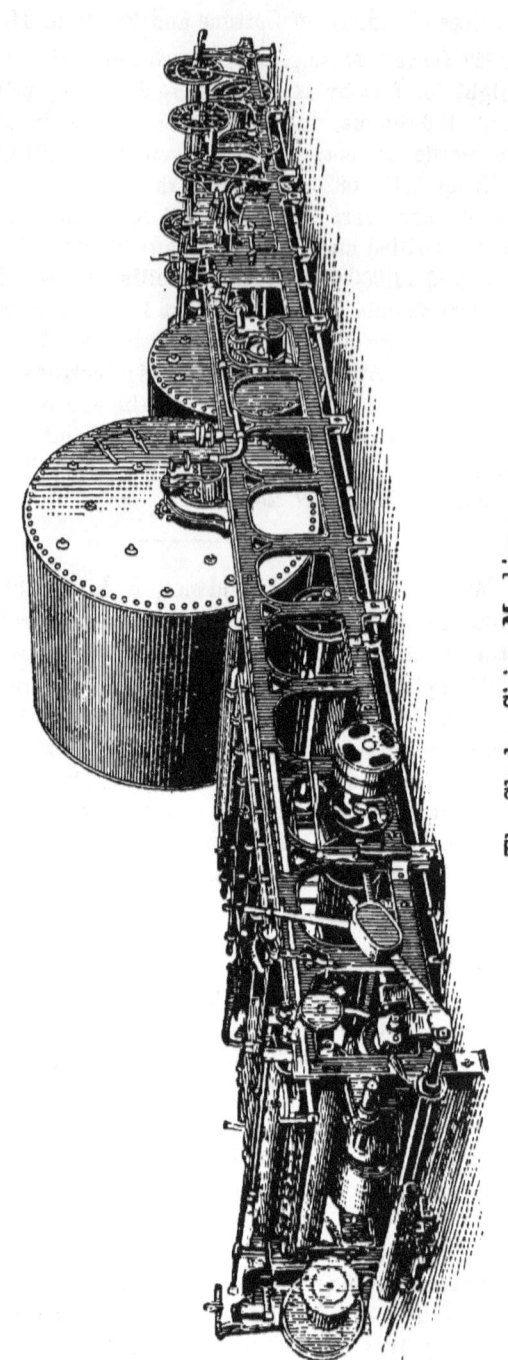

The Slasher-Sizing Machine.

Duties on Cotton Yarns in Foreign Countries.

In Russia the duties on cotton yarns range from £1 15s. 6d. per cwt., unbleached, No. 45 and below, to £3 9s. for twisted yarns of two or more threads. In Germany they run from 6s. 1d. per cwt. for numbers up to 17, single, bleached, up to £1 15s. 7d. for cable twist and sewing thread. In Holland all kinds are free; in Turkey all pay 8 per cent. ad valorem; in Sweden, Norway and Denmark the tariffs are simple, and, save for sewing thread in Sweden, low; the same is the case for Belgium. In France the tariff is very complicated, and very high in some instances. It ranges from 6s. 1d. per cent. to £7 6s. 4d., the latter being the rate for unbleached twisted, of above 170,500 metres to the half millogramme; single unbleached, twisted unbleached, bleached, dyed or clouded, warped (bleached, unbleached and dyed), and thread in balls or reels, are all different categories. In Portugal the duties begin at £1 10s. 10d. and go up to £4 4s. 7d.; in Spain they run from £1 10s. up to £3 11s. 2d.; in Italy from 7s. 4d. to £2 4s. 8d.; in Austria from 6s. 1d. to £1 15s. 7d.; in Switzerland from 5¼d. to 14s. 3d., and in Greece from 19s. 3d. to £2 8s. Although the United States tariff has not such a minute classification as that of France, it is even more remarkable in another direction. The duty on thread and yarn varies, not with the length of a thread to a particular weight, or with the bleaching or dyeing, twisting or otherwise, but with the value. Where the yarn does not exceed 25c. a pound in value, the duty is £2 6s. 8d. per cwt., which in the most favorable conditions possible would be 50 per cent., and might be 75, 80 or 90 per cent. The duty goes on rising as the value per pound rises, until for thread or yarn of the value of 80c. to $1 per pound the duty is £11 4s. per cwt., which is about 50 per cent. under the best circumstances. About a dollar per pound the duty is 50 per cent. ad valorem.

Value of American Cotton Crop of 1889.

It is estimated that the cotton crop of the South of 1888-9 was worth anywhere from $325,000,000 to $350,000,000.

European Exports of Cotton Yarns and Cotton Tissues.

The following table shows the exports of cotton yarns and cotton tissues from the principal European countries Austria-Hungary, Germany, France, Great Britain—during the years comprised between 1881 and 1885, inclusive:

Articles.	Austria-Hungary.	Germany.	France.	Great Britain.
	Francs.	Francs.	Francs.	Francs.
Cotton Yarn.				
1881.......	2,000,000	42,000,000	2,500,000	394,700,000
1882.......	2,200,000	40,200,000	2,700,000	385,700,000
1883.......	2,500,000	32,000,000	2,200,000	405,000,000
1884.......	2,200,000	28,000,000	2,200,000	416,500,000
1885.......	2,200,000	23,000,000	3,200,000	355,700,000
Cotton Tissues.				
1881.......	18,500,000	148,200,000	88,500,000	1,952,000,000
1882.......	16,200,000	183,800,000	97,700,000	1,888,500,000
1883.......	20,500,000	180,700,000	89,600,000	1,887,200,000
1884.......	18,000,000	192,500,000	89,200,000	1,766,700,000
1885.......	17,000,000	188,200,000	102,200,000	1,652,000,000

Old and New Cotton Mills.

The erection of a cotton mill or factory at the present time is on a far more comprehensive scale than in the early days of manufacturing. The new cotton mills, covering large areas and constructed on the principle of good light, temperature and ventilation, are as widely different from the old style as the modern house is from the dwelling of the mediæval age. The old mills were almost wholly of a narrow type, while many of the textile establishments now erected vary from 100 to 125 feet in width, being necessary in many cases for the high stories characteristic of the present building age.

Perhaps the most noticeable difference in the modern mill structure, to the ordinary observer, is the unusual facilities for natural light. Light from combustion is comparatively poor and costly. In many of the weaving departments of mills built years ago and poorly windowed, the constant use of gas or oil for lighting purposes so overheats the air that the ordinary operative loses physical vigor. In a wide mill, with high stories, the windows must be necessarily large in order to secure good natural light, occupying at least 40 per cent. or more of the side walls, and leaving but little width of the brick work between them.

Price of British Cottons Exported to United States and other Countries in 1833.

The following statement shows the average *declared* price per piece and per yard, and yards in piece, of British cottons exported to United States in 1833.

Description.	Length of each piece.	Average price per piece. s. d.	Averarge price per yard. s. d.
Dimity	60 yards.	26 3	5¼
Quiltings and Ribs	60 "	52 6	10½
Lawns and Lenos	20 "	10 10	6½
Calicoes, Printed	28 "	11 11½	5⅛
Calicoes, Plain	24 "	7 4	3½
Cambrics and Muslins	20 "	10 5	6¼
Cotton and Linen, Mixed	40 "	11 4	3¼
Ginghams	20 "	10 5	6¼
Imitation Shawls	12 "	6 3	6¼
Nankeens	50 "	17 8½	4¼
Velveteens	60 "	52 6	10½
Lace	40 "	10 10	3¼
Tecks, etc.	50 "	25 5	6¼
Damasks	36 "	24 9	8¼
Counterpanes		6 0	6 0 each
Shawls	Dozen	6 3	6¼
Tapes	"	1 9	2
Hosiery	"	11 0	10½ pair.

— *Official Custom Returns of Great Britain*

Prices of American Cotton Goods in 1789-91.

According to the statement of Almy & Brown, of Providence, R. I., who were among the pioneers of cotton manufacturing in this country, the following were the selling prices of the goods produced by them from June 6, 1789, to Oct. 15, 1791:

	s. d. s. d.	
Corduroys	3 6 to 4 0	per yard.
Royal Ribs, Denims, etc.	3 0 to 4 0	"
Cottonets	2 6 to 3 0	"
Jeans	2 0 to 2 6	"
Fustians	1 8 to 2 0	"
Thickets	4 0 to 4 4	"
Fancy Cords	3 6 to 4 0	"
Velvirets	4 0 to 4 4	"

Average Selling Price of Ordinary Plain Cotton Cloth in England from 1814 to 1833.

The average selling price throughout the year of one piece of calico (plain cotton cloth, 24 yards to piece), in Manchester, England, from 1814 to 1833, according to the British official returns, and the approximate value per yard, in U. S. money of to-day, are given below.

Years.	Average price per piece in Manchester, Eng. £.	s.	d.	Approximate value in U. S. currency of to-day, per yd. Cents.
1814	1	4	7	25.58
1815	0	19	8¾	20.54
1816	0	16	8½	17.37
1817	0	16	1	16.75
1818	0	16	8½	17.37
1819	0	13	9	13.91
1820	0	12	1½	12.62
1821	0	9	8¼	9.75
1822	0	9	3½	9.66
1823	0	8	11¼	9.29
1824	0	8	5¾	8.77
1825	0	8	5¼	8.77
1826	0	6	3¼	6.52
1827	0	6	6	6.75
1828	0	6	5¼	6.68
1829	0	5	8	5.54
1830	0	6	3¼	6.52
1831	0	6	2¼	6.43
1832	0	5	8	5.54
1833	0	6	2	6.41

Price of British Printed Cotton Cloth Exported to U. S. from 1827 to 1832.

British Customs statistics give the average declared price per yard of printed cotton cloth exported to the United States in the years named, as follows:

Years.	Price per yard. Declared value. Pence.	Equal in U. S. currency of to-day, per yd. Cents.
1827	9	18
1828	8¾	17½
1829	9½	19
1830	8	16
1831	7½	15
1832	6	12

The Cotton Power Loom.

The machine required for weaving plain cotton cloth in which each end of weft and twist is interwoven alternately, and on the face of which no figure is shown, is simple. The warp yarn is contained on a *beam*, the weft is placed in a *shuttle*, and the loom consists of the necessary frame work and mechanism for holding the warp in the required position, passing the weft between alternate warp threads.

A general view of the cotton power loom is given in the following cut:

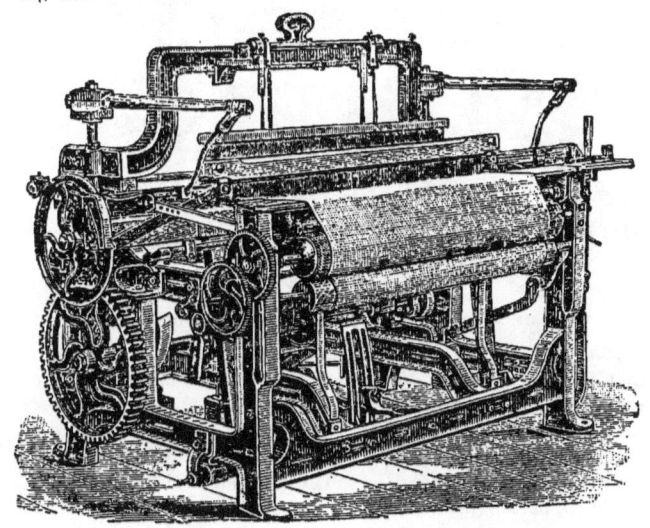

FRONT VIEW OF POWER LOOM FOR WEAVING PLAIN COTTON CLOTH.

In the process of weaving it is necessary to hold the warp somewhat tightly, each portion at the same tension, and to obtain this condition the cloth is pulled forward by the taking-up roller as it is woven, but the warp is held back by the friction of weighted chains or ropes on the *collars* of the beam. The warp passes upwards from the beam, over the back rest, and thence to the back of the *healds;* between the back rest and healds are the *lease rods*—a large one, with a smaller rod nearer the healds. By means of these rods the warp is separated into equal portions, two ends passing alternately over or under the thick rod; those passing over the thick one also passing under the thin rod. The rule commonly observed for four healds is to have the ends passing the first and third heald over the thin rod, and those drawn through the second and fourth, over the thick rod, and consequently under the thin one. The first heald is the one nearest the front of the loom; that is, 1, 3, 2, 4, and applies to plain cotton cloth, although the first and second healds are worked as one, and the third and fourth together.

Respecting the two ends which pass together at the lease rods, the one through the front heald is to the left of the one through the third heald; whilst with the other couples the end through the more forward heald is to the left of the other.

As will be seen by looking at the accompanying illustration, which gives the back view of a power loom for weaving plain cotton cloth, the healds are suspended on each side of the *heald-roller*, *A*, by means of straps and cords, which are shown in the cut.

BACK VIEW OF A POWER LOOM FOR WEAVING PLAIN COTTON CLOTH.

The portion of the heald roller supporting the back healds is larger than for the front ones; this is to make the former when lifted make the *shed* at the same angle as the front healds. Below are seen the crank shaft, *B*, and the *tappet* shaft, *C*, driven from it at exactly half the speed. The latter shaft bears the picking plates, *H*, and shedding tappets, *K*. The *slay*, supported by the slay-sword, *D*, on the rocking shaft, is shown also. It carries the reed at *E*, held in position by the slay cap, *F*. The back rest at *G*, over which the warp passes, and the weight levers and driving pulleys are also noticeable parts. The cloth is woven pick by pick, and the whole action of the loom may be confined in repetitions of the operations contingent on putting in one *pick*. Supposing the warp to be in position and the machine in running order, the first movement is to open the warp into two parts, and is called *shedding;* the second is to pass the shuttle through the opening thus made, called picking; and thirdly, to beat up the weft close to the pick last put in—technically, to fill the cloth. In addition to these, auxiliary movements are taking place for winding on the woven cloth, keeping it distended and checking the motion of the loom in case of accident.

EXPLANATORY NOTE.

Beam is the flanged roller on which the warp yarn is wound.
Counts.—A system of indicating the fineness of yarn.
Fell.—The edge of the fabric (in the loom) which has most recently been woven.
Harness. Am. }
Heald. Eng. } The arrangement of leashes.
Pick.—The insertion of a thread of weft.
Selvage.—The sides of a fabric.
Shed.—The opening made in the warp for the passage of the shuttle.
Slay.—Lay or lathe.
Tappet.—Scotch for wiper

Prices of Cottons in 1859, 1860, 1887 and 1889.

The first column gives the jobbers' prices in March, 1859; the second column, jobbers' prices in March, 1860; the third column, agents' prices for June, 1887; and the fourth column, jobbers' prices for the month of October, 1889. The omissions of prices in the third and fourth columns in some instances are owing to the fact that there has been a change in the tickets or qualities of the goods, and in some cases the goods are no longer made.

BROWN SHEETINGS AND SHIRTINGS.

	March, 1859. *Cents.*	*March*, 1860. *Cents.*	*June*, 1887. *Cents*	*Oct.* 1889. *Cents.*
Agawam F, 36-in	7½	....	6½	....
Amoskeag A, 36-in	9	9	....	....
Appleton A, 36-in	9	8½	7	6¾
Atlantic A, 36-in	9	8¾	7¼	7
Graniteville EE, 36-in	8¼	....	6½	6¼
Great Falls E, 36-in	7¾	....	7	6¾
Indian Head, 36-in	9	8⅝	7¼	6¾
Indian Head, 30-in	7	...	....	6¾
Indian Head, 40-in	11½	...	10½	10
Massachusetts A, 36-in	7¼	7¾	....	6½
Nashua R, 36-in	8¼	8½	6¾	7
Nashua O, 30-in	7	7¼	5¾	....
Pepperell E, 39-in	9¼	9½	7	7
Pepperell R, 36-in	8¾	9	6½	6½
Pepperell O, 33-in	8¼	....	6	6
Pepperell N, 30-in	7½	7¾	5¾	5¾
Pocasset Canoe, 36-in	9	....	6½	6¾
Stark A, 36-in	9	....	7¼	7
Waltham, 39-in	9½	....	...	....
Waltham, 51-in	12	....	....	....
Waltham, 58-in	14½	....	....	...
Waltham, 77-in	20	....	....	....
Waltham, 87-in	23	....	....	....
Waltham, 97-in	26	....	....	....
Indian Orchard W, 33-in	7¾	...	....	....
Indian Orchard B, 30-in	8¼	....	....	...

BLEACHED SHEETINGS AND SHIRTINGS.

Amoskeag, 32-in	8¼		....	....
Amoskeag, 37-in	10½	11½	.	....
Amoskeag, 42-in	11¾	12½	....	....
Amoskeag, 46-in	12¼	13½	....	....
Amoskeag Z	...	8¼	....	....
Blackstone A, 36-in	10	10	7½	7¼
Boott R 30-in	6½	....	5	5¼
Boott S	9	9¼	....	....
Boott W	11½	....	....	....
Great Falls A, 36 in	9	9¼	....	....
Great Falls Q, 36-in	12½	....	....	....
Great Falls M, 33-in	8¾	9	6¼	6¾
Harris, 36-in	9½	....	....	....
Hope A, 36-in	9	....	7½	7¼
Hill	11	11½	8¼	7¾
Hill, 32-in	10	10½	....	7¼

Prices of Cottons in 1859, Etc.—Continued.

(Bleached Sheetings and Shirtings.—Continued.)

	March, 1859 *Cents.*	*March,* 1860. *Cents.*	*June,* 1887. *Cents.*	*Oct.* 1889 *Cents.*
Lonsdale, 36-in.	10½	11¾	8¾	8
Masonville, 36-in.	11½	....	8¾	8½
Slaterville, 36-in.	9½	10½	....	....
New York Mills	15	15½	11	10
Waltham, 42-in	10	11	....	....
Waltham, 46-in.	12	....	....	....
Waltham, 54-in.	15½	15½	....	....
Waltham, 72-in.	21	23½	....	....
Waltham, 81-in.	24	27	....	....
Waltham, 90-in.	28	30	....	....
Wamsutta, 36-in.	12½	13	11	10
Wamsutta, 40-in.	14½	15	14	....
Wamsutta, 45-in.	15½	16½	16	14½
Warren, 36-in.	9¾	11½	....	11
Wauregan WT, 36-in.	11½	13	8¾	9¼
White Rock, 36-in.	....	13	8	8
Pepperell, 6-4.	....	16	14½	13½
Pepperell, 8-4.	....	23	18	18
Pepperell, 9-4.	....	26	20	20
Pepperell, 10-4	....	30	22½	24
Utica Steam Cot. Mills, 36-in	....	10	11	8½
Utica Steam Cot. Mills, 5-4.	....	15½	15	13½
Utica Steam Cot. Mills, 6-4.	...	18½	17½	15½
Utica Steam Cot. Mills, 9-4.	....	30	25	22½
Utica Steam Cot. Mills, 10-4.	....	33	27½	24½

BROWN DRILLS.

Amoskeag brown	8¾	....	....	....
Amoskeag bleached	9½	....	....	....
Amoskeag blue	10½	....	....	....
Laconia brown	9½	....	6¾	6¾
Laconia bleached	10	....	7¼	....
Laconia blue	10½	....	10½	10
Massachusetts	8¾	....	6¾	6¾
Pepperell	9½	....	6¾	6¾
Stark	9½	....	6¾	7
Suffolk	9	....	6½	6¾
Boott	9½	....	6¾	6½

BROWN DENIMS.

Amoskeag A	14½	15	14	13
Columbian XXX	10	10	12	10
Otis AAA	10	10	12½	10
Pearl River	14	14½	13½	12½
Warren BB	9½	9½	9½	9
York	15	14½	13½	12½

CORSET JEANS.

Amoskeag, colored	9¼	....	....	....
Amoskeag, bleached	9½	....	....	....
Pepperell, colored.	9	....	8¼	8
Pepperell, bleached	9½	....	8¼	8
Naumkeag, colored	9½	....	7½	7
Naumkeag, bleached	9¼	....	7½	7
Laconia, colored	9¼	....	6½	6½
Laconia, bleached	9½	....	6½	6½

Prices of Cottons in 1859, Etc.—Continued.

(Bleached Sheetings on l Shirtings.—Continued.)

HICKORY STRIPES.

	March, 1859. Cents.	March, 1860. Cents.	June, 1887. Cents.	Oct. 1889 Cents.
Amoskeag	11	....	9½	9½
Boston	9¾	....	7¾	6½
Jewett City	9¼	....	7½	7¼
Thorndike	8½	....	9½@10	9½

TICKINGS.

Amoskeag ACA, 32-in	16½	17	14	12½
Amoskeag A, 32-in	13	13½	13	11½
Amoskeag B, 32-in	11½	12½	12	11
Amoskeag C, 32-in	11	11½	11½	10½
Amoskeag D	10	10½	11	9½
Amoskeag awning, 32-in	11	11½	13	15
Conestogo A, 30-in	9½	9½	....	....
Conestogo AA, 30-in	10½	10½	....	....
Conestogo HT, 30-in	11½	11½	....	....
Conestogo XX T, 30-in	12½	12½	....	....
Conestogo CCA, 30-in	14½	14½	13	11
Hamilton, 30-in	11½	11¾	11	10
Methuen, 32-in	14	14½	12½	12
Pearl River, 32-in	15½	15½	13½	12
Thorndike A	9½	9½	8	7¼
York, 30-in	12½	12½	....	12
York, 32-in	16	16	....	14

COTTON FLANNELS.

Amoskeag A, brown	11½	....	14	13
Amoskeag B, brown	11¼	....	13	12
Amoskeag A, bleached	14	....	15	14½
Amoskeag B, bleached	13½	....	14	13
Hamilton F, brown	10	....	10½	9
Hamilton BF, bleached	10½	....	....	10

COTTON BAGS.

Stark A, 2-bush	25	....	21	20½

PRINTS.

Allens	10	9½	5½	6
American	10	9½	5½	6
Gloucester	9½	....	5½	6
Conestoga	9½	....	5½	....
Garner	9½	....	5½	6
Merrimack D	10	9½	6	6½
Merrimack W	10½	....	6½	....
Spragues	10	9½	....	....

GINGHAMS.

Lancaster staples	10	....	7½	6
Glasgow	10	....	7	
Manchester	9½	....	6¾	5½

British Exports of Sewing Thread.

In 1888 the total quantity of sewing thread exported from Great Britain was 21,719,100 lbs., valued at £3,180,885. The figures for the previous year, 1887, were 20,392,000 lbs., valued at £2.979,184.

Location of the Cotton Trade of Great Britain

The bulk of the cotton trade in England is found in Lancashire, and it is the chief and most absorbing occupation of cities and towns like Manchester, Liverpool, Preston, Blackburn, Bolton, Bary, Wigan, Oldham, Chorley, Barnley, Padinam, Accrington, Middletown, Bacup, and countless villages.

The chief cotton centres of Scotland are Glasgow, Paisley, and a few of the Ayrshire towns.

Loss of Weight in Bleaching Cotton.

In bleaching cotton it loses a portion of its weight, because the bleaching process is, in all cases, *substractive*. It loses much resinous and coloring matter, often amounting from 10 to 12 per cent. On dyeing, etc., on the contrary, it acquires a portion of the drugs employed, because this process is *additive;* and as much as 10 to 15 may be added to the weight of the raw yarn, by its passage through the various coloring processes.

Cotton Crops of Egypt.

The following is a tabulated statement of the cotton crops of Egypt from 1873 to 1888, inclusive. The weight of the bale is 750 pounds:

1873-4	413,611	2,575,648
1874-5	348,802	2,206,443
1875-6	466,894	2,982,287
1876-7	438,536	2,817,482
1877-8	403,270	2,605,453
1878-9	254,342	1,677,749
1879-80	471,726	3,202,051
1880-1	409,101	2,794,321
1881-2	425,315	2,930,962
1882-3	326,077	2,267,863
1883-4	380,801	2,265,531
1884-5	501,686	3,564,717
1885-6	407,970	2,901,607
1886-7	418,372	2,983,123
1887-8	413,891	2,942,638

Cotton Factories.

The accompanying illustration gives a fair representation of the modern cotton factory:

A MODERN COTTON FACTORY.

The general height of the cotton mills in this country (that is, those built prior to the late war) is three to four stories with an attic, but some mills since then, or more recently, are five, six and even more stories, with plain roof.

The height of cotton mills in Scotland is six stories, with plain roof. Those in England are from six to eight stories high.

Inventor of the Cotton Gin.

Eli Whitney, the inventor of the cotton gin, died on Jan. 8, 1825, and was buried in the cemetery of New Haven, Conn. His tomb is after the model of Scipio's at Rome. It is simple and beautiful, and promises to endure for years. It bears the following inscription:

ELI WHITNEY,

The inventor of the cotton gin.

Of useful science and arts, the efficient patron and improver.

In the social relations of life, a model of excellence.

While private affection weeps at his tomb, his country honors his memory.

Born December 8th, 1765.—Died Jan. 8th, 1825.

Adulterated or "Loaded" British Cottons.

British cotton goods are still sold fully loaded, and sometimes so much so that it is hardly fair to call them cotton, when that material can scarcely be considered the chief constituent of them. According to a British textile authority: "They will probably continue to sell so long as they constitute our cheapest textile; but if any of the efforts to find a new fibre, or to improve the processes in those in use, were to be rewarded with success, the English sized calicoes would have had their day. There is no doubt that ingenuity in bleaching and finishing has been brought to such a degree that the marketable cotton cloth now covers a multitude of sins, and that a third-class article can be brought almost to equal in appearance a cloth of the best quality."

Differences in Textile Fibres.

The textile fibres, cotton, wool, silk, flax and hemp differ considerably from each other in their structure. The first three consist of definite and entire filaments not divisible without decomposition; the last two consist of fibrils bundled together in parallel directions which are easier separated into much more minute filaments. These bundles are bound together by parenchymatous rings, from which they are freed by operations of heckling, spinning and bleaching. The downy filaments are cylindered tubes, growing in that state, but get more or less flattened in the maturation and dyeing of the wool. They are shut off at both ends, and their flattened diameters vary from 1-500 to 1-1000 of an inch, according to the quality.

The filaments of wool, when seen through a powerful microscope, have somewhat the appearance of a shale, with the edges of its scales turned out a little from the surface so as to make the profile line of the sides like a fine saw, with the teeth sloping in the direction from the roots to the point. Each fibre of wool seems to consist of serrated rings imbricated over each other like joints. The teeth differ in size and prominence in different wools, as well as the annular spaces between them, the latter being in general from 1-2000 to 1-3000 of an inch, while the diameter of the filament itself may vary from 1-1000 to 1-1400. The cocoon-silk threads are twin tubes laid parallel in the act of spinning and glued with more or less uniformity together by the varnish which covers their whole surface. Each filament of this thread varies in diameter from 1-800 to 1-2500 of an inch, the average breadth being 1-1000 ; but it is variable in different silks.

Early History of Calico Printing.

The art of impressing colored patterns or designs on white cotton cloth seems to be as old almost as history itself. Herodotus speaks of a people on the shores of the Caspian Sea who painted the forms of animals on their garments with vegetable dye. Indeed, calico printing has been one of the industries of India for centuries, and from there it was introduced into Europe. It was brought to England in 1696, but it was not practiced in Lancashire until about 1768, as its introduction encountered great opposition from the silk weavers. As early as 1720 a law was passed by Parliament prohibiting the wearing of all printed calico whatsoever, although ten years later, by special act of legislation, the manufacture and wearing of printed cloth made of cotton weft and linen warp was permitted. In 1744 Parliament allowed cloth made entirely of cotton to be printed, but so many burdensome restrictions surrounded its manufacture that no very great progress was made until 1831, when all the oppressive laws relating to it were repealed.

As early as 1824 the product of printed cottons in the New England States amounted to 60,000 yards per week, and in 1860 the product of print cloths in the same States aggregated 271,800,871 yards, or 5,223,000 yards per week, which indicates how rapid has been the progress made in this industry in this country. England and the United States are the largest producers of calico in the world, although France and Germany make considerable quantities. Calico printing involves a variety of very nice operations :

1. Calendering, or making the cloth smooth and even.
2. Fixing the colors, *i.e.*, the use of substances which have an affinity for both fibre and color.
3. Patterns, madder styles, by printing ·the mordant in figures and subsequently producing the colors in dye liquors ; padding, bronzing indigo, pencil blue, China blue styles, etc., by printing one component of the color and then passing the cloth through a solution of the other component ; steam colors, spirit colors, aniline black, etc., by printing the color together with the mordant, and developing it by air or steam ; resist styles, by printing reserve pastes which protected certain portions of the cloth and prevent the fixing of the color in the subsequent dyeing operations ; discharge styles, by discharging the color from portions of the cloth previously dyed.

Processes Cotton Cloth in the Gray Undergoes Before It Becomes Printed Calico.

When the plain, unbleached cloth is received at the print works, it undergoes the following processes before it can be delivered to the agents as a print:

1, Shearing; 2, singeing; 3, bleaching; 4, preparing; 5, drying; 6, winding; 7, printing; 8, drying; 9, steaming; 10, ageing; 11, soaping; 12, washing; 13, drying; 14, clearing; 15, drying; 16, starching; 17, drying; 18, inspecting; 19, calendering; 20, winding; 21, measuring; 22, folding; 23, pressing; 24, boxing.

To secure good results, high, artistic talent is necessary in the designing department, supplemented necessarily with personal direction, based upon good artistic judgment and practical knowledge of trade wants.

The engraving department must also make fine mechanical work to transfer to the rollers the designs, so they will print perfectly, while the color maker must develop the delicate tones required to make the harmony and blending of colors necessary to make the finished article a success.

In the processes following the printing, such as steaming, calendering, etc., the same skillful treatment is necessary as in the preceding work; and in the final work of inspection, folding, pressing, and ticketing, great care is necessary to put the fabric into the most attractive form for selling.

How Indigo Prints are Made.

Patterns on indigo-dyed goods are produced either by resisting or by discharging; the first method is not so largely used now as formerly, as by the discharging process better and neater impressions can be obtained.

The dyeing of cotton cloth in the indigo vat has not experienced much change of late years, except that the continuous dyeing machines have come more prominently into use in preference to the round vats formerly employed.

The machinery now mostly in use consists of a square tank, generally imbedded in the ground, through which the cloth is passed in its full width over a system of rollers. As a rule, the reduction on the indigo is effected in tubs, and then the necessary quantity is added to the dye vats. After dyeing, the goods are scoured to remove the lime and other impurities, and well washed and dried, and are then ready for the discharging.

Bleaching Printing Cloth.

The first operation the gray pieces have to undergo before they are bleached is the

STAMPING.—This is necessary in order that the goods can be recognized after they have been bleached. Then follows the stitching of the pieces to each other, end to end, in order to form a long ribbon, by means of which the cloth is treated in a continuous way.

As is well known, cotton cloth contains on its surface a certain amount of light down, consisting of the ends of cotton fibre, and this will have to be removed before the goods are bleached. The removal of this down is of special importance if the goods are afterwards intended to be printed, since these small filaments of cotton would interfere with the formation of clean prints.

This down is removed during the operation of

SINGEING.—This is performed on specially constructed machines, working on the principle of passing very rapidly the pieces over red-hot plates, revolving hot cylinders or gas-burners, which only burn off the small outstanding filaments without touching the cloth, if the operation is well conducted. The gas-singeing machine is now mostly employed, but plate or cylinder singeing still does very good service, and among the newer methods recommended may be mentioned the singeing by electricity.

The goods are washed thoroughly on the washing machine and then allowed to steep or lie in a heap all night. A kind of fermentation sets in, which allows the sizing materials to be removed.

LIMING.—This operation consists in passing the pieces in a continuous way through milk of lime, the proportion of which has been so arranged that the cloth takes up about five per cent. of lime to the weight of cotton.

SCOURING OR BOILING.—The pieces are then brought into the kiers by means of machinery. In these they are so arranged that they fill up all the space of the kiers in a regular way, boys entering the vessels and helping in the laying of the cloth in the apparatus by means of sticks.

As a rule, all the operations of bleaching are performed on cloth folded up in the form of a rope, this being a very convenient form, especially for running the pieces from one apparatus or machine through the other, but in some cases the cloth is worked quite open, and spread out to its full width.

Cost of Weaving Print Cloths in England and America.

The cost of weaving printing cloths in England and America is given as follows:

	28 in., 56 reeds, 14 picks (64x63) 58 yards.		28 in., 60 reeds, 16 picks (64x64) 58 yards.	
ENGLAND.	Cents.	Pence.	Cents.	Pence.
Ashton Under-Lyne...	24.68	12.34	27.70	13.85
Blackburn....	25.04	12.52	29.06	14.53
Stockport............	25.04	12.52	29.48	14.74
Hyde...............	25.28	12.68	29.30	14.65
General Average.......	25.00	12.50	28.88	14.44
AMERICA.				
Rhode Island.........	16.82	8.41	Unknown.	
Providence...........	17.26	8.63	22.30	11.15
Fall River............	19.96	9.98	23.20	11.60
Lowell................	19.96	9.98	23.20	11.60
General Average......	18.50	9.25	22.90	11.45

The weight of a cloth 28 inches, 56 reed, 14 picks, 58 yards long, is 7 pounds and 4 ounces, and the cost of weaving in wages per pound, is 0.898 cent, or 0.449d. less in America than in England, while the difference in favor of America in a cloth 28 inches, 60 reed, 16 picks, 58 yards long, weighing 8 pounds and 4 ounces, is 0.726 cent, or 0.363d. per pound. American print cloth is made of coarser yarn than the English, the usual counts being about No. 29 for warp and No. 36 for weft, while in England they are respectively about No. 31 and No. 41.

The usual production at Fall River and Lowell for each loom, per week of sixty hours, is 5½ pieces of 28-inch, 16x16 (64x64), 45 yards, making each loom earn for its attendant 99c., or 4s 1½d. It is quite an ordinary thing for eight looms to be worked by one weaver. Printing cloth in America is 28 inches wide and in England 32 inches wide. The former being made of coarser yarn and the latter of finer, makes the foregoing a fair comparison.

Two Kinds of Cotton Goods Printers.

In both England and this country there are two kinds of cotton goods printers—those who sell direct to the merchants themselves, and those who print the cloth for merchants at piece price.

Principal Colors, etc., Used in Dyeing and Printing Cotton Cloth.

The aniline colors are divided into basic and acid coloring matters; the basic products are those which are neutral salts—the combination of an acid with base of the dyestuff itself—while the acid colors are those which have been obtained on the bases of the aniline colors by means of sulphuric acid. As a general rule much faster shades are obtained by means of the basic aniline colors, and these are also much more employed in printing on cotton cloth than the acid colors.

Of the colors which can be fixed by steaming, we have, in the first instance, the pigments, then the aniline or coal tar colors, and the dyewood extracts, among which may be mentioned indigo and some mineral colors.

The pigments are fixed by means of albumen, the principle of their fixation relying on the fact that albumen becomes coagulated by the action of steam, and thus keeps the pigments impressioned in the coagulated substance and permanently fixed on the fibre, so that they cannot be removed either by washing or soaping. The thickenings only react in a mechanical way by keeping the colors on the spots for which they are intended, and preventing them from running.

The new class of azo dyestuffs (unlike the others derived from coal tar) can be applied on cotton without the aid of mordants, and in a single bath. The azo colors are, without doubt, the richest class of colors derived from coal tar, and have been found especially useful for cotton yarns.

Mineral colors are fixed on cotton in two ways—as ready-made pigments, by the aid of a fixing medium, such as albumen, etc., or by applying first the mordant, and afterwards developing the color in another bath. They form a very important group, not so much for printing purposes as in producing white patterns on colored cotton goods, but some of them are largely employed in the finishing processes. They include white pigments, yellow pigments, metallic powders, red pigments, green pigments, blue pigments, prussiate blues, brown pigments, blacks and grays, etc.

Natural organic coloring matters include logwood, red woods, madder, cochineal, yellow dyestuffs, Persian berries, fustic, tumeric, annatto, cutch or catechu, aloes, indigo, etc.

Coal tar colors represent the benzole colors (principally aniline)—aniline, magenta, soluble blues, diphenyl amine, methyl violets, Hoffman's violets, crystal violets, methyl green, methylene blue, æthylene blue, safranine, phosphine, indulines, neutral red and neutral violets, Bismarck brown, chrysoidine, flavantine, etc.

Azo colors are victoria blue—auramine, red coraline, the eosines—the soluble azo colors (new class of azo colors)—indo-phenol, artificial indigo, alizarin, alizarin orange, alizarin blue, gallein, cerulein, etc.

Mordants comprise alumina mordants, iron mordants, chromium mordants, tin mordants, copper mordants, lead mordants, manganese mordants, zinc mordants, arsenic mordants, antimony mordants, vanadium compounds, cereum salts, dunging material, astringents, or tanning materials, soaps, oils, prepared oil mordants, solvents, etc.

In some kinds of calico, pieces containing much white are bleached after printing in order to clear the white. This is done by passing the pieces through a weak chlorine bath, and then directly through a steaming box; then washed, and either dried or starched, as the case may be. The pieces are often slightly blued with ultramarine.

In some cases the mordants are first printed on calico, and the colors fixed by dyeing.

Thickening or sizing materials include the various starches—dextrine, gums, tragacanth, albumenoid matters, caseine or lactarine, glue, gelatine, etc.

Dyewood extract colors are an important class of coloring matters which are even now very largely used in printing; in fact, from these the steam or extract style derives its name. The most important of these is the logwood extract, which is employed in very large quantities for the production of steam blacks, and in a smaller way for the production of compound shades.

Steam mineral colors are chrome yellow, cadmium yellow, iron buff, steam prussiate blue, steam manganese brown, etc.

Oxidation colors are aniline black colors and chromed colors, such as calectin, logwood black, Prussian blue, etc., chrome yellow, etc.—*Antonio Sansome.*

Calico Printing Machine.

The Calico Printing Machine consists of a large *drum*, revolving on its axis. The drum is covered with several layers of a coarse cloth called *lapping*, in order to form a kind of elastic cushion. Against this drum is pressed the engraved *copper cylinder*, which receives the color from a wooden cylinder, covered with cloth, and revolving or dipping in the *color trough*. In order to remove the surplus color from the copper roller, the so-called *doctor* is supplied. The latter is simply a sharp blade, which is pressed at an angle on the roller, and scrapes off all the color from the roller except that which is contained in the engraving. In order to remove any loose threads or filaments the so-called *lint-doctor* is also supplied, working on the other side of the roller, opposite to the color-doctor.

TWELVE-COLOR CALICO PRINTING MACHINE.

Cloth to be printed passes between the engraved copper roller and the drum, and, in order to have an elastic under layer, it is supplied with the *blanket*, which is a thick, strong cloth, generally made of pure wool, and which is arranged as an endless web, both ends being carefully sewn together. For keeping the blanket clean the *back cloth* is allowed to go between the blanket and the printing cloth. The back cloth is simply formed of gray cloth, which has to be bleached and printed in its turn.

The three cloths—that is, the blanket, the back cloth and the *printing cloth*—go through at the same time between the drum and the printing roller. The latter gives the color in the engraving over to the printing cloth next to it, and this giving up is caused, first, by the pressure of the printing roller against the drum, and secondly by the action of the lapping and the blanket, which, by forming a kind of elastic cushion, press the print cloth into the engraved cavities of the roller and force the cloth to absorb the color, which is prevented spreading over by the pressure asserted at the time.

For each color one roller is necessary, and therefore a pattern containing more than one color or shade requires a separate roller for each, each roller, of course, containing the engraving of the color it has to give up to the cloth, and must be supplied with the other accessories of doctor, color-trough, cylinder, etc.

Additional Points about Calico Printing.

It is generally desired to make the dye or colors on calico as permanent as possible, so that they may resist the action of water, soap, soda, and other articles in ordinary domestic use for washing garments, etc., and in this respect cotton, woolen and silken goods vary greatly. The two latter have ordinarily a great affinity for vegetable coloring, with or without the aid of mordants. Cotton, on the other hand, has little or none independent of mordants ; and, even with them, the colors it receives have little permanency when compared with that shown in dyed stuffs of an animal origin. This fact is familiarly known in the loss of color which even the best dyed cotton dresses, furniture hangings, etc., undergo in the operations of repeated washing. However, the discovery and utilization of coal tar colors in dyeing and printing on cotton have greatly modified or changed the process formerly employed. The latter have the singular property of not requiring a mordant; hence, in nearly every case, they are directly transferred to the cloth, etc., by a simple immersion of it in a suitable solution of the dye.

FIXING COLORS ON COTTON CLOTH.

To fix the colors derived from a vegetable source on calico, *mordants* are used. They usually consist of some mineral substance, as the sulphate of iron or copperas, chloride of tin, acetate of lead, alum, etc. They act by uniting with coloring matter of the plant, rendering it insoluble, so as to prevent its being washed away from the article thus dyed.

The mordant is only applied in places where a certain color is to be produced. The mordants are fixed on by paste, etc., at certain portions of the cloth, and this being passed through a tub containing the coloring matter, they affect only those parts which have been covered with them, so as to permanently dye them.

Any number of vegetable colors may be produced in calico printing by a proper application of mordants, and subsequent immersion in a solution of vegetable coloring matter. Superfluous color is generally removed by a weak solution of chloride of lime and abundant washing in water.

PRINTED COLORS AND DYED COLORS.

In some instances the mordants are first printed on calicoes and the colors fixed by dyeing, in others by printing and then steaming. Indeed, the method of fixation of the different coloring matters in printing vary considerably according to the nature of the dye-stuffs, but they can be divided into two distinct classes, comprising—

1st. Printed (direct) colors.
2d. Dyed colors.

The dye colors are produced either by first printing with mordants, then fixing and dyeing in a bath with coloring matters; or the cloth is dyed all over and designs produced by the resisting or discharging processes. The printed or direct colors are applied at once on the cloth, and fixed by different methods, relying either on the steaming, oxidation, or reduction process, etc., and are therefore styled steam or oxidation colors.

All dyestuffs capable of being fixed on cotton cloth by means of mordants can be employed for dyeing cloth on which the mordants are printed, and this plan is sometimes followed, but not so much since the development of steam colors.

AGEING, DUNGING AND FIXING PROCESSES.

The *ageing process* has for its object the decomposing of the acetates, so that acetic acid is driven off and a basic insoluble product is deposited on the fibre. For this the steam ageing apparatus is now successfully used, the cloth passing rapidly through it, and exposed for about two minutes to a temperature of 185° F.

The ageing process is followed by the so-called *dunging* or *fixing process*. This operation consists simply in passing the cloth in a continuous manner through an apparatus or cistern containing the dunging liquors. The object of this is—first of all to complete precipitation of the insoluble compound on the fibre, and at the same time the removing of the thickening, and also any portion of the mordant which has not been fixed on the fibre. The brightening process consists in treating the cloth with a so-called *acid* soap.

TOPICAL, RESIST AND DISCHARGE PROCESSES.

At times colors are printed on calico *topically;* that is, they are applied, mixed with gum, etc., directly on the cloth. By this method the dye is imprinted on at once, and no further manipulation is required. On the other hand, *resists*, or substances which prevent the action of the dye on cloth, are used; and places so marked return a white appearance, or that of the "ground" already dyed.

Another method which is often employed in calico printing is that of "*discharging.*" If, for example, a piece of black cotton cloth be marked over by blocks covered with a paste containing tartaric or citric acid, wherever the latter touches the cloth, its color will be removed or "discharged," and thus white spots are produced on the black ground. Numerous modifications of this principle with other discharging agents, and various coloring matters, are of frequent use for producing colored patterns on an even-dyed ground.

In *the discharging process* the goods are padded all over, or on one side only, with mordant and dried, and afterwards the discharge is printed on, which, by dissolving the iron or alumina mordant where it is applied, prevents any color from being formed there, and therefore causes the production of white spots on colored grounds when the goods are dyed in alizarin, etc.

Still another method is found in cases where the same mordant produces various colors with different coloring matters.

EXTRACT STYLES.

The steaming method is generally known as the *extract style*, and, as a rule, the majority of alizarin steam colors —reds, pinks, purples, chocolates, browns, etc.—are fast, being printed on cloth previously prepared with oleine or alizarin oil. Alizarin reds and pinks are also printed with alumina mordants, purples with iron, and chocolates with mixtures of iron and alumina mordants. In fact, alizarin is fixed on calico by two distinct methods, either by dyeing or printing. In the latter case steaming is necessary for the development of the shades.

PADDING AND MADDER STYLES.

The so-called *padding styles* in calico printing are, in reality, a modification of the madder styles or alizarin dyed colors, and, although not used so largely as formerly, are still employed in print works to a certain extent.

The *madder styles*, which were at one time very largely used, have not been much in vogue the last few years, but prints in which dyed alizarin red enters have been, and are now, very extensively produced, especially for designs of red and aniline black on white grounds.

In printing works the practice of steaming varies considerably. While aniline colors generally are steamed, sometimes at about four pounds pressure, alizarin steam reds are sometimes steamed at much higher pressure, some printers maintaining that at much higher pressure better colors are the result.

Starchy substances are generally employed as thickeners, or as sizing or finishing materials in printed cottons, such as wheat starch, rice starch, Indian or maize starch, potato starch or farina starch, wheat flour, gums, albumens, glues, gelatines, etc.

PIGMENTS AND RED WOODS.

The pigment colors now generally used are the following:

First in importance is *ultramarine*, then *chrome orange*, *chrome* and *cadmium yellow*, *chrome green*, *vermillion*, *buff* or *oxide of iron*, *ochre*, *burnt sienna*, *lampblack*, etc. These can be fixed by steaming, as also the aniline or coal tar colors and the dye wood extracts.

Red woods are not now often used as self-colors, but they are still used to a great extent in compound shades, principally for the production of chocolates, browns, etc.

Since the lowering in price of artificial alizarin the chocolates derived from the red dye-wood have lost a great deal of their importance, the more so as the production of these chocolates with alizarin, on red or purple colors of the print works, are mixed together, the shades being modified according to requirement by the addition of dye wood extracts, etc. The extracts of dye woods are also very extensively used for the production of fancy or light shades of great variety.

COAL TAR COLORS.

The coloring matters derived from coal tar are of three kinds: The *benzol colors*, which comprise all the aniline dyes, and also the carbolic acid or phenol dyestuffs; the *naphthaline colors*, which comprise the azo products, and the *anthracene* derivatives, principally alizarin, etc.

Coal tar colors now form the most important class of dye products used in printing. For calico printing the aniline and the anthracene colors are of the utmost importance, while those derived from naphthaline, principally the azo colors, are only employed to a moderate extent in printing, on account of the difficulty or impossibility of obtaining fast shades with these products.

One of the great difficulties at first experienced in the printing of aniline was the liability of the color either to turn to a greenish hue by exposure, owing to the effect of the sulphurous acid, or the danger of rottening the fabric. These difficulties, however, are not so much encountered now as formerly.

MINERAL COLORS, ETC.

Mineral colors are fixed on cotton in two ways—as ready-made pigments, by the aid of a fixing medium, or by applying first the mordant and afterwards developing the color in another bath.

The dyeing of cotton cloth in the indigo vat has not experienced much change in late years, except that the continuous dyeing machines have come more prominently into use in preference to the round vats formerly employed.

White patterns under aniline black are now often produced by padding the goods with aniline black color, then printing on alkaline resist, and afterwards exposing the goods to ageing in the usual way.

The acid colors are not so much employed in calico printing as the aniline basic dyestuffs; the aniline blues, however, are pretty largely used, and they supply shades which will stand even lukewarm soaping, and are also very bright, but they do not come up in the point of fastness.

Iron steam blacks are not now so much employed as formerly. There are now some logwood preparations which yield some very good steam blacks.

DYEWOOD, EXTRACTS, ETC.

Indeed the most important of the dyewood extracts in calico printing is still the *logwood extract*, which is employed in very large quantities for the production of steam blacks, and in a smaller way in the production of compound shades.

The brands of alizarins generally used for steam reds are those of yellow shades, because they give a color which is more pleasing to the eye, as can be easily understood.

Turkey red goods, obtained by the discharging process after dyeing, are produced in very large quantities. The cloth is first of all dyed Turkey red, and then the patterns are produced by discharging, and thus whites, yellows, blues, greens and blacks are obtained on red grounds.

Violets and greens produce deep blue colors on calicoes, and are extensively used for the purpose in print works, but the shades obtained are not as bright as those produced by some other methods.

Olive greens are very largely employed in steam color printing, and are mostly produced by means of logwood, berry extracts, etc.—*Extracts from " Calico Printing."*

Price of Domestic Ginghams in 1818.

Extract of letter from Samuel Slater, Jr., of New Povidence, R. I., to J. & M. Brown, Philadelphia, Pa., August 14, 1818:

" A Providence friend of mine sent me a letter to-day which he had recently received from his correspondent in Philadelphia, stating that you, he and others, could not obtain more than about *thirty* cents for good ginghams, on a credit of four to six months."

The Calender.

This is a machine for smoothing or hot-pressing cotton fabrics between rollers to give them a glossy appearance. The domestic processes of starching and ironing afford simple illustration of the object and result of calendering. The mangle effects the same object as the flat-iron, and is a near approach in construction to the calendering machine. The latter was originally of wood. Hollow iron and copper cylinders are used where heat as well as pressure are required, the cylinders being heated by steam passed through the interior, or by red-hot heaters; but it is desirable that one of the cylinders shall be of a material combining considerable hardness with a degree of elasticity; for this purpose solid paper cylinders are used.

Before the final calendering the fabric is flatly smoothed by passing over warm cylinders. Cotton goods are starched with flour, thickened with plaster of Paris, porcelain clay, etc., to give them the appearance of stoutness, which of course vanishes when the article is washed. The fabric is then simply passed between plain cylinders, which produces the desired effect by flattening the threads; when, by means of a cylinder with a pattern raised upon it, the amount of this flattening is unequal on different parts of the cloth, the effect known as *watering* is the result. *Glazing* is produced by the rollers being made to move with different velocities, so that one side of the fabric is rubbed as well as pressed by the roller whose surface moves with greater rapidity. A copper roller is used for glazing, so hot that if the machine stops it burns the goods.

Finishing Printed Cottons.

The finishing of printed cotton fabrics is a very important question, as upon the way the goods have been finished depends, to a great extent, their saleable value. With the exception of Turkey red prints, and some kind of indigoes, all printed goods are subjected to the finishing operations.

The finish varies considerably, according to the styles, and especially according to the markets for which the goods are intended; and finishing is a branch of industry which can only be learned by practice, therefore we shall only treat of the principle here, and indicate the apparatus usually employed. For some goods no stiffening is required, while for others a starching all over is necessary; but prints are, as a rule, only starched at the back. In some instances a lustre is required on the cloth, while on others only a matt finish is wanted.

The *starching* of prints all over is performed on the starching machines, and is still in principle the old arrangement of a frame supporting three rollers, one of brass or copper between two of hard wood. The cloth, after passing through a trough, is squeezed by passing between the copper and the wooden rollers to remove the excess of starch; the cloth is then dried on the drying machine, and in order to give smoothness is passed through the mangle or calender. The starch is simply prepared by boiling starch in a pan, often only by direct steam in a tub, and can be made thinner or thicker according to requirements.

Sago flour and potato starch are, as a rule, preferred by the finisher, but mixtures are found in the market suitable for special purposes. In boiling the starch a low temperature gives better results than a hard boiling. To impart a more pleasing appearance to goods containing white, a small quantity of blue, principally ultramarine, is added to the starch, and, as a rule, also a softening, such as soap, tallow, etc., and for some purposes glycerine, which is the best material that can be used for the purpose. Often China clay and other white pigments are added to the starch, in order to give artificial weight and to fill the cloth.

The *back starching* machine is largely used now in the finishing of modern prints; it relies on the principle of a roller revolving in a starch trough, taking up starch on its surface, and giving it to the cloth, which is passed in full width over it. The drying of this back starched cloth is also performed on the cylinders or tins, which are provided with a special arrangement of skeleton wooden cylinders, in order to allow only the surface without the starch to touch the heated cylinder until the starch is sufficiently dry to be passed to the set of cylinders in the ordinary manner.

The Stretching.—For widening the pieces which have been stretched only in the direction of the length by the different operations of bleaching and printing, several arrangements are devised, working on different principles, such as with grooved cylinders, etc., or on the principle of widening, or as in the so-called *stentering machine,* by the arrangement of a long frame, the widening performed by means of endless traveling bands containing pins or clamps on both sides of the pieces.

The *Calender* is of different construction, but it consists in principle of an intermediate iron bowl, and two other bowls, generally made of paper or compressed cotton, which assert a very heavy pressure on the cloth, which passes around the iron bowl, and consequently between this and consecutively one and the other of the bowls, which assert a heavy pressure on the intermediate iron, one by means of screws or other suitable arrangements.

The iron bowl is generally made hollow, in order that it may be heated by steam, or sometimes by means of heated cannon balls or gas.

The *friction calender or mangle,* which is often required to impart a higher gloss to the goods, works on the principle of two paper bowls, with an iron one on top, and this latter, besides asserting a heavy pressure on the other two, is made to revolve at a higher speed than they do, and thus a friction is caused on the cloth.— *Cotton Mfg.*

Engraved Copper Cylinder and Blocks in Calico Printing.

Baines thus describes the engraved copper cylinder used in calico printing:

"A polished copper cylinder, several feet in length (according to the width of the piece of cotton cloth to be printed), and three or four inches in diameter, is engraved with a pattern round its whole circumference, and from end to end; it is then placed horizontally in the press, or printing machine, and, as it revolves, the lower part of the circumference passes through the coloring matter, which is again removed from the whole surface of the cylinder, except the engraved pattern, by an elastic steel blade, placed in contact with the cylinder, and reduced to so fine and straight an edge as to take off the color without scratching the copper.

"The color being thus left only on the engraved pattern, the piece of cotton cloth is drawn tightly over the cylinder, which revolves in the same direction, and prints the cloth. After the piece is printed it passes over several metallic boxes, heated by steam, which dry it. A piece of cloth may be thus printed and dried in one or two minutes, or in even shorter time, which, by the old method, would have required the application of the block 448 times.

"Two, three, four, or even twenty cylinders may be used at the same time in one machine (according to its size and construction), each cylinder having engraved upon it a different portion of the pattern, and being supplied with a different color. The piece of cloth passes over them successively, and receives the entire pattern almost in the same moment. To produce the same effect by hand-block printing would require 896, 1,344, 1,792, or 2,240 applications of the blocks, according as two, three, four or five cylinders are employed."

First Cotton Goods Made in England.

The first cotton goods of English make in which both the warp and weft were wholly or entirely of cotton, were made at Derby, in 1773. After a considerable quantity of these goods had been made, the manufacturers discovered that an existing law imposed not only a double duty upon them when printed, but also prohibited the sale of them in the home market.

How Copper Rollers for Printing Calico are Engraved.

The copper roller used in the calico printing machine is a hollow cylinder, from $\frac{1}{2}$ inch to $1\frac{1}{2}$ inches in thickness, and is mounted on an iron axis to revolve and be pressed against the iron drum of the machine. The engraving of copper rollers is done sometimes by hand, but more often by mechanical or chemical process. The mechanical method, or mill engraving, relies on the following principle : The pattern to be engraved is cut by hand on a small cylinder of soft steel, which is then subjected to the process of hardening, and the design is then produced on another soft steel cylinder by a heavy rolling pressure on specially constructed machinery. The second cylinder is then utilized to produce the design on the copper roller, on which it is pressed by heavy pressure on suitable machines, when the copper, being softer, easily takes the impression, the design being repeated all over the roller wherever required. In the chemical process, or etching method, the copper roller is covered all over with a layer of varnish, on which the design is cut through by a sharp point moved by means of a pentagraph machine, according to the design required; the varnish is removed by the sharp point, and the copper is laid bare. The roller is then immersed, or rather allowed to revolve for a short time in a bath of weak nitric acid—sometimes along with chromic acid, when the copper is, to a certain extent, dissolved in the portions not protected by the varnish— and etched to a sufficient depth to carry the necessary amount of color. It is finally washed and dried, and after the varnish has been removed the roller is, if necessary, polished, and is ready for printing.

No Sheetings, Shirtings, Ginghams, etc., Made in the United States Before 1790.

According to the most reliable historical and manufacturing authorities, no cotton sheetings, shirtings, ginghams, or checks, were made in the United States prior to the year 1790. All such classes of goods then used by our people were imported, being of English manufacture, and of linen warp, with cotton weft.

Steam Styles of Prints.

Many Print Works doing steam styles have left off the boiling in lime, which was usually the first treatment in bleaching, contenting themselves with a good soda boil and an increased strength of bleaching powder before the final scouring, and the result is their whites are only passable. The goods will do for the lower class of steam work, but alizarine red and pinks do not show up well. The cloth is not thoroughly bottomed, and will not serve for dyed styles. It seems true, what old bleachers maintain, that for a thorough cleansing from the bottom, the lime boil is quite necessary.

Progress in Cotton Spinning and Weaving.

Great progress has been made in this country in spinning and weaving fabrics of Nos. 60 to 100, such as lawns and fine dress goods; also spinning fine yarns for spool cotton. Yarns as fine as 80 to 180 are now spun on ring-spinning frames, which are being more largely used for warp-spinning than any other. This machine was invented here, and is now also used in Europe. Yarns as fine as 550 are spun on mules for three-cord sewing cotton. The cotton factories of the Carolinas and Georgia are said to have twice the advantage of Lancashire that New England possesses.

Cloth Selvages.

Nothing adds more to the appearance of a piece of cloth than a good selvage. Whether the cloth is to be used by the consumer in a gray, or in some finished state, a good selvage is equally a desideratum. "In those countries where gray calicoes are used for clothing, without passing through the hands of tailors or dressmakers, where civilization has made more or less progress, an even, clean selvage is, necessarily, of vital importance. In goods which undergo some process of finishing before they are purchased by the consumers, the qualities required to form a perfect selvage have to be considered from another standpoint. In these goods the selvages are usually cut away when the material is being made up into a garment. Ladies, however, when purchasing goods, whether made of silk, wool or cotton, hesitate before buying a piece of material which is bordered by even one ragged selvage, rightly judging that a manufacturer who would be content to produce cloth thus imperfectly made, could not be trusted to turn out pieces free from imperfections between the selvages."

Influence of Light on Dyed Colors.

The chemical activity of the sun's rays is well known, and certain unstable mordant solutions seem to be decomposed and precipitated more readily under the influence of light. It is not surprising, therefore, to find that light should also have a very marked effect upon dyed colors. Under the prolonged influence of light and air almost all colors fade, and according to their relative behavior in this respect they are broadly divided into two classes, namely, those which are "fast to light" and those which are "not fast to light."

Each of the colored rays of the spectrum possesses a different fading power. White light is the most active, then follow the yellow, blue, green, orange, violet and red rays. Direct sunlight is more energetic than diffused daylight. The light of the electric art acts in the same sense as sunlight, but is less powerful.

According to the best authorities on colors, the presence of oxygen and moisture assists very materially in the fading action of light, so that even some fugitive colors, dyed, for example, with safflower, annatto, orchid, do not fade if exposed to light in dry oxygen, or *in vacuo*.

Definition of Tones, Scales and Hues of Colors.

TONE of a color is intended exclusively to designate the various modifications which that color, in its greatest intensity, is capable of receiving from *white*, which *lowers* its tone, or of *black*, which *heightens* it.

SCALE is applied to the assemblage of tones of the same color thus modified. The pure color is the normal tone of the scale, that is, if the normal tone does not belong to a scale of which all the tones are made dull with black.

HUE is applied exclusively to the modifications which a color receives from the addition of a small quantity of another.

Colors are distinguished as *pure, broken, reduced, gray* or *dull*. Pure colors are those termed *simple*, as red, yellow, blue, and those which result from their binary compounds, orange, green, violet and other hues.

Broken colors are the pure colors mixed with black, from the tone of the lightest to the deepest.—*Chevreul*.

Electricity in Printing Cottons.

The application of the electrical current to the production of coloring matters, or for the fixation of dyestuffs in dyeing and calico printing, according to Sansone, has attracted considerable attention in the last few years at the hands of chemists.

"The application of electricity for the developing or fixing coloring matters is based upon the chemical processes largely·utilized in printing, viz., oxidation and reduction, and when it is remembered that both processes can be separately effected by the electrical current, we can easily imagine that all the colors which can be produced by oxidation or reduction ought to be obtained by the electrical process.

"Consequently we have of the oxidation colors or of the methods relying on oxidation, the following: Analine black, persulphocyanogen yellow (canarin), the discharge of indigo or turkey red, and the formation of some coloring matters, such as alizarin from anthraquinone, etc., the bleaching of vegetable fibres and formation of oxycellulose being also possible by the same process.

"In the reduction processes, of course, is concluded the preparation of an indigo vat for dyeing, and the investigator has also tried to print indigo in a direct way on calico, by utilizing the reducing action of the current in the color box. He has also aimed at producing an electrical printing machine, by which colors could be fixed on calico by the electrolitic direct process, but, as said before, we must wait awhile before we can pass any judgment over the feasibility of electrical application in calico printing.

"So far, however, electricity has been utilized in calico printing, but in a different manner from the galvanoplastic processes, and depositing either copper or iron shell rollers, thus producing printing rollers with a copper layer at a very low cost; or for the commonly called galvanizing process, by coating the ordinary copper roller with a thin layer of nickel, in order to render them more liable to stand acid colors. The gilding of copper rollers has scarcely ever been employed, but considering the low cost of depositing a very thin film of gold, which can be done by the modern galvanoplastic process, it is a matter well worth trying for those rollers which are used for printing very acid colors."

Calico in the Form of Sateen.

Calico in its new form and under the name of sateen, is the same fabric, with the same material and process of printing, except that sateen is woven on three, four or five harness, which enables the manufacturer to make what is called a warp or satin face. French sateen is, in weaving parlance, "quarter satin"—both these fabrics take their name from the method or manner of weaving. Satin is woven on sixteen harness, with fifteen threads up every time a filling pick is thrown in; while sateen is woven on four harness, usually with three-warp threads up every time a filling pick goes in.

Cotton Industry of the World in 1888.

The following figures are given for the spindles, looms and thread-spindles of the industrial countries of the world in 1888: Spindles—England, 42,740,000; European Continent, 23,380,000; United States, 13,525,000; East India, 2,490,000; total, 82,135,000. There were besides, in Canada, Mexico and South-America some 600,000, and in Japan, 100,000; grand total, 82,825,000. On the European Continent, Germany occupied the first place with about 5,500,000 spindles, France being second with 5,200,000. The total number of mechanical looms in Europe in 1888 was estimated at 1,000,000, of which about 600,000 were in England.

Effect of Heat on Cotton Fabrics.

Recent experiments have shown that cotton may be heated to 248 deg. F., for three hours, without apparent injury. The same may be said of printed cottons. The same temperature, however, will, if continued for a longer period, slightly change the color of cotton, but will not otherwise injure it.

Cotton Consumed in Manufacturing.

The estimated annual consumption of cotton in England, for the past ten years, has been 1,416,440,000 pounds, as against 770,343,200 pounds for the United States. England requires rather more cotton than all the rest of the Continent of Europe put together, the total of the combined countries amounting to no more than 1,295,600,000 pounds annually.

STARCH MANGLE. BACK STARCHING MACHINE. DRYING CYLINDERS. Finishing Machine.

Early British Cotton Industries.

The quantity of cotton imported into England, according to the custom-house returns of that country, from 1701 to 1800, inclusive, is given as follows:

Years.	Pounds.	Years.	Pounds.
1701	1,985,868	1751	2,976,610
1701 to 1705—av.	1,170,881	1764	3,870,392
1710	715,008	1771 to 1775	4,764,589
1720	1,972,805	1776 to 1780	6,766,613
1730	1,545,472	1790	31,447,605
1741	1,645,031	1800	56,010,732

EXPORTS OF COTTONS FROM 1701 TO 1800.

The value of British cottons exported from 1701 to 1800, inclusive, was as below:

OFFICIAL VALUE.

Years.	£.	Years.	£.
1701	23,253	1764	200,354
1710	5,698	1766	220,759
1720	16,200	1780	355,060
1730	13,524	1787	1,101,457
1741	20,709	1790	1,662,359
1751	45,986	1800	5,406,501

COTTON CONSUMED IN ENGLAND IN 1787.

The purposes for which cotton was used in the year 1787 are thus stated:

	Pounds.
Calicoes and Muslins	11,600,000
Fustians	6,000,000
Mixtures with silk and linen	2,000,000
Hosiery	1,500,000
Candlewicks	1,500,000
Total	22,600,000

VALUE OF ENGLISH COTTON MANUFACTURES IN 1767 AND 1787.

The value of English cotton manufactures in 1767 and 1787 is shown in the annexed table:

1767	£ 600,000
1787	3,304,371

The above shows an increase in the twenty years of 5½ fold. In 1787 the number of cotton mills in England was 119, and in Scotland, Wales, and Isle of Man, 24, making altogether 143 mills or factories.

ENGLISH AND SCOTCH COTTON POWER LOOMS IN 1820 AND 1829.

In 1820 and 1829, the number of cotton power looms in England and Scotland was given as below:

	1820.	1829.
In England	12,150	45,500
In Scotland	2,000	10,000
Total	14,150	55,500

COTTON POWER LOOMS OF GREAT BRITAIN IN 1833.

In 1833 the showing of cotton power looms in Great Britain was as follows:

In England	85,000
In Scotland	15,000
Total	100,000

EARLY RESTRICTIONS ON CALICO PRINTING IN ENGLAND.

As regards calico printing in England, the business was subjected to onerous duties and vexatious excise regulations from its infancy to 1831.

In 1700, Act 11 and 12, William III., Cap. 10, forbade the introduction of Indian printed calicoes into England, for domestic use, either as apparel or furniture, under penalty of £200 on the wearer or seller; other acts for the same purpose were passed at a later date. In their petition to His Majesty's Privy Council for trade in 1831, the natives of Bengal, India, state that Bengal cottons, when used in England, are charged with a duty of 10 per cent. There was also levied up to that time in England an excise duty on English printed calicoes of $3\frac{1}{2}$d. per yard.

In 1712 Parliament imposed an excise duty of 3d. per square on "calicoes printed, stained, painted, or dyed," and in 1714 the duty was raised to 6d. per square yard. In 1720 Parliament prohibited the use or wear of any printed or dyed calicoes whatsoever, whether printed at home or abroad, and even of any goods in which cotton found a part; excepting only "calicoes dyed all blue, and muslins, neck cloths, and fustians."

In 1736 (by the 9th, George II., C. 4,) so much of the act of 1720 was repealed as forbade the use or wear of printed goods of a mixed kind containing cotton; and thenceforth cloths were made and printed of linen warp and cotton weft, probably approaching in appearance to calicoes.

In 1774 Parliament removed the prohibition as regards English calicoes and allowed them to be printed on paying an excise duty of 3d. per square yard. In 1779 and 1782 three several additions of 5 per cent., making on the whole 15 per cent., were made to that duty.

DUTIES ON COTTONS AND MIXED GOODS IN 1784.

In 1784, the Act 24, George III., C. 40, laid a new duty on all cottons and mixed goods of 1d. per yard, of bleached or printed, under 3s. per yard in value, and 2d. on all above that value—in addition to the former duties of 3d. per yard; and 15 per cent. additiona was charged on new duties as well as on the old.

In 1785, owing to the opposition of the cotton manufacturers, a short bill (25, Geo. III., C. 24,) was passed by Parliament, repealing all the new duties imposed by the previous bill on the linen and cotton manufactures. By the 25, Geo. III., C. 72, all cottons, muslins, and stuffs of which cotton formed a part, when printed, painted, dyed, or stained, were made liable to an additional duty of 2d. per yard, if of the value of 1s. 8d. and not more than 3s. per yard; and to a duty of 4d. per yard, if worth more than 3s. The addition of 15 per cent. was also charged upon these duties, as well as upon the duty of 3d. per yard imposed in 1774. Therefore the duties stood thus:

ADDED DUTIES ON COTTONS IN 1785.

	Duty imposed in 1774. Per yard.	Additional imposed in 1785. Per yard.	15 per cent. on the whole. Per yard.	Total Duty. Per yard.
Above the value of 1s. 8d., and not above 3s. per yard......	3d.	2d.	$\tfrac{3}{4}$d.	$5\tfrac{3}{4}$d.
Above the value of 3s. per yard.	3d.	4d.	$1\tfrac{1}{5}$d.	$8\tfrac{1}{5}$d.

CONSOLIDATION OF BRITISH CUSTOMS IN 1787.

On the consolidation of the British customs in 1787 all former duties were repealed, and cotton, linen, or mixed goods of any kind were subjected to a duty of $3\tfrac{1}{2}$d. per square yard, when printed or dyed. The whole duty was returned by drawback on the exportation of the goods. At the same time, foreign calicoes and muslins were charged with a duty of 7d. per square yard, when printed or dyed in Great Britain.

The duties fixed in 1787 continued till 1831, when, on the earnest representations of the calico printers, they were entirely remitted, and released the trade from the shackles of the excise.

BRITISH CALICOES AND MUSLINS PRINTED IN 1796 AND 1800.

The calicoes and muslins printed in Great Britain in 1796 and 1800 were as follows:

IN ENGLAND.	Rate of Duty.	1796. yards.	1800. yards.
Foreign calicoes and muslins.	7d.	1,750,270	1,577,536
British " " "	3½d.	24,363,240	28,692,790
IN SCOTLAND.			
Foreign calicoes and muslins.	7d.	141,403	78,868
British " " "	3½d.	4,258,557	4,176,939

EXPORTATION AND CONSUMPTION OF BRITISH CALICOES, ETC., IN 1814, 1820, AND 1830.

The accompanying table gives the printing, home consumption, and exportation of British calicoes, muslins, etc., in 1814, 1820, and 1830. (The average duty per piece was 5s., which, when exported, was refunded).

Years.	Printed. Pieces.	Consumed at home. Pieces.	Exported. Pieces.
1814	5,192,228	1,868,068	3,324,160
1820	5,456,196	1,728,340	3,727,820
1825	8,140,876	2,015,972	4,082,684
1830	8,596,952	2,281,512	6,315,440

SELLING PRICES OF COTTON IN ENGLAND IN 1780.

In 1780, the prices at which cotton sold in England are given as follows:

	Per Pound. s. d.
Berbice	2 1
Demarara	1 11 to 2s. 1d.
Surinam	2 0
Cayenne	2 0
St. Domingo	1 10
Tabago	1 9
Jamaica	1 7
Isle of Bourbon	7 6 to 10s.

Three Operations in Dyeing Cotton.

The dyeing of cotton usually requires three distinct operations, namely, the impregnation of the fibre: first with tannic acid, secondly with nitrate of iron, stamic chloride, or tartar emetic, and thirdly, with the solution of coloring matter.

Cotton Manufacturing Districts of Great Britain.

Blackburn is the most northern of those districts in England which take an important part in the cotton goods industry. It takes the lead in Lancashire, with regard to its importance as an exclusively cotton manufacturing town, says Prof. Brooks. The class of goods made there are of a plain character, principally shirtings, mulls and jaconets, while a large number of looms are engaged on dhooties.

Darwen weaving industry is of a similar character, and there is a fair trade in yarn by several sale-spinning mills.

Preston and Chorley have a connection with goods of a distinctly finer and more "fancy" character, such as leno, velveteen, damasks, embroidery and brocades, while the plain trade, including the well-known home made shirting, is important. Here also the spinning trade is comparatively small, the yarns spun being 40—80's T and 40—90's W.

Burnley is remarkable for the recent increase of cotton manufacturing within its borough, and has a most extensive trade in Burnley printers and shirtings, with a few heavy twills ranking second to Blackburn in quantity produced.

Accrington, Harwood and district have a plain trade, but in yarns the goods are of a much finer character than other plain districts. A large business is done in the better classes of printers for the supply of the local print and dyeworks.

Bolton has centered in it the spinning of medium fine yarns, 40—200's, from Egyptian cotton, also the manufacture of heavy fancy goods, especially Alhambras, Marseilles, and other counterpanes and towels, with some finer fancies of leno, damasks and velvets, although many mills are to be found engaged in Blackburn goods.

Haslingden, Bacup, Rawtenstall, and many smaller districts in East Lancashire are engaged in manufactures of coarse and heavily-sized goods, shirtings, T-cloths, wigans and domestics.

Manchester, while being pre-eminently the English market of the manufactured cotton goods, is also known as the locality where the finest yarns known to commerce are spun, i.e., yarns from Egypt and Sea Island cottons, 80—200's in twists and 80—350's in weft. The finer numbers, however, are not used for the ordinary purposes of manufacturing, their consumption being divided between the lace curtain manufactories of Nottingham and the great sewing thread factories.

The weaving trade of Manchester consists of checks, ginghams, Harvard and Oxford shirtings mostly.

Oldham is the spinning town. Here the coarsest yarns, 4-24's, made out of the waste from finer mills, have their spinning centre, and here the spinning of medium yarns from American cotton has made the name of the town familiar wherever English cotton yarn is known.

Rochdale depends mainly on the coarse trade, 12-24 wraps (water T) made from Indian cotton, together with some mule spinning up to 30-40's. The weaving of the heaviest cotton goods from waste, twills, sheets, T-cloths, velveteens, fustian and cords is here carried on.

Mossley, 30-50's, wrap yarn; Shaw Lees, Royton, Dukinfield, Ashton, Heywood and Hyde, may be placed in the same category as Oldham, minus the waste trade.

Stalybridge spins 30-150's.

Stockport has good trade in spinning, as high as 150's gassed and doubled yarns with varied weaving, including the well-known Turkish towels.

Cotton weaving extends no further into Yorkshire than Todmordeo, and about 2,000,000 spinning and doubling spindles are in use about Halifax, Brighouse, Sowery Bridge and district, these being employed on yarns for dress fabrics made of a mixture of cotton and worsted, as well as for cotton and hosiery in the Nottingham and Leicester districts.

In Scotland the cotton trade is confined to the counties of Lanark, Renfrew and Ayr. The doubling spindles there are on the increase, especially for the Paisley thread trade. The weaving department is also increasing, there being in 1888 in the three counties 28,853 looms, as compared with 20,963 in 1856. Superior classes of cloth are made for the home trade—fine reeds, fine muslin, plain and figured—and the manufacture of Turkey reds is also extensive.

In Ireland there are three cotton-spinning firms, three cotton-weaving firms, and one both spinning and weaving, with a total of 70,900 spindles and 2,501 power looms.

Summarizing the different classes of work into which the cotton industry of England is divided, we may allot to the coarse plain trade the Rossendale Valley and Rochdale, locating the medium plain trade in Blackburn, Burnley and Darwen, with the finest plain goods in Accrington and Preston, the light fancy trade in Preston, Chorley and Ashton, and the heavy fancy in Bolton and Bury.—*British Cotton Mfg.*

Varieties of British Cotton Cloth.

The principal makes of British cotton cloth are given by C. P. Brooks, M. S. A., as follows:

SHIRTINGS.

Shirtings are heavily-sized goods, 125 per cent. not being unusual. The widths vary from 38 to 50 inches, length always $37\frac{1}{2}$ yards, long stick. Reed and pick from 12 square to 16x15. These goods are made to weight thus: A 39-inch, 16x15, weighs 8 lb.; a 45-inch, 9 lb.; a 50-inch, 10 lb. Various kinds are made, some medium-sized. What is known as Indian shirting is the heavy-sized class.

Shirtings are exported to India, China, Japan, Turkey, Italy, Levant. A good class is made, bleached, and exported to Egypt, Japan, India and China, as white shirtings.

DHOOTIES.

Dhooties are shirtings ornamented by stripes of gray or colored yarn, and in suitable lengths for Hindoo loin cloths. The stripes are of a varied character in gray dhooties, being simply tape edges formed by cramping gray or bleached yarn at the selvage. In colored dhooties, stripes of vari-colored warps are introduced about an inch from the edge of the cloth, and varying from $\frac{1}{2}$ an inch in width to 4 inches, sometimes being introduced at intervals all across the piece.

A range of dhooties includes all widths from 22 to 50 inches, and the length of scarf varying from 2 yards in the smaller size to 5 yards in the larger. A scarf is the distance between the headings, which in these goods is very extensive, sometimes reaching to 20 inches in length at the junction of the two scarfs:

A Range—22 inches and 23 inches....2-yard scarf.
        24   "   25   "   ....$2\frac{1}{2}$ "   "
        26   "   28   " 3   "   "
        29   "   32   "   ....$3\frac{1}{2}$ "   "
        35 inches................ 4   "   "

The higher widths being variously $4\frac{1}{2}$ or 5 yards.

Dhooties are made up in about 40-yard lengths; thus a piece 44 inches wide would contain 4 double scarfs. The yarns employed vary similarly to shirtings, from 30s to 40s warp, 36s to 60s wefts.

HINDOO AND JAVANESE CLOTHS.

The dress of a male Hindoo consists of a dhootie containing 4 square yards, a doputta of 8 square yards, and a turban of 12 square yards, while in addition the Hindoo woman wears a sarrie, a similar cloth to the dhootie. India is the recipient of the dhooties in greatest quantity. Savongs go to Java; patadiongs to the Philippines.

To this class of shirtings belong long-cloths, mediums, wigans (plain and twill), double wraps and twills. Export long cloths are plain goods, shirting style, 36 yards long, generally 36 inches wide, 12 square, medium size.

T CLOTHS, MEXICANS AND MADAPOLLAMS.

T-cloths are always 24 yards in length, of coarse yarns, heavily sized, from 28 to 32 inches wide, 12x10 to 16x16, 4 lb. and 6 lb. in weight.

Domestics for export are from 28 to 39 inches, 60, 72, 80 or 96 yards. Warp, 18-24's; weft 16-40's; and from 14 to 16 reed and pick; medium to heavy size. A better class is made for the home trade.

Mexicans are of better quality than the foregoing, and are always above 17x17 reed and pick, yarns, twist, coarse; weft, medium; medium size; 28 to 32 inches in width.

Madapollams are lighter in reed and pick than the foregoing, being about 11 and 12 square: width 28 to 32 inches, and similar in length to the T-cloths and Mexicans; sized medium.

TURKEY REDS AND PRINTERS.

Dyeing and printing cloths form an important department.

Turkey reds, like printers, are cloths of good quality. Shirting counts and widths, but about twice the length; pure size.

Printers, Burnley make, sometimes dubbed Burnley lumps, are 32 inches, 116 yards, 16x16, 32's to 50's yarn. Quality important, yarns good, lightly sized, warps even and hard twisted, weft free from unevenness, snarls, etc.

Glossop printers, 36 inches, 19x22; 50 yards, $11\frac{3}{4}$ lbs.

These are not the only descriptions of printers, coarse cloth of varied dimensions being required, which, when stamped with patterns of every conceivable style, are exported to India, Persia, Italy, Brazil, Levant, Java and Japan.

TANJIBS, JACONETS, MULLS, CAMBRICS, ETC.

In light goods, tanjibs, jaconets, mulls and cambrics may be classed together.

Tanjibs are the coarsest; 30 to 50 inches wide, 38 yards long, 32s to 40s; lightly sized.

Jaconets and nainsooks are finer; 39 to 44 inches, 14x14 to 16x16, 32s to 50s; always 20 yards long.

Mulls are somewhat similar in style; 39 to 50 inches wide, 20 yards, 16x16 to 20x20, from 60s to 100s, yarn; pure size.

Cambrics are the finest of the group, generally wide from 24 square to 36 square, 80s to 160s, yarn; pure size.

Turkey, India, China, Japan, Roumania, the Levant, Egypt are all customers for these four cloths.

Book and tarletan muslins are very fine home trades.

A variety of cambric called embroidery cloth is largely made in some districts. It is of first-class quality, usually about 50 inches wide and cut up into short lengths.

SHEETINGS, GINGHAMS, CHECKS, ETC.

Sheetings are very wide goods—60 to 100 inches. The yarns are coarse, generally 12s to 20s, although fine sheetings are frequently made.

Waste plains are coarse goods woven with yarn spun from waste.

Ginghams, checks, zephyrs, although colored goods, are of plain weave and of unclassifiable dimensions.

Other plain cloths, needing little remark in consequence of their unimportance, are:

	Inches.	Yards.	Square.
Tarletan Muslin	52	40	13
Chambray	28	30	27x22
Hair-cord Muslin	59	24	20x22

Wrapped one twofold and one fine single.

| Blue Mottle | 27 | 96 | 16x11 |

Blue warp, white weft.

Victoria lawns, fine goods and Taffechelas, formerly important goods, are now in little request.

DRILLS, ETC.

Cotton cloths other than plain:

Drills—Heavy 3-shaft twills, narrow, heavily sized. Exported chiefly to China; few to Cyprus, Levant, Turkey and Brazil.

CRETONNES, JEANS, SATEENS, ETC.

Cretonnes—Printed twill, made from coarse waste wefts, finer warps, various widths, generally narrow. Home trade; also exported to Turkey and British colonies.

Jeans—Finer 3-shaft twills, plain borders, narrow, for printing or finishing.

Sateens—5-shaft broken twills, 30 to 36 inches, 75 to 90 yards, 70 to 96 reed, 40 to 80 picks, 36s to 80s weft.

Velveteens—Narrow, heavy-picked cloths, from 90 to 120 to the quarter-inch, yarns fine and best quality, 80 to 100 yards. Home trade and general export.

CORDS, FUSTIANS, CORDUROYS, ETC.

Cords, Fustians, Corduroys—Heavy, figured cloths, 20s yarn, 90 to 140 picks* to a quarter-inch, 70 to 90 yards.

Brocades—Fancy jacquard goods; 36 inches, 75 yards; 72 to 96 reed, 20 to 26 picks.

Doriah Stripes—Cloth carrying crammed stripes—not in color—are often narrow, 26 to 30 inches, 10 yards long, 12 to 30 reed by 13 to 14 picks; yarn, 40s to 50s T, and finer wefts.

Leno—Narrow, generally 30 inches, 24 to 40 yards, very variable in reed and pick; yarns.

In white check we find:

Figured Checks—30 to 36 inches, 13x16 to 18x20; 12 yards single cuts.

	Inches.	Yards.	
Satin check	40	32	16x20
Tape check	36	24	22x20
	37	48	20x24

STANDARD MAKES OF BRITISH COTTONS.

	Width.	Length.	Reed and Pick.	Yarn or Pick.	Weight Lbs.
Shirtings	39	37½	16x15	30– 36s	8¼
T-cloths	32	24	14x14	......	6
Mexicans	32	24	18x18	......	7
Jaconets	44	20	14x14	40– 50s	..
Mulls	50	20	20x20	80–100s	..
Domestics	29	80	14x14	18– 18s	..
Dhooties	44	40	16x15	30– 40s	..
Printers	32	116	16x16	32– 50s	..

---

* Where reed and pick are given, it must be understood as referring to a quarter of an inch, unless otherwise specified. Thus—12 x 10 means 12 ends and 10 picks in a quarter of an inch, or 48 ends and 40 picks per inch.

American Cotton Plant.
(SHORT STAPLE.)

This species of cotton is cultivated in the United States. Its stem rises to the heighth of two or three feet, then divaricates into boughs, which bristle with hairs. The leaves are also hairy on their inferior surfaces, and are three or five lobed. The upper leaves are entire or heart-shaped; the petroles are velvety. The flowers near the extremities of the boughs are large and somewhat dingy in color. The capsules are ovate, four-celled, and nearly as large as a moderate sized apple, and yield a fine silky cotton of short staple. The seeds are greenish.

Cotton Manufactures of France.

In 1880 France exported cotton yarns and cotton fabrics, as follows:

	Value.
Cotton Yarns	$725,258
Cotton Fabrics	$15,822,999

The cotton mills or factories of France in 1878, according to the report of the French government published in that year, represented the following:

Cotton spinning mills	417
" spinning and weaving	76
" weaving	564
Total	1,058
They employed operatives: Men	44,092
Women	33,513
Children	19,483
Total	97,088
Cotton spindles: In operation	4,552,392
Not in operation	281,734
Total	4,834,126
Cotton power-looms: In operation	57,828
Not in operation	4,322
Total	62,150
Cotton hand-looms	50,578

In 1880 there were imported into France cotton yarns to the value of $6,319,792, and cotton fabrics, $13,284,83.

German Cotton Manufacturing Interests.

According to the most reliable German statistical authorities, the cost of cotton mills in that country in 1877 varied from $10.59 to $15.47 per spindle.

The official statistics of the German Empire, about the same date, make the following exhibit:

Cotton hand spindles	1,613,318
" self-acting spindles	4,602,103
" water "	862,135
" twist "	548,060
" weaving looms, Jacquard power	16,333
" " " " hand	9,852
" " " power	111,046
" " " hand	29,948
" bobbin machines, power	1,588
" " " hand	304
" embroidery machines, power	76
" " " hand	1,344
" bobbinet " power	455
" " " hand	202

According to the census report of Germany in 1875, there were in that country at that date, the following:

Cotton spinning and weaving factories	104,619
Cotton operatives	296,827

From the annexed statement it will be seen that in the foregoing enumeration, what we would term petty or household enterprises, are dignified in Germany with the title of "factories."

In cotton weaving alone 97,588 establishments employed 203,489 operatives.

Cotton factories, which employed more than 5 hands in each, had an aggregate of 4,265,336 spindles.

Cotton Industries of Norway, Sweden, Austria, Switzerland, Holland, Belgium, Spain and Italy.

The following is given as about the number of cotton spindles in Sweden and Norway, Austria, Switzerland, Holland, Belgium, Spain and Italy in 1880:

Countries.	Number Cotton Spindles.	Pounds Cotton per Spindle.	Total Consumption Pounds Cotton.
Sweden and Norway	305,000	65	19,825,000
Austria	1,555,000	67	104,185,000
Switzerland	1,850,000	25	46,250,000
Holland	230,000	60	13,800,000
Belgium	800,000	50	40,000,000
Spain	1,750,000	46	80,500,000
Italy	800,000	56	44,800,000
Total	7,290,000		349,360,000

Capacity of Some of our Cotton Bagging Mills.

The capacity of the cotton bagging factories in Alabama is said to be sufficient to supply the demand for cotton bagging in this country. In 1889 these mills were turning out 30,000 yards a day, which can be increased to 45,000 yards per day. The cotton bagging which they produce is said to weigh about three-quarters of a pound to the yard of forty-four inches wide, and the cost of the same per bale of cotton to the planter averages somewhere in the neighborhood of eighty cents.

Tenuity of Cotton Fibres.

Some idea of the tenuity of the cotton fibres may be formed when it is remembered that 14,000 to 20,000 individual filaments of American cotton only weigh one grain, so that there are about 140,000,000 to every pound, and each hair only weighs on the average about the 1-17000 part of a grain, and if the separate fibres were placed end to end in a straight line, one pound would reach 2,200 miles.

How to Distinguish Cotton from Flax.

To distinguish cotton from flax, dip the mixture in a boiling solution of caustic potassa, and let it remain for two minutes. The flax will assume a dark yellow color, while the cotton will be a light yellow, or nearly white.

Russian Cotton Industry.

The cotton industry of Russia is without exception the most important trade of that country, as will be seen from the annexed synoptical table:

Name of the government or province.	No. of mills				Number of spindles		Number of power looms	
	1877		1887					
	Spinning	Weaving	Spinning	Weaving	1877.	1887.	1877.	1887.
Petersburg	13	10	12	11	750,120	791,978	6,606	8,554
Moscow	18	35	24	34	640,426	960,706	16,283	24,205
Vladimir	10	29	11	36	402,698	537,594	13,421	90,987
Tver	4	5	5	6	210,656	235,184	5,053	6,139
Jaroslav	1	1	2	1	103,550	189,744	944	1,002
Ziasan	1	3	1	4	95,189	140,800	349	1,093
Smolensk	1	1	1	1	26,676	66,292	500	780
Kostroma	..	9	1	15	....	30,192	3,675	6,716
Tiflis	..	..	1	1	....	10,800	.....	.....
Kazan	1	1	..	..	5,564	....	35	.....
Kalouga	1	..	..	..	4,200	....	.....	.....
Kherson	..	..	1	1	....	10,638	.....	122
Poland	9	6	13	8	216,640	505,622	4,417	10,572
Perm	1	1	.	.	2,500	....	75	.....
Balt. provs	4	3	4	6	281,488	348,362	2,016	2,237
Finland	3	2	3	2	56,576	84,864	1,192	1,225
Total	67	106	79	123	2,796,283	2,912,806	54,566	84,516

The cotton weaving establishments in Russia give employment to over 80,500 hands, the total annual production being estimated at 56,000,000 roubles.

About 360,000,000 pounds weight of cotton are annually imported into Russia, being mainly derived from America and Egypt. The territory acquired in Central Asia by Russia is well suited for the cultivation of cotton.

Cotton Industries of Syria.

One of the most important articles produced by the native population of Syria is what is known as "mabroum," a thin cotton tissue with a loose weft, which serves for making clothing. It is stated that in former times as much as 300,000 pieces of this material used to be produced in Damascus annually, but this branch of the textile industry has been gradually transferred to Homs, Hama and Broussa, and the quality of the goods has already deteriorated considerably.

Cotton Mills of Brazil.

Twenty of the cotton mills of the Empire are located in the province of Minas Geraes, twelve in Sao Paulo, fifteen in the city and province of Rio de Janiero, and the rest are scattered throughout the country. The largest is the Brazil Industrial Factory, which is located at Macacos, in the province of Rio de Janiero, which runs eight hundred looms and employs five hundred hands. The capital stock of the company is $1,650,000, and the shares are now quoted at about fifteen per cent. below par. The company is in debt and has issued debentures to the amount of $550,000, on which it pays interest to the amount of $19,000 every six months.

Another large factory is the Petropolitana, also in Rio de Janiero, whose capital is $1,100,000, and which has recently enlarged its plant to the value of over $3,500,000. The Rink Factory in Rio de Janiero is another large mill in which $800,000 capital is invested, and employs four hundred workmen. It produces an annual average of 1,300,000 yards of cotton goods, 220,000 yards of woolen goods, and 65,000 yards of felt.

Canadian Cotton Goods Industry.

In the year 1879 the quantity of raw cotton brought into Canada to be manufactured into fabrics was only 7,243,413 lbs., while in 1887 the quantity imported reached 30,971,170 lbs., an increase of 23,737,657 lbs. In 1879 the imports of gray and bleached cotton fabrics into Canada from Great Britain and the United States amounted to 12,771,896 yards, of the value of $971,685. The importation of this class of cottons in the fiscal year 1888 was only 1,634,190 yards, of the value of $174,873.

Swiss Cotton Industry.

In 1889 there were in Switzerland 92 spinning firms, running 1,722,299 spindles, or 119,094 spindles less than in 1884; there were 58 firms engaged in the doubling branch, running 73,545 spindles, or 8,455 spindles less than in 1884; 65 firms were engaged in the production of white or gray woven goods, running 16,800 looms, or 304 more than in 1884; and 44 firms were engaged in the production of colored goods (regattas, ginghams, etc.), running 6,921 looms, or 196 less than in 1884.

Kinds and Qualities of Cotton Produced Throughout the World.

Cotton in commerce is known by its color, the length of its staple or fibre, and its strength and fineness. A white color is generally considered to be characteristic of an inferior quality. The cotton of Smyrna, Cypress, Salonica, and all parts of the Levant is distinguished by its white color. The chief part of the North American cotton is also white, viz.: New Orleans, Tennessee, Alabama and Georgia Upland. Yellow, when not the effect of accidental wetting, or the result of an inclement season, is an indication of fineness and strength. The cotton of the West Indies and South America is called yellow, but its color is not quite yellow, and inclines more to a cream color. East India cotton has a slight tinge of orange. The fine Georgia Sea Island, though not properly a yellow cotton, has a faint but decided tinge of yellow, which distinguishes it from the white short staple of America.

The following gives a synopsis of the general character, together with varieties of the same, cultivated throughout the world:

AMERICAN (U. S.) COTTON.

Upland Cotton is produced in the inland districts of Virginia, North and South Carolina, Georgia, Tennessee, Alabama, Mississippi, Texas, and other States. It is generally a light, flimsy cotton, of a weak and very unequal staple, and having one intermixture of long fibres.

New Orleans Cotton is superior to the Upland, and has the preference, on account of its clean, soft and glossy appearance. It is rather short in staple, but is even and strong, and is easily incorporated with other cottons of a long staple. It is grown on the banks of the Mississippi and Red rivers, and is exported in very large quantities to the British and French markets, where it ranks in price and quality equally with the Brazil cotton. Upland, Alabama and Tennessee rank next to New Orleans; they are soft, short, and weak in staples

SOUTH AMERICAN COTTON.

Pernambuco Cotton has a fine, long staple, is clean and pretty, of a uniform quality, and is much esteemed by carders and spinners. It is principally used for hosiery.

Maranham Cotton is rather inferior to the Pernambuco, is not of such an even quality, nor so clean; it is very similar to good Demerara, and is used for the same purposes.

Bahia Cotton is very much like the Maranham, and obtains the preference sometimes on account of being cleaner and more even in the length of the staple.

Rio Cotton.—This is a very inferior cotton, having a brown color, and containing much spill; it is generally used for the same purposes as the low West Indian.

Surinam Cotton has a long, fine staple; it is clean, has a yellowish color, and is a superior cotton. It is used in the manufacture of hosiery.

Cayenne Cotton has a fine, good, clean staple, and is preferable to the Surinam cotton; it is used for the same purposes.

Demarara Cotton.—This cotton has deteriorated very much in quality since the colony has been in possession of the English. The best has a fine, strong, silky staple, and is much esteemed. The inferior kinds are rather brown, dirty, and much mixed.

Berbice Cotton.—The quality of this cotton has fallen off very much within the last few years. The best descriptions of it have a good staple, and are fine, silky and clean; but latterly there is a great deal of it brown, dirty and mixed.

Carthagena Cotton has a very long staple; but is weak, stringy, and rather dirty,

Giron Cotton is of a brown color, has a fair staple, and is generally pretty clean.

Cumana Cotton is inferior to the Giron in its staple, and not so clean.

Caraccas Cotton is also inferior to the Giron, and contains more dirt.

La Guayra Cotton is not as good as the Cumana, but better than the Caraccas, and not so dirty.

WEST INDIA COTTON.

The cotton which comes from the numerous islands comprising the West Indies, is of various qualities; but in general it is a strong, coarse article, irregular in the staple, and only adapted to the manufacture of the stouter fabrics of cloth, to which it is mostly applied. It is totally unfit for the manufacture of fine goods.

Among the various islands the best cotton is raised in some of the Bahamas, Barbadoes, Hayti, Curacoa, Grenada, St. Vincent, Guadaloupe and Tobago. In these islands, however, there is not so much cotton raised now as formerly.

EAST INDIA COTTON.

Bourbon Cotton is the most even in its quality of any of the different varieties; has a fine, silky staple, and is very clean. It is, with the exception of Sea Island, the most valuable produced.

Surat Cotton has a very fine but exceedingly short staple. It is generally very dirty, containing leaves and sand. It is the lowest priced cotton in the market, and is used in the manufacture of coarse, low-priced goods.

Bengal Cotton is very much like the Surat, but still shorter in the staple. It is generally cleaner, and sells for about the same price as Surat.

Madras Cotton is mostly raised from Bourbon seed, and is sometimes not unlike it in staple. It is generally dirty, and contains much smell, which diminishes its value. It is worth but little more than Surat.

TURKEY, LEVANT AND EGYPTIAN COTTON.

The *Smyrna, Cypress* and *Salonica Cottons* are of a short, mossy character, and rather dirty. They are used chiefly in making candle wicks, etc.

Egyptian Cotton is a very superior cotton, of a yellowish color, not as fine and silky as the Sea Island, and ranks next to it in price and quality. It is, however, somewhat irregular in staple, and prepared in a bungling, slovenly manner. No description of cotton loses less in carding, and it incorporates freely with cotton of a shorter staple, such as New Orleans Upland, etc. The best and cleanest of the cotton is generally used by the manufacturer for spinning a superior quality of fine yarn.

AFRICAN COTTON.

In Africa the cotton plant is found growing wild on the borders of the Senegal, Gambia and Nigir rivers; in Abyssina, Guinea, Sierra Leone, Timbuctoo, and generally throughout the interior.

Sea Island Cotton has also been successfully cultivated in Tiji, Tahito, Queensland, Australia and Polynesian Islands.

Varieties of American Cotton.

American cotton may be divided into two great sections, the "smooth" and the "hairy leaved" kinds, or, in the language of science, *Barbadense* and *Hirsuum*; the chief of these two in commercial excellence being Sea Island and New Orleans respectively.

The Hirsutae, or hairy cottons, are more or less covered with a distinct clothing of hairs. The blossoms are white or faintly primrose in color in one race, or sub species, obscurely spotted at the base, and in form widely expanded or patulous; the boll is smooth on the surface, and wanting the depressions peculiar to the other species. The Hirsute group are also found with seeds black or naked, often from the effects of bad cultivation, but in other instances from the natural habit of the plant.

The longest fibre cotton is Sea Island, averaging 1⅝ inches in length and chiefly spun into 150's and 400's yarns, although, for experimental purposes, it has been spun as high as No. 2150.

The best variety of our even-running cotton is Orleans of the mean length of 1 1-16; is largely used for weft, while Texas, though shorter, is, from its strength, generally used for warp yarn.

Cotton grown on the Uplands of Alabama, Mississippi, Louisiana and Arkansas has a staple of ¾ to ⅞ inch. That from "Bottom" and "Swamp" lands averages 1 to 1⅛ inches. A good deal of "Extra" or "Fancy" Stapled Cotton with staple measuring 1⅛ to 1⅝ inches, is grown in these States. These Extra Stapled Cottons (known as "Benders," "Peeler," "Allen," etc.), together with the Cotton from the "Bottoms," make the average length of staple about as given in the above table.

The South Carolina Sea Island Cotton is of rather better quality than that grown in Georgia and Florida.

The property which the cotton fibres have of holding together when the yarn is spun, is not due to any scale or beard, as in the case of wool, but to the fact that the fibres have a natural twist in them, and when the cotton is pressed and twisted together these twists are forced together, just as two spiral springs would be if pressed together.

Characteristics of Some Cotton Textures.

The beauty or excellence of some cotton cloths consists in the closeness of their texture, that of others in the openness and regularity of the intervals between the warp and weft threads.

Sea Island Cotton Plant of Georgia.

(LONGEST STAPLE KNOWN.)

This cotton is raised on the sea coast of Georgia and the small islands which form the neighboring archipelago. Though not decidedly yellow, it has somewhat of a dull butter tint, which distinguishes it from white cotton. It is remarkable for its long staple, the filaments being three times longer than those of the Indian cotton. It has a silky softness. It is sometimes dirty, but the well cleaned and the best is preferred to every other quality for spinning fine yarn. The reason of this superiority appears to be the cylindrical-spiral form and equability of its filaments, which facilitates their torsion into a uniform thread.

Technical Classification of Cotton.

The fiber of cotton, when young, is a thin hollow cylinder, filled with liquid, which, in ripening, disappears and the cylinder contracts into a flat band, with thickened edges, and assumes more or less of a twist. It is this peculiar form which allows, in short cotton, the fibre to be easily spun. "Short staple" more exactly or technically signifies a length under 0.98 inches, or 25 millimeters ; "medium" means 0.98 to 1.117 inches, or 25 up to 30 millimeters ; "long staple" denotes 1.18 to 1.57 inches, or 30 to 40 millimeters ; "extra" represents 1.58 inches, or 40 millimeters or more.

The general average for the United States is given in the following table :

	Least.	Medium.	Most.	Extra.	All.
Length—Inches	0.91	1.07	1.32	1.72	1.10
Millimeters	23.03	27.09	33.44	43.63	27.89
Width—1.1000 inches	0.93	0.91	0.88	0.80	0.91
1.1000 mil.	23.60	23.20	22.40	20.40	23.00
Strength—Grains	134.30	121.80	126.50	109.90	125.60
Grams	8.70	7.96	8.20	7.12	8.14

Average Length of American Cotton.

The average length of the staple of the cotton raised in the various Southern States is given as follows :

North Carolina	$\frac{3}{4}$ @ $\frac{7}{8}$ inches.
South Carolina	$\frac{3}{4}$ @ $\frac{7}{8}$ "
Georgia	$\frac{3}{4}$ @ $\frac{7}{8}$ "
Florida	$\frac{3}{4}$ "
Alabama	$\frac{7}{8}$ "
Mississippi	1 "
Louisiana	1 "
Texas	1 "
Arkansas	1 "
Tennessee	$\frac{3}{4}$ @ 1 "

It is said, however, that the cotton grown on the Uplands of Alabama, Mississippi, Louisiana and Arkansas usually has a staple of $\frac{3}{4}$ to $\frac{7}{8}$ inch, while that from the "bottom" or "swamp" lands averages 1 to $1\frac{1}{8}$ inches. Extra stapled cotton, known as "Benders," "Reeler," "Allen," etc., having a staple measuring $1\frac{1}{8}$ to $1\frac{3}{8}$ inches, is also grown in these States. The staple of Texas cotton ranges from $\frac{3}{4}$ to $1\frac{1}{4}$ inches, according to the different sections of the State.

Cost of Raising Cotton per Pound.

Advances are sometimes made on growing cotton crops in credits from one-half to three-quarters of their estimated value, and insurance is also occasionally effected when the seed is put in the ground. However, the latter is usually made when the cotton reaches the gin. As regards the cost of production per pound of cotton, various estimates are given, based upon the yield in 1879-80. These vary from 5 @ 6c., 7 @ 7 1-2c. to 8 @ 10c. per pound, and in nearly every instance are based on the major portion of the necessary supplies being bought elsewhere, and not raised on the plantation.

It is said, however, by reliable testimony, that when supplies are produced with cotton under good management, the cost of raising cotton per pound ought not to range wider than from 3 to 6 cents. The former figure, however, is very low; the estimates undoubtedly presume a perfection of management in detail in culture that is difficult to practically carry out without labor being especially tractable. Indeed, a well known planter, who produces cotton on a large scale, gives it as his opinion that with cotton at 10 @ 11 cents per pound, and the cost of production 8 @ 9 1-2 cents per pound, the farmer simply makes a living, if he raises his own provisions, but makes no money if he has to buy the latter. Cotton lands, according to their location and fertility, vary all the way in value from $1 to $50 per acre, the mean range being about $5 to $20 per acre. Land that will produce 1,000 pounds of seed cotton to the acre is generally valued in the neighborhood of $40 per acre.

Cost of Cotton Spindles.

In 1860 the whole number of cotton spindles in the United States was 5,235,000, costing for a No. 25 yarn mill, from $16 to $20 per spindle. The value of a bale of cotton prior to the war ranged from $40 to $50. During the war it rose to over $900 per bale. Standard printing cloths, now costing about 3 1-2 cents per yard, were then worth about 33 cents. In 1880 there were 10,653,435 cotton spindles in the United States, and for No. 25 yarn mill, cost $14 to $18 per spindle. Since then new mills have been costing as high as $30 to $40 per spindle.

Cost of Shipping Cotton at Various U. S. Ports.

The comparative tables of the cost of shipping a cargo of cotton from eight of the leading cotton ports of the country is given in the accompanying tables. They are made by a Southern authority who has given the subject much consideration. The estimates are based on a vessel of 2,000 tons burden, having a carrying capacity of 5,000 bales:

NEW ORLEANS.

Fixed charges	$96 00
Compressing, 65c. per bale	3,250 00
Stowing, 55c. per bale	2,750 00
Harbormaster's dues	20 00
Pilotage	50 00
Pilotage (extra)	175 00
Wharfage	240 00
Quarantine	30 00
Total charges	$6,611 00

NEW YORK.

Fixed charges	$96 00
Stowing, 65c. per bale	2,750 00
Harbormaster	10 00
Pilotage	100 00
Wharf dues	13 00
Quarantine	14 00
Total charges	$2,983 00

BALTIMORE.

Fixed charges	$96 00
Compressing, 30c. per bale	1,500 00
Stowing, 45c. per bale	2,250 00
Pilotage	100 00
Quarantine	15 00
Total charges	$3,961 00

NORFOLK.

Fixed charges	$96 00
Compressing and stowing	6,000 00
Harbormaster	30 00
Pilotage	80 00
Wharfage	20 00
Total charges	$6,226 00

SAVANNAH.

Fixed charges	$96 00
Compressing, 35c. per bale	1,750 00
Stowing, 50c. per bale	2,500 00
Harbormaster	20 00
Pilotage	125 28
Wharfage	5 00
Total charges	$4,511 28

CHARLESTON.

Fixed charges	$96 00
Compressing, 65c. per bale	3,250 00
Stowing, 40c. per bale	2,000 00
Harbormaster	20 00
Wharfage	20 00
Total charges	$5,386 00

MOBILE.

Fixed charges	$96 00
Compressing, 65c. per bale	3,250 00
Stowing, 55c. per bale	2,000 00
Pilotage	175 00
Wharfage	200 00
Quarantine	30 00
Total charges	$6,501 00

GALVESTON.

Fixed charges	$96 00
Compressing, 50c. per bale	2,500 00
Stowing, 55c. per bale	2,750 00
Pilotage	80 00
Lighterage, 35c. per bale	1,750 00
Total charges	$7,176 00

Cotton Picking.

The season of cotton picking commences in the latter part of July and continues, without intermission, to the Christmas holidays. The work is not heavy, but becomes tedious from its sameness. Each hand is supplied with a basket and bag. The basket is left at the head of the "cotton row;" the bag is suspended from the picker's neck by a strap, and is used to hold the cotton as it is taken from the boll. When the bag is full it is emptied into the basket, and this routine is continued throughout the day. Each hand picks from 250 to 300 pounds of seed cotton each day; however, some negroes of extraordinary ability go beyond this amount.

Ethics of Cotton Buying.

A large part of the export business in cotton at all the various United States ports is done by selling future contracts for specific months' shipments to spinners or others, and by covering with purchases of corresponding months' deliveries in New York. When the month of shipment comes round the actual cotton is bought and the futures are sold.

Cost of Cotton in Lowell and Lancashire.

Cotton brought from the interior towns of Texas cannot, it is stated, be carried to Liverpool by way of Galveston or New Orleans so cheaply as it can be by way of New York or Boston. Assuming the average bale to weigh 500 pounds, at 10 cents per pound, we have the following comparative costs of the same at Lowell, Mass., and at Lancashire, Eng.:

LOWELL, MASS.

	Per Bale.	Per Cwt.
Cost of cotton in Texas, 500 lbs. at 10 cts.	$50 00	$
Freight to Lowell in a covered, locked car, in which the cotton is protected from rain, mud and other causes of waste, at 70 cts. per 100 lbs.	$3 50	
	$53 50	$10 70

LANCASHIRE, ENGLAND.

	Per Bale.	Per Cwt.
Five hundred pounds, at 10 cts., including all local charges	$50 00	$
Freight from Texas to Liverpool at $1.10 per 100 pounds	$5 00	
Insurance at 3-8 of 1 per cent. on $56	.21	
Transhipment in Liverpool to Lancashire, 1-4 per cent. per pound	$1 25	
	$56 96	$11 39
Advantage of Lowell over Lancashire	$3 46	.69

Percentage of Different Lengths in Staple of Cotton.

	Per Cent.
Short or under 0.98 long	24
Medium, or from 0.98 to 1.17 inches long	55
Long, or from 1.18 to 1.56 inches long	16
Extra, or 1.57 inches, or more	5

The "extra" and "long" are said to correspond with the Gossypium Maritimum; the "short" and "medium" to Gossypium Hirsutum and Gossypium Herbaceum.

In length of fibre the maximum of cottons falls in South Carolina to 1.966 inches, and in Florida to 1.910 inches. In Upland or short staple cottons, California stands first, being 1.699 inches; Georgia second, 1.552 inches; Alabama third, 1.427 inches, and Texas fourth, 1.380 inches, while Virginia and North Carolina hold fifth place.

In width of fibre, with the exception of California and Missouri, all the widest fibre comes from the Uplands. The strongest fibre comes from Louisiana, and the next in strength from Alabama.

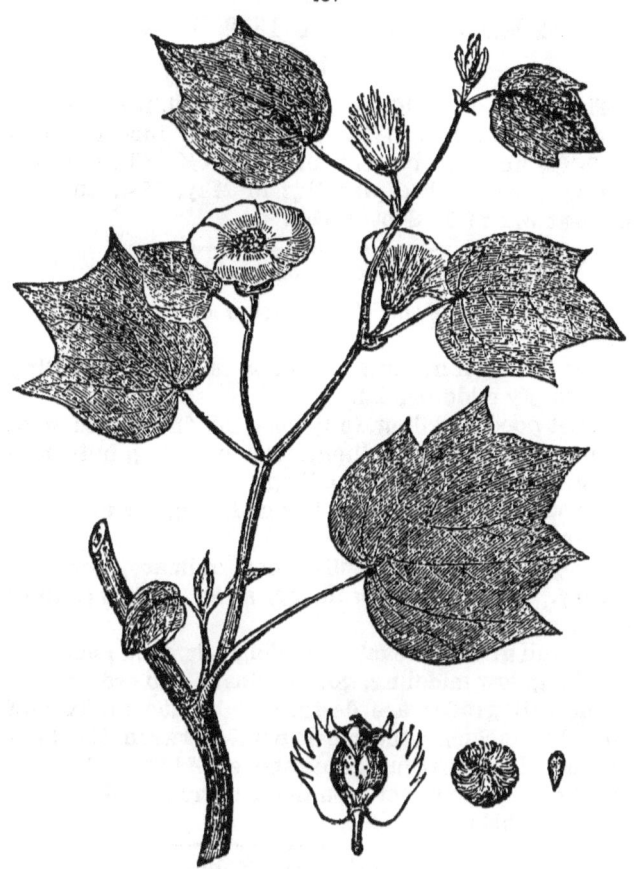

West Indian Cotton Plant.

This species of cotton is supposed to be a native of the American Continent. It is a shrub five or six feet high. Its stems and branches are smooth, and the leaves have a polished surface. The lower leaves have five lobes, the upper three. These are entire, acute, and have three glands on their back surfaces. The flowers, which are very large, have a deep yellow color. The capsule is also large, and produces a large body of cotton. The seeds are black. This is the species in most general cultivation in the West India Islands.

There is also in the West Indies and elsewhere a cotton-bearing tree called the *Umbrella tree*, which attains to the height of 100 feet. The produce of the latter, however, is of so short and brittle a fibre that it is unfit for spinning or any other purpose, except stuffing pillows and beds.

Price of Middling Cotton in 1859, 1860, 1887 and 1889.

The price of Middling Cotton, April 1, 1859, was 13c and on April 1, 1860, 11⅞c. The price in June 1887. was 11 7-16c, and the present price is 10¾c. The lowest cotton ever touched was 5½c in May, 1848, and the highest was $1 85. Sept, 1, 1864.

Classification of Cotton in New York.

The following is the cla-sification of cotton in New York:

Fair, barely fair, strict middling fair, fully middling fair, barely middling fair.

Strict good middling, fully good middling, good middling, barely good middling, strict middling, fully middling, middling, barely middling.

Strict low middling, fully low middling, low middling, barely low middling.

Strict good ordinary, fully good ordinary, good ordinary, barely good ordinary, strict ordinary, fully ordinary, ordinary.

The full grades are fair, middling fair, good middling, middling, low middling, good ordinary, and ordinary.

The half grades are designated by the prefixes of "barely," meaning the mean point between the half-grade and the next full grade above, and "fully," meaning the mean point between the half-grade and the next full grade below.

Highest and Lowest Prices for Middling Upland Cotton in New York and Liverpool in the Seasons Named.

Season.	*New York.*		*Liverpool.*	
(Beginning Sept. 1 and ending Aug. 31)	*Highest. Cts.*	*Lowest. Cts.*	*Highest. d.*	*Lowest. d.*
1882-83............	12 15-16 Sept. 1	10 April 4	7⅛ Sept. 1	5 7-16 July 14
1883-84............	11 15-16 April 14	10⅛ Sept. 1	6 7-16 June 9	5⅝ Sept. 1
1884-85............	11½ Feb. 26	9¾ Oct. 24	6 3-16 Sept. 1	5 7-16 Oct. 22
1885-86............	10 5-16 Sept. 1	8 13-16 Feb. 26	5 9-16 Oct. 5	4 11-16 Feb. 27
1886-87............	11 7-16 May 31	9⅛ Nov. 4	6 June 6	5⅛ Sept. 1
1887-88............	11⅜ Aug. 14	9 7-16 Oct. 3	5¾ Dec. 28	5⅛ Oct. 3
1888-89............	11½ Aug. 20	9⅝ Oct. 17	6⅝ Aug. 31	5⅜ Dec. 31
1889-90............	......	......	......	......

Average price for Middling Uplands in Liverpool for year 1889, 5 55-64d.

Cotton Production of the World Prior to 1880.

The following statement, which was prepared some years previous to the census report of 1880, and incorporated in it, gives an approximate account of the quantity of cotton consumed in each country of the world, when the population of many countries was upon a much smaller basis than at present. The table, however, gives a very good general idea of the relative consumption of cotton per capita in each:

The entire production of cotton in the world was estimated as follows:

	Pounds.
Imported into and consumed in Europe	2,217.000,000
Consumed in United States	628,000,000
Native consumption in India, China, etc.	1,360,000,000
Total as above	4,205,000,000
Native consumption in Turkey	20,000,000
Native consumption in Africa (1 lb per head).	200.000,000
Native consumption in South America, etc.	40,000,000
Received by Persia from Bokhara, etc.	15,000,000
Total crop of the world	4,480,000,000
Equal to bales of 400 lbs	11,200,000

Of which about one-half is grown in the United States, and one-half of the whole is spun in England.

Our Long-Stapled Cotton.

With the demand for finer cotton fabrics of varied design, our manufacturers have been obliged to resort to such stapled cotton as will meet their wants. Our Sea Island variety answers the purpose in many particulars where very fine numbers are required to be spun, but its high price often militates against its use in cases where a cheaper cotton can be advantageously employed. About one-half of the Sea Island crop is now consumed in this country, while fourteen years ago less than an eighth part was thus disposed of. The average export price of Sea Island cotton for 1887-88 was 23.8c. per pound. This renders it too high in cost for many of our manufacturers, yet a long-stapled cotton must be had, and Egyptian cotton has been found to supply the want to good advantage at 5 to 7c. a pound less.

The average Sea Island staple is 1¾ inches long, while the Egyptian staple is 1½ inches long. The 1½ inch staple Egyptian readily spins to 80s yarn, and even finer, for weft purposes. The finer grades of brown cotton engage the principal attention of the planting interests of Egypt, and it may be noted that the much larger portion of our importations of cotton goods consists of those made from Egyptian cotton, the like of which can be and ought to be manufactured in this country.

Cotton Centre of the United States.

New Orleans, La., lies in the meridian west of Greenwich. Taking this as the dividing line we find that in 1850 27.4 per cent. of the cotton crops of the country were produced east of it, and 72.6 per cent. west. Texas and Arkansas had not then begun their development, and New Orleans, as a consequence, lay west of the cotton producing centre of the country. That it controlled so large a proportion of the trade at that time was due to the lack of railroads in the South, and to the facilities that the Mississippi and its tributaries offered for transportation. It was about that date that the movement of population and cotton production moved rapidly southward and westward, with the following result:

	Cotton raised west of 90 deg. W. Per cent.	Cotton raised east of 90 deg. W. Per cent.
1850	72.6	27.4
1860	57.0	43.0
1870	55.9	44.1
1880	53.3	46.7
1885	50.1	49.9
1886	49.4	56.6

Just as the population of the country moved westward, until the centre of the population has reached Cincinnati, so the staple has traveled in the same direction, until the meridian of New Orleans has now become the centre of cotton production, and that city is the most central point on the Continent to this great Southern crop. However, the centre of maximum production has been located by the Census at a point on the Mississippi where the three States of Mississippi, Louisiana and Arkansas join.

Old and New Cotton Gin.

Whitney's saw-gin is a vast improvement on the Hindoo *churka*. It comprises a series of circular saws, mounted on a frame, and turned by a fly-wheel; nearly in contact with it, rotates another cylinder, mounted with brushes; and the cotton, drawn between the two, is deprived of its seed by the action of the saw teeth against the brushes. The improved Macarthy gin is said by far to be the most complete machine for this purpose. In it, after traveling along an endless apron, the cotton is seized by a spiked roller, partially opened, and transferred by a vibrating comb to other rollers studded with blades.

Comparative Cost of Compressing and Stowing Cotton.

The comparative cost of compressing and stowage at the various ports named is given as follows:

	Compressing per bale.	Stowage per bale.
New Orleans	65	55
New York	..	55
Baltimore	30	45
Norfolk	65	55
Savannah	35	50
Charleston	65	40
Mobile	65	55
Galveston	50	55

In point of compressing and stowage (with the exception of Charleston, in the latter) it would appear that Baltimore is the cheapest port in the country from which to ship cotton in quantity. In the matter of harbor-masters' fees, pilotage, lighterage and wharfage charges, the exhibits of cost at the various ports are as follows:

	Harbor-master.	Pilotage.	Lighterage.	Wharfage.	Total.
New Orleans	$20 00	$195 00	$.....	$240 00	$455 00
New York	10 00	100 00	.....	13 00	123 00
Baltimore	.....	100 00	.....	......	100 00
Norfolk	30 00	80 00	.....	20 00	130 00
Savannah	20 00	125 28	.....	15 00	160 28
Charleston	20 00	......	.....	20 00	40 00
Mobile	.....	175 00	.....	200 00	375 00
Galveston	.....	80 00	17 50	......	97 50

The foregoing present facts that are of considerable interest to domestic manufacturers, as well as to exporters of cotton. Besides, they show the necessity of a lower and more equable adjustment of these charges, as well as those for compressing and stowage, if certain of these ports wish to hold a fair share of the trade of the country in raw cotton.

Freight and Insurance on Cotton.

In 1880 cotton was shipped from Texas to Liverpool via Boston, for $1.10 per 100 lbs., 70 cents being allowed for land carriage and transphipment in Boston, and to steamship 40 cents. The rate of marine insurance was 3-8 of 1 per cent. and the cost of handling in Liverpool and transportation to Manchester was not less than 1-4 per cent. per pound. Contracts in 1880 were made for bringing cotton from Texas to factory cities of New England at 70 cents per 100 lbs.

Cotton Supply, etc., of the World in 1889-90.

The estimated consumption and supply of cotton for the season 1889-90 is as follows:

	Estimated Requirem's. 1889-90. Bales.	Actual Consumpt'n. 1888-9. Bales.	Actual Consumpt'n. 1887-8. Bales.
American,	7,386,000	7,098,000	6,983,000
East Indian	1,640,000	1,536,000	1,398,000
Sundries	770,000	768,000	980,000
Total	9,796,000	9,402,000	9,361,000
Average weight	453 lbs.	453 lbs.	439 lbs.
Bales of 400 lbs.	11,088,000	10,648,000	10,279,000
Great Britain	3,977,000	3,770,000	3,842,000
Continent	4,205,000	4,069,000	3,796,000
U. S., Canada, etc.	2,906,000	2,809,000	2,641.000
Total as above	11,088,000	10,648,000	10,279,000

Consumption of Cotton in Southern Mills.

The consumption by Southern mills for 1886-7 and 1887-8 was as follows:

	1887-8.	1886-7.
Virginia	21,802	18,331
North Carolina	76,360	66,678
South Carolina	111,003	99,970
Georgia	133,877	129,702
Florida		160
Alabama	32,712	22,565
Mississippi	17,107	13,274
Louisiana	9,907	8,454
Texas	544	180
Arkansas	1,474	1,115
Tennessee	36,437	34,986
Missouri	2,052	2,200
Kentucky	12,815	6,837
Total	456,090	401,452

Capital Earnings and Dividends of Some New England Cotton Mills.

The following is a statement of the capital stock, earnings and dividends of some New England cotton mills for 1888:

	Capital.	Earnings.	Dividends.
Wampanoag	$750,000	$157,550	$86,350
Chace	500,000	115,000	37,500
Granite	400,000	136,000	64,000
Flint	580,000	102,858	58,000
Barnard	330,000	53,000	24,750
Merchants	800,000	125,720	60,000
Narragansett	400,000	67,143	32,000
King Philip	1,000,000	137,105	60,000
Union	750,000	237,000	187,500
Sagamore	600,000	133,000	78,000

Cotton Plant in Bloom.

The above cut shows the cotton plant in bloom.
No. 1. Represents the blossom.
No. 2. The flower.
No. 3. The same flower, second day.
No. 4. The same flower at night.
No. 5. The "burr" or involucre.
No. 6. The young boll.
No. 7. The boll bursting.
No. 8. The boll nearly ripe.
No. 9. The boll ripe; cotton perfect.
No. 10. The cotton blown by the wind.

Cotton, from the Arabic word *Kotôn*, is the spontaneous production of all the inter-tropical regions. Of the four great materials assigned by Providence for human clothing, it is believed that none was assigned to Europe. To Asia was given all—cotton, flax, the sheep and the silk-worm.

Comparative Values of Different Kinds of Cotton.

In estimating the value of different kinds of cotton, a manufacturing authority places them in the following order: Best Sea Island, Egyptian, Bourbon, Pernambuco, Cayenne, Bahia, Maraham, Surinam, Demerara, Berbice, Bahama, Grenada, Curacoa, Barbadoes, and the West Indies generally; Giron, and the best Spanish; New Orleans, Upland, Tennessee, Alabama, Smyrna, Cypress, Salonica, Jamaica, St. Kitts, and the inferior West Indies; Carthagena, Caracas and the inferior Spanish; Madras, Bengal and Surat.

Acreage in Cotton in the Ten Cotton-Growing States for a Series of Years.

ACCORDING TO THE UNITED STATES AGRICULTURAL BUREAU.

Season.	North Carolina.	South Carolina.	Georgia.	Florida.	Alabama.	Mississippi.	Louisiana.	Texas.	Arkansas.	Tennessee.
1879–80	625,915	944,649	1,591,958	101,650	1,892,698	2,055,040	1,321,977	1,934,973	1,177,516	762,925
1880–81	973,537	1,527,959	2,878,851	237,875	2,563,095	2,260,796	916,674	2,478,054	1,147,274	816,495
1881–82	1,061,155	1,619,639	2,994,005	263,082	2,639,988	2,351,228	914,174	2,676,298	1,181,632	840,990
1882–83	1,050,543	1,587,244	2,844,305	260,402	2,534,338	2,233,844	887,524	2,810,113	1,110,790	815,760
1883–84	1,050,543	1,618,989	2,872,748	257,779	2,610,420	2,278,521	931,900	3,034,922	1,188,545	807,602
1884–85	1,061,049	1,716,128	2,958,930	268,110	2,740,941	2,392,447	922,581	3,186,668	1,259,857	815,678
1885–86	1,082,268	1,767,612	3,077,287	273,472	2,823,169	2,535,994	987,162	3,505,335	1,373,244	823,885
1886–87	1,082,268	1,749,936	3,015,741	281,676	2,794,937	2,586,714	1,006,905	3,750,708	1,400,709	832,073
1887–88	1,066,301	1,622,185	2,941,486	262,616	2,809,599	2,548,674	1,066,854	3,960,327	1,388,658	855,799
1888–89	1,071,633	1,646,518	2,970,901	259,990	2,851,743	2,592,001	1,088,191	4,158,343	1,416,431	881,478
1889–90	……	……	……	……	……	……	……	……	……	……

Raw Cotton Consumed by the World.

The following is the estimated consumption of raw cotton by the various countries of the world, both gross and per capita of population prior to 1880:

Countries.	Population.	Raw Cotton Consumed. Pounds.	Per head.
The world............	1,408,396,000	3,163,600,000	2.26
Russia................	86,260,000	142,500,000	1.65
Sweden and Norway.	6,291,000	24,800,000	3.94
Denmark..............	2,023,000	......	....
Germany.............	42,727,000	249,100,000	5.83
Austria...............	37,331,000	101,300,000	2.71
Holland..............	4,130,000	13,800,000	3.34
Belgium...	5,336,000	43,200,000	8.09
Switzerland..........	2,776,000	42,500,000	15.30
France...............	36,906,000	230,000,000	6.23
Spain and Portugal...	21,275,000	79,900,000	3.75
Italy and Malta......	26,948,000	52,800,000	1.96
Greece................	1,450,000	......	....
Turkey,Roumania,etc	15,353,000	......	....
	286,806,000	979,900,000	3.39
Russia	86,260,000	142,500,000	1.65
Rest of Continent	202,546,000	837,400,000	4.11
Great Britain	34,180,000	195,700,000	5.72
Total, Europe	322,986,000	1,175,600,000	3.63
Turkey, Persia, etc...	24,540,000	......	....
India	250,000,000	295,000,000	1.18
China................	435,000,000	1,000,000,000	2.29
Japan................	33,620,000	65,000,000	1.98
Siam, Java, etc.......	12,500,000	......	....
Total, Asia........	755,660,000	1,360,000,000	1.7
Egypt and N. Africa	17,000,000	......	....
West, S. and E. Africa	13,000,000	......	....
Interior of Africa	200,000,000	......	....
Total, Africa......	230,000,000	......	....
U. S. and Canada	48,850,000	628,000,000	12.85
Cent. and S. America and West Indies......	43,250,000	......	....
Total, America...	92,100,000	628,000,000	6.82
Australia	2,650,000	......	....

Common sheetings and shirtings require about seventy or eighty picks, or threads, to the inch, which, in a power-loom driven by 200 revolutions a minute, would make about five yards per hour.

Average Weight of American Cotton Bales.

The average weights of American cotton bales (on a basis of the six successive seasons ending with 1888) are as follows:

	Pounds.
North Carolina	466
South Carolina	473
Georgia	477
Florida	477
Alabama	497
Mississippi	490
Louisiana	482
Texas	513
Arkansas	500
Tennessee	495

General average for the United States, according to the above, is about 485 pounds to the bale.

General Method of Planting Cotton.

The general method of planting cotton may be described as follows: The seed is sown on ridges, surrounded with furrows, for the purpose of draining off the superfluous water. Sowing time extends from the beginning of March to the end of April, the early part of the latter month being considered the most eligible, because of there being less danger to the young plants from the occurrence of frost—that fearful bane to the cotton planter. After the plants have attained a moderate height they are thinned out, so as to remove those that promise badly and to leave sufficient space between those that are vigorous; this space varies from about ten to twenty inches. The soil is carefully weeded and the plants are still further thinned, if their luxuriant growth should require that process as the season advances.

As the summer approaches, and when the frost has disappeared, the crop is liable to injury from heavy rains and the attacks of a caterpillar which feeds voraciously on the leaves of the plant. The blossom then appears, varying in color from yellow to red, and lastly dark brown. The pod succeeds, and about August the picking season commences, which lasts for some months. The appearance of a pod bursting is very beautiful as it rests on the plant, being varied by the contrast of the color of the cotton with the green leaves of the shrub, and the beautiful flower, either fully opened or opening on the stems.

Exports of British Cottons to U. S., from 1831 to 1846.

The following gives the exports of British cotton thread, cotton yarns, plain and printed calicoes, cambrics, muslins, etc., to the United States from 1831 to 1846, inclusive. (From British official statistics):

Years.	Cotton yarn. Pounds.	Cotton thread. Pounds.	Plain cotton cloth. Yards.	Printed and dyed cotton cloth. Yards.	Muslins and cambrics. Yards.
1831	250,539	304,099	21,094,267	27,961,642	392,490
1832	159,730	144,187	12,435,595	13,599,285	189,668
1833	156,024	324,117	15,852,212	12,290,631	295,208
1834	89,844	373,583	12,406,857	19,713,345	883,705
1835	131,060	496 754	23,875,102	43,980,284	815,789
1836	205,369	481,325	17,065,042	32,028,305	869,715
1837	357,432	191,287	5,554,139	13,902,683	604,513
1838	265,983	450,951	11,389,241	22,262,242	627,374
1839	117,557	855,710	11,194,870	22,439,785	628,623
1840	242,855	391,575	7,439,463	17,775,607	335,172
1841	220,068	567,000	11,957,053	26,025,281	585,121
1842	45,160	284,506	5,120,403	15,691,333	285,915
1843	103,199	388,779	7,736,295	7,720,651	430,174
1844	39,717	509,069	9,661,820	12,008,635	600,402
1845	69,507	423,999	12,412,981	13,097,851	1,034,216
1846	81,663	422,462	10,640,215	13,556,509	587,059

Cotton Looms of the United States in 1887.

The number of cotton looms in the United States in 1887 was as follows:

Alabama	2,255	Mississippi	1,946
Arkansas	52	Missouri	394
California	...	New Hampshire	41,646
Connecticut	18,912	New Jersey	4,115
Delaware	1,196	New York	14,606
Florida	...	North Carolina	6,931
Georgia	10,193	Ohio	123
Illinois	678	Pennsylvania	15,561
Indiana	1,695	Rhode Island	37,953
Kentucky	613	South Carolina	6,666
Louisiana	1,593	Tennessee	3,003
Maine	20,256	Texas	362
Maryland	3,328	Utah	22
Massachusetts	119,373	Vermont	1,344
Michigan	132	Virginia	2,329
Minnesota	...	Wisconsin	1,024
Total			308,101

Cotton Looms in other Countries in 1888.

The total number of mechanical cotton looms in May, 1888, in Europe, was estimated at 1,000,000, of which about 600,000 are in England.

Exports of American Cottons in 1887 and 1888.

The exports of domestic cottons to the various foreign countries during the years 1887 and 1888 were as follows:

UNCOLORED COTTONS.

	1887. Yards.	1888. Yards.
China	49,416,891	78,360,170
South-America—		
Chili	9,802,509	5,514,655
Argentine Rep.	4,335,031	4,494,773
Venezuela	1,892,213	2,195,601
Brazil	2,145,385	2,634,214
U. S. Colombia	1,518,776	1,620,436
Peru	2,720,524	477,162
Uruguay	619,327	1,021,261
Ecuador	422,138	773,106
Other	244,203	290,086
Great Britain	8,425,426	7,104,419
Africa	7,141,984	7,824,558
West Indies	2,980,400	4,294,696
East Indies	6,175,718	2,591,214
Central America	3,562,988	3,358,609
Asia	1,595,520	2,583,792
Mexico	1,975,139	1,837,505
Germany	1,360,344	1,076,877
British North America	942,907	1,282,899
Azores, Maderia, etc.	884,244	767,224
Japan	683,340	699,432
Hong Kong	155,369	206,586
British Possessions not included above	6,013,373	3,841,653
Other countries	752,930	1,358,146
Total	115,766,679	136,809,074
Value	$7,812,047	$9,256,486

COLORED COTTONS.

Mexico	14,121,638	10,508,533
South America—		
Brazil	5,038,989	5,490,853
Venezuela	5,604,955	7,045,215
U. S. Colombia	3,317,809	4,176,756
Argentine Republic	1,533,448	7,925,096
Ecuador	2,791,227	4,544,124
Chili	602,833	2,085,197
Peru	306,423	991,261
Uruguay	646,609	1,331,696
Other	190,104	412,912
West Indies—		
Hayti	8,990,982	6,476,639
Cuba	395,104	1,712,975
San Domingo	1,417,329	3,135,819
British	1,096,786	1,361,974
Dutch	917,088	1,424,109
Danish	153,767	216,555
Porto Rico	189,536	59,765
Hawaiian Islands	1,099,586	1,015,094
Central America	2,869,048	3,043,726
England	859,121	2,885,869
British Honduras	305,743	212,799
Portugal	3,000	....
French Colonies	614,567	826,068
Germany	455,076	1,240,504
Other points	835,178	670,074
Total	54,446,936	67,793,013
Value	$3,522,612	$4,003,772

Different Staples of Cotton.

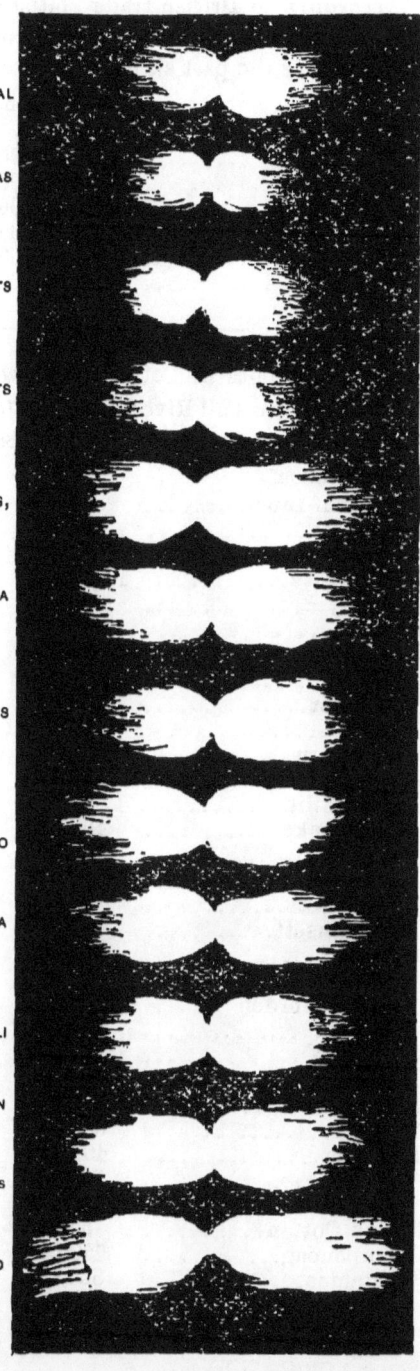

INDIAN COTTON, VIZ.:
(GOSSYPIUM INDICUM)
1 BENGAL

2 MADRAS

3 COMMON SURATS

4 PRIME SURATS

N. AMERICAN, VIZ.:
(GOSSYPIUM BARBADENSE)
5 WEST INDIES UPLANDS, DEMERARA, BERBICE AND SMYRNA

6 MOBILE AND ALABAMA

7 NEW ORLEANS

S. AMERICAN, VIZ.:
(GOSSYPIUM PERUVIANUM)
8 BAHIA AND MACEIO

9 MARANHAM AND PARA

10 PERNAMBUCO, ARACALI AND CEARA

11 PERUVIAN
N. AMERICAN, VIZ.:
(GOSSYPIUM BARBADENSE)
EGYPTIAN, SAME SIZE AS PERUVIAN
(LONG STAPLE)

12 SEA ISLAND

Production and Exportation of British Cotton Goods.

According to British trade statistics, the production and exportation of cotton yarn goods in the United Kingdom for the past six years were as follows:

Year.	Production. Pounds.	Export. Pounds.
1880	1,300,600,000	1,082,000,000
1881	1,345,800,000	1,183,100,000
1882	1,352,300,000	1,115,900,000
1883	1,420,000,000	1,176,000,000
1884	1,387,200,000	1,163,200,000
1885	1,272,800,000	1,115,600,000

Profits of Cotton Manufacturing.

In thirty-two Fall River mills the following dividends for the quarter ending April 30th, 1889, were declared:

Corporation.	Capital.	Per Cent.	Amount.
American Linen	$800,000	3	$24,000
Barnard	330,000	2	6,600
Bourne	400,000	4	16,000
Border City	1,000,000	3	30,000
Barnaby	400,000	4	16,000
Chace	500,000	2	10,000
Conanicut	120,000	1½	1,800
Davol	300,000	2	6,000
Fall River	180,000	3	5,400
Flint	580,000	3½	20,300
Globe Yarn	900,000	2	18,000
Granite	400,000	6	24,000
King Philip	1,000,000	1½	15,000
Laurel Lake	400,000	3	12,000
Merchants	800,000	2½	20,000
Mechanic	750,000	1½	11,250
Metacomet	228,000	2	5,760
Narragansett	400,000	2	8,000
Osborn	600,000	3	18,000
Pocasset	800,000	2	16,000
Richard Borden	675,000	2	13,500
Robeson	260,000	2	5,200
Sagamore	900,000	2½	22,500
Shove	550,000	2	11,000
Slade	550,000	1½	8,250
Stafford	800,000	2	16,000
Seaconet	400,000	4½	18,000
Tecumseh	500,000	2½	12,500
Troy C. and W	300,000	6	18,000
Union Cotton	750,000	5	37,500
Wampanoag	750,000	4	30,000
Weetamoe	550,000	2	11,000
Totals	$17,933,000	2.71	$487,560

Manufactured Cottons Consumed by the World.

Some years ago a prominent statistical authority in Europe made the following tabular statement of the manufactured cottons consumed by the world:

	Goods imported from Great Britain.		Total Consumption.	
	Pounds.	Per head.	Pounds.	Per head.
The world	1,041,700,000	0.74	4,205,300,000	2.98
Russia	2,600,000	0.03	145,100,000	1.68
Sweden & Norway	8,000,000	1.27	32,800,000	5 21
Denmark	5,000,000	2.47	5,000,000	2.47
Germany	65,200,000	1.52	314,300,000	7.35
Austria	7,900,000	0.21	109,200,000	2.92
Holland	43,000,000	10.41	56,800,000	13.75
Belgium	17,400,000	3 26	60,000,000	11.35
Switzerland	....	....	42,500,000	15 30
France	19,900,000	0.54	249,900,000	6 77
Spain and Portugal	25,700,000	1.21	105,600,000	4.96
Italy and Malta	51,100,000	1.59	103,900,000	3.85
Greece	6,900,000	4.75	6,900,000	4.75
Turkey, Roumania, etc.	37,000,000	2 40	37,000,000	2.40
Total	289,700,000	0.99	1,269,600,000	4.38
Russia	2 600,000	0.03	145,106,020	1.68
Rest of Continent	287,100,000	1.41	1,124,500,000	5 52
Great Britain	....	....	195,700,000	5.72
Total Europe	289,700,000	0.89	1,465,300,000	4.52
Turkey, Persia, etc.	38,000,000	1.54	38,000,000	1 54
India	330,000,000	1.32	625,000,000	2 50
China	100,000,000	0 23	1,100,000,000	2.52
Japan	20,000,000	0.59	85,000,000	2 52
Siam, Java, etc.	30,000,000	2.40	30,000,000	2 40
Total Asia	518,000,000	0.69	1,878,000,000	2 48
Egypt and N. Africa	34,000,000	2 00	34 000,000	2.00
W., S. and E. Africa	28,000,000	2.15	28,000 000	2.15
Interior of Africa	....	....	....	....
Total Africa	62,000,000	0.26	62,000,000	0.26
U. S. and Canada	22,000,000	0.45	650,000,000	13.30
Cen. & So. America & West Indies	135,000,000	3.12	135,000,000	3 12
Total America	157,000,000	1.70	785,000,000	8.32
Australia	15,000,000	5 66	15,000,000	5.66

As early as 1793 British muslins were said to be equal in appearance to those of India, while the patterns were far more elegant. and the cost was less than one-third.

Annual Crops, Exports and Home Consumption of Cotton Since 1841.

Season.	Total Crop.	Exports.	Home Consumption.	
			Northern. Mills.	Southern. Mills.
1841-42	1,684,000	1,465,000	268,000	......
1842-43	2,379,000	2,010,000	325,000	......
1843-44	2,030,000	1,629,000	347,000	......
1844-45	2,394,000	2,084,000	389,000	......
1845-46	2,100,000	1,667,000	423,000	......
1846-47	1,779,000	1,241,000	428,000	......
1847-48	2,423,000	1,858,000	532,000	75,000
1848-49	2,840,000	2,228,000	518,000	112,000
1849-50	2,204,000	1,590,000	488,000	107,000
1850-51	2,415,000	1,989,000	404,000	60,000
1851-52	3,126,000	2,444,000	588,000	111,000
1852-53	3,416,000	2,528,000	650,000	153,000
1853-54	3,075,000	2,319,000	592,000	145,000
1854-55	2,983,000	2,244,000	571,000	135,000
1855-56	3,065,000	2,995,000	633,000	138,000
1856-57	3,094,000	2,253,000	666,000	154,000
1857-58	3,257,000	2,590,000	452,000	143,000
1858-59	4,019,000	3,521,000	760,000	167,000
1859-60	4,861,000	3,774,000	793,000	186,000
1860-61	3,849,000	3,127,000	650,040	193,000
1861-65	......	......	......	......
1865-66	2,278,000	1,555,000	541,000	127,000
1866-67	2,233,000	1,557,000	573,000	150,000
1867-68	2,599,000	1,656,000	800,000	168,000
1868-69	2,434,000	1,447,000	822,000	173,000
1869-70	3,114,000	2,179,000	777,000	80,000
1870-71	4,347,000	3,168,000	1,072,000	91,000
1871-72	2,974,000	1,957,000	977,000	120,000
1872-73	3,848,000	2,676,000	1,063,000	138,000
1873-74	4,130,000	2,811,000	1,192,000	128,000
1874-75	3,831,000	2,674,000	1,071,000	130,000
1875-76	4,632,000	3,232,000	1,220,000	134,000
1876-77	4,474,000	3,028,000	1,302,000	127,000
1877-78	4,774,000	3,356,000	1,345,000	151,000
1878-78	5,074,000	3,4f6,000	1,375,000	198,000
1879-80	5,761,000	3,864,000	1,574,000	223,000
1880-81	6,606,000	4,565,000	1,713,000	230,000
1881-82	5,456,000	3,551,000	1,677,000	287,000
1882-83	6,950,000	4,724,000	1,759,000	313,000
1883-84	5,713,000	3,917,000	1,537,000	346,000
1884-85	5,706,000	3,920,000	1,437,000	318,000
1885-86	6,575,000	4,336,000	1,781,000	385,000
1886-87	6,499,000	4,445,000	1,687,000	422,000
1887-88	7,046,833	4,627,502	1,859,009	456,090
1888-89	6,938,290	4,742,347	1,834,310	479,781
1889-90	......	......	......	......

Cost of "Woven Wind" Muslins.

At two places in Bengal, India—Sonar-ga and Vickrumpoorn—muslins are made by a few families so exceedingly fine, that four months are required to weave one piece, which sells at from 400 to 500 rupees. When this muslin is laid on the grass and the dew has fallen on it, it is no longer discernible.

Estimated Number Cotton Spindles in Europe on Sept. 30 of the Year Named.

	Great Britain.	Continent.	Total Europe.
1883	42,000,000	22,450,000	64,450,000
1884	42,750,000	22,650,000	65,400,000
1885	43,000,000	22,750,000	65,750,000
1886	42,700,000	22,900,000	65,600,000
1887	42,740,000	23,180,000	65,920,000
1888	42,740,000	22,380,000	66,120,000
1889	....	....	....

Estimated Number of Working Cotton Spindles in the United States on Sept. 1, in the Years Named.

Years.	Northern States.	Southern States.	Total U. States.
1880	10,095,000	484,000	10,679,000
1881	10,625,000	750,000	11,375,000
1882	11,350,000	800,000	12,150,000
1883	11,800,000	860,000	12,660,000
1884	12,250,000	1,050,000	13,300,000
1885	12,250,000	1,125,000	13,375,000
1886	12,250,000	1,150,000	13,500,000
1887	12,300,000	1,200,000	13,550,000
1888	12,275,000	1,250,000	13,525,000
1889	12,725,000	1,450,000	14,175,000

Statistics of Special Cotton Mills in 1880.

Below we give the mills which were employed in working raw cotton. waste or cotton yarns into hose, webbing, tapes, fancy fabrics, or mixed goods or other fabrics, which are not sold as specific manufactures, either of cotton or wool. Some of these mills worked both fabrics, but belonged more in the class of cotton manufactures than in that of woolen manufactures:

	Eastern States.	Middle States.	Southern States.	Western States
Establishments..	70	161	11	7
Capital...........	$3.970,803	$6,616.645	$381,500	$255,500
Spindles........	15,348	34,922	9,072	——
Looms..........	897	2 804	234	——
Operatives......	3,169	9,271	271	181
Cotton consumed bales.....	9,006	27,794	684	3,114
Cost............	$578,705	$1,600,358	$39,016	$189,366
Wages paid operatives.......	$877,007	22,898,931	$66,024	$34,947
Value of product.	$5,539,192	$12,760.128	$235,395	$325.058

Cotton Manufactures of the United States in 1880.

The statistics of cotton manufactures in the United States for the year 1880, make the following showing:

Establishments	756
Capital invested	$208,280,346
Spindles	10,653,435
Looms	225,759
Employees	174,659
Wages paid	$42,040,510
Cotton consumed, bales	1,570,344
Cotton consumed, lbs	750,343,981
Cost of cotton consumed	$86,945,725
Value of all materials used	$102,206,347
Pounds of goods manufactured	607,264,241
Yards of goods manufactured	2,273,278,025
Value of total product	$192,090,110

The foregoing were subdivided among the different geographical sections of the country as below:

New England States.

Factories	439
Spindles	8,632,087
Looms	184,701
Average number of yarns	30
Capital invested	$156,754,690
Hands employed	127,185
Wages paid	$32,170,861
Cotton consumed, lbs	541,373,880
Cotton consumed, bales	1,129,498
Value of cotton consumed	$63,069,434
Value of materials used	$74,290,026
Cotton goods manufactured, lbs	432,744,610
Cotton goods manufactured, yards	1,813,478,967
Value of entire product	$143,363,030

Southern States.

Factories	161
Spindles	542,048
Looms	11,898
Average number of yarns	11
Capital invested	$17,375,897
Hands employed	16,741
Wages paid	$2,750,956
Cotton consumed, lbs	84,528,757
Cotton consumed, bales	182,349
Value of cotton consumed	$8,890,408
Value of all materials used	$9,999,145
Cotton goods manufactured, lbs	68,858,265
Cotton goods manufactured, yards	148,058,675
Value of entire product	$16,356,598

Middle States.

Factories	139
Spindles	1,391,164
Looms	27,318
Average number of yarns	22
Capital invested	$31,014,759
Hands employed	28,367
Wages paid	$6,613,260

Cotton Manufactures of the United States in 1880.
CONTINUED.

(Middle States Continued)

Cotton consumed, lbs	108,329,428
Cotton consumed, bales	228,729
Value of cotton consumed	$13,258,526
Value of materials used	$16,191,758
Cotton goods manufactured, lbs	93,574,519
Cotton goods manufactured, yards	289,762,256
Value of the entire product	$29,389,286

Western States.

Factories	17
Spindles	88,136
Looms	1,842
Average number of yarns	12
Capital invested	$3,135,000
Hands employed	2,366
Wages paid	$505,403
Cotton consumed, lbs	15,119,916
Cotton consumed, bales	29,768
Value of cotton consumed	$1,657,367
Value of all materials used	$1,725,418
Cotton goods manufactured, lbs	12,086,847
Cotton goods manufactured, yards	21,978,127
Value of the entire product	$2,981,196

Eastern States.

Material consumed, bales	1,129,498
Material consumed, lbs	541,373,880
Cost	$63,169,434
Value of all materials	$74,290,026
Goods manufactured, lbs	432,744,610
Goods manufactured, yards	1,813,478,967
Total product	$543,363,030

Middle States.

Material consumed, bales	228,729
Material consumed, lbs	109,321,428
Cost	$13,258,526
Value of all materials	$16,191,758
Goods manufactured, lbs	93,574,519
Goods manufactured, yards	289,762,256
Total products	$29,289,286

Southern States.

Material consumed, bales	182,349
Material consumed, lbs	84,528,757
Cost	$8,890,408
Value of all materials	$9,999,145
Goods manufactured, lbs	68,858,265
Goods manufactured, yards	148,058,675
Total products	$16,356,598

Western States.

Material consumed, bales	29,678
Material consumed, lbs	15,119,916
Cost	$1,627,357
Value of all materials	$1,725,418
Goods manufactured, lbs	12,086,847
Goods manufactured, yards	21,978,127
Total product	$2,981,196

Magnified Fibres of Cotton.

The following is the explanation of the accompanying cuts:

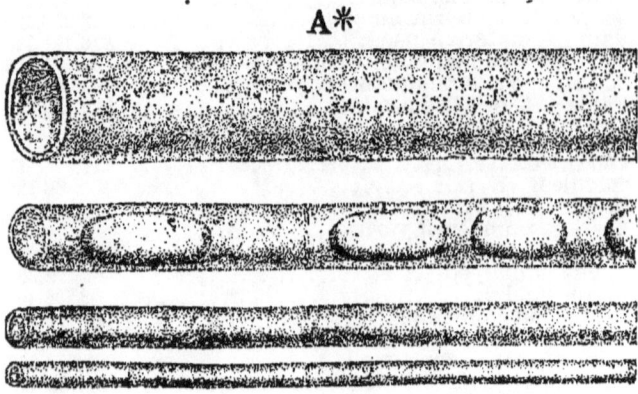

FIBRES OF UNRIPE COTTON.

A.—Fibres of the unripe cotton. In that state the fibres are perfect cylindrical tubes. A* is a fibre, represented as seen under water, indicating that the water had gradually entered and enclosed several air-bubbles, proving the tube to be quite hollow and without joints.

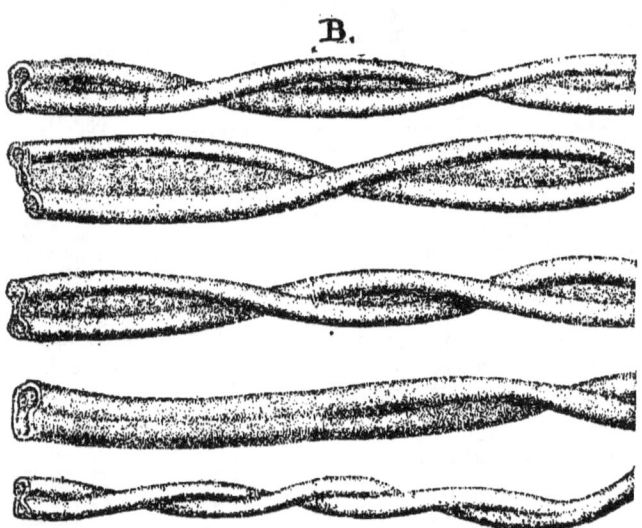

FIBRES OF RIPE COTTON.

B.—The first two fibres are from ripe cotton and are already twisted, though the pod or capsule is not yet burst, and is still on the growing plant. The other three fibres are of raw cotton prepared for manufacture.

C.

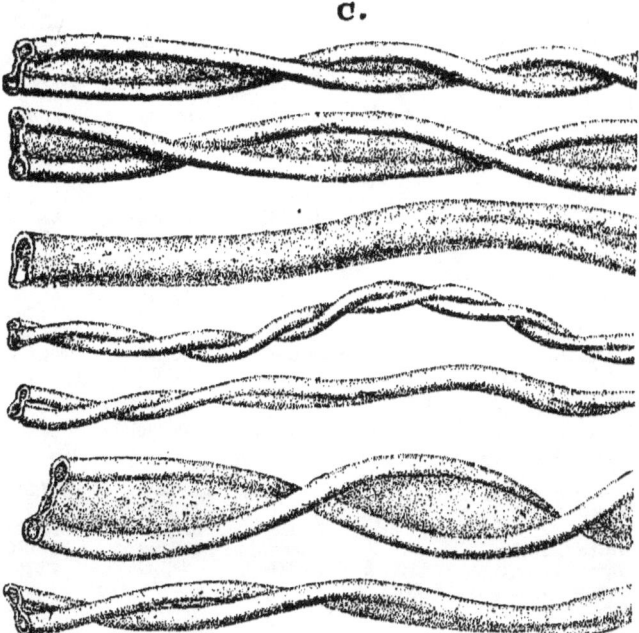

FIBRES OF UNRAVELLED THREADS OF MANUFACTURED COTTON.

C.—Various fibres of unravelled threads of manufactured cotton.

The fibres of cotton in the above drawings represent $\frac{1}{100}$ of an inch in length, and are magnified 400 times in diameter. In thickness those fibres vary from $\frac{1}{800}$ to $\frac{1}{3600}$ of an inch. The twists or turns in a fibre of cotton are from 300 to 800 in an inch.

How Sewing Cottons Are Made.

Sewing cottons are made by "doubling" the yarn produced generally by the throstle-frame, a modification of which is also employed for this purpose. Sometimes six threads are combined in pairs, so as to give great strength for sewing purposes.

Cotton Spindles in the United States in 1889.

The accompanying table gives the number of cotton spindles in the United States in 1889, as compared with 1880 and 1887:

	1880.	1887.	1889.
Alabama	49,432	104,791	96,647
Arkansas	2,015	6,400	13,700
California	....	*No returns	*No returns
Colorado	....	....	....
Connecticut	936,376	1,092,524	1,023,928
Dakota	....	....	....
Delaware	46,188	67,706	61,714
Florida	816	816	1,300
Georgia	198,656	406,330	442,148
Idaho	....	....	....
Illinois	4,860	27,000	26,000
Indiana	33,396	59,896	61,868
Iowa	....	....	6,000
Kansas	....	....	....
Kentucky	9,022	27,500	42,500
Louisiana	6,096	44,028	61,168
Maine	695,924	824,432	812,722
Maryland	125,706	176,800	176,800
Massachusetts	4,236,084	5,330,120	5,905,875
Michigan	5,100	5,500	....
Minnesota	1,708	....	....
Mississippi	18,658	47,050	54,800
Missouri	19,302	17,500	17,500
Montana	....	....	....
Nebraska	....	....	....
New Hampshire	944,053	1,180,648	1,207,312
New Jersey	232,221	351,068	351,068
New York	561,658	631,676	619,472
North Carolina	92,385	227,348	321,070
Ohio	13,327	28,152	26,152
Oregon	....	....	....
Pennsylvania	425,391	452,735	445,962
Rhode Island	1,746,539	1,856,982	1,948,958
South Carolina	82,334	232,692	351,040
South Dakota	....	....	....
Tennessee	35,736	100,277	116,783
Texas	2,648	5,174	17,734
Utah	432	576	288
Vermont	55,081	63,868	62,775
Virginia	44,340	68,912	79,612
Washington Territory	....	....	....
West Virginia	....	....	....
Wisconsin	10,000	32,480	32,128
Wyoming Territory	....	....	....
Total	10,653,435	13,470,981	14,385,024

* One Mill.

Cotton Spindles of other Countries in 1889.

According to the most reliable reports, the cotton spindles of the world, not including the United States, in 1889, represented the following:

England, 42,740,000; European Continent, 23,380,000; East India, 2,490,000; Canada, Mexico and South America, 600,000, and Japan, 100,000. On the European Continent Germany occupies the first place with about 5,500,000 spindles, and France next with 5,200,000.

Our Cotton Factories in 1791, 1805, 1812 and 1817.

Samuel Wilkinson, of Connecticut, says:

"Nearly all the cotton factories in this country, from 1791 to 1805, were built under the direction of men who had learned the art or skill of building machinery in Mr. Samuel Slater's employ. Mr. Slater used to spin both warp and filling on the water frame up to 1803. The operations of manufactories up to 1817 were confined to spinning yarn only, which was put out in webs and woven by hand-loom weavers. Mules for spinning filling had not then been introduced. The cotton used to be put out to poor families in the country and whipped on cords, stretched on a small frame about three feet square, and the motes and specks were picked out at four to six cents per pound, as it might be, for cleanness.

"In 1812 each spindle in Rhode Island and Massachusetts produced yarn enough weekly to make two and a half yards of cloth of the value of 30 cents per yard."

Only 1,000 Bales of Cotton Consumed in Manufacturing in the United States in 1805.

In 1805 the total consumption of cotton by the manufactories of the United States was a little more than 1,000 bales.

Metric System of Length.

The metre, the unit of length, is the ten-millionth part of a line drawn from the pole to the equator.

1 millimetre = $\frac{1}{1000}$th of a metre = 0.03937 inches.
1 centimetre = $\frac{1}{100}$th of a metre = 0.39370 inches.
1 decimetre = $\frac{1}{10}$th of a metre = 3.93708 inches.
1 metre = as above = 3.2809 feet.
1 decametre = 10 metres = 10.9363 yards.
1 hectometre = 100 metres = 109.3633 yards.
1 kilometre = 1,000 metre = 0.62138 miles.

Cotton Manufacturing in the South and North Compared.

According to some authorities the South has several advantages over the North and Northeast as a manufacturer of cotton. Some of these are given as follows:

1. Proximity to raw material.
2. A superior climate.
3. Cheaper power.
4. Lower cost of rent and living.
5. Lower wage scales.
6. Less liability of strikes.
7. Cheaper buildings.
8. Less expense for heating mills.
9. Saving on freight.

The dividends paid in 1888 by many Southern mills ranged between the extremes of 4 and 28 per cent., while the average was $11\frac{1}{2}$ per cent.

As to wages, it would seem that in large Southern manufacturing centres the scale of prices does not materially vary from those prevalent in the Northern mills, there being possibly 5 to 10 per cent. advantage in favor of Southern mills, which is probably made up to the Northern mills by superior expertness.

The smaller cotton mills at country points in the South get labor for 20 to 25 per cent. less than the scales in vogue at the great centres both North and South, and it is safe to say that the average paid in the South for the same hands is 15 per cent. below the Northern average.

The Draw-Loom.

So long as a fabric is plain, like shirtings, sheetings, etc., the hand loom will suffice to weave it; but if it is figured, an additional apparatus is necessary. In this case the warp threads, instead of being raised alternately, are raised two or more together, then one only, then two or more, according to the exigencies of the pattern. Hence, two healds will not suffice; there must be other mechanism for raising the warp threads in some prescribed order. A *draw-boy* was at one time employed for this purpose. But as the excellence of the work depended on the right group of healds being pulled up at the right time, and as a boy could not always be relied upon here, an improvement called the *draw-loom* was devised, which insured something like mechanical precision in this work.

Philadelphia Cotton Manufactures in 1782.

The following advertisement is from the *Pennsylvania Gazette* of April 3, 1782. The advertiser is said to have been the first one to make "jeans, fustians," etc., in America:

> *Philadelphia Manufactures*—suitable for every season of the year, viz: Jeans, Fustians, Coatings, &c., to be sold by the subscriber at his dwelling house and Manufactory, in South Alley, between Market Str. and Arch Str., and between Fifth and Sixth Streets, on Hudson's Square.   SAMUEL WETHERILL.

Cotton Thread of American Origin.

The *New York Transcript* (1831) contains the following correspondence, dated South Oxford, Slaterville, R. I., November, 1831:

"Here resides Samuel Slater, the patriarch of manufactures in this country. It is only known to a few that the world is indebted to this gentleman for the discovery of cotton thread. In 1794, while spinning a quantity of Sea Island cotton, the evenness and beauty of the yarn attracted the attention of Mrs. Slater. The question arose, if this is doubled and twisted, why will it not make good sewing thread? The experiment was made, and, in order to be fully satisfied of the result, a sheet was made with one-half of linen thread and the other half with cotton. It was immediately put into use, and the first thread that gave way was the linen. From this period he commenced the manufacture of thread, and it soon spread into England, France and other European countries, where it is generally supposed to be of English origin."

How Cotton Yarns Are Measured.

Cotton yarn is measured as follows: 54 inches, 1 thread; 4,320 inches, 80 threads, 1 lea or rap; 30,240 inches, 560 threads, 7 lea, 1 hank, 840 yards. One spindle of 18 hanks is 15,120 yards. A reel is 54 inches in circuit. The "number" of a yarn is the number of hanks, of 840 yards each of that yarn, weighing 1 pound, thus: Of No. 60 yarn, 60 hanks, 840 yards long, weigh 1 pound. Of No. 70 yarn, 70 hanks, 840 yards long, weigh 1 pound. Of No. 80 yarn, 80 hanks, 840 yards long, weigh 1 pound.

Production of Cotton Goods in Philadelphia in 1788.

Samuel Wetherill, Chairman of the Committee of Manufactures, in his report to the Board of Managers of the Pennsylvania Society for Promoting Manufactures and Useful Arts, says that, from April 12, 1788, to Aug. 23, 1788, twenty-six looms had wrought the following goods:

Jeans	2,959½ yards.
Corduroys	197½ "
Federal Ribs	67 "
Beaver Fustian	57 "
Plain Cottons	1,567½ "
Linen	725 "
Tow Linen	1,337½ "
Total	6,911 "

"Besides in the looms there are 200 yards of jeans, corduroys, cottons and linen, and of manufactured goods they have sold at this time (Aug. 23, 1788,) of jeans, dyed cotton and linen yarn, fine and tow linen, etc., to the amount of £448, 5s., 11½d.

"In addition to the enumerated articles manufactured to the 23d of August, 1788, the following were made up to November 1, 1788:

Jeans	759½ yards.
Corduroys	383½ "
Flowered Cotton	39 "
Cottons	2,095 "
Flax Linens	123 "
Tow Linens	494 "
Bird Eye	123 "
Total	4,017 "

"And about 240 yards of different kinds of goods now in the looms, the whole amounting to 11,367 yards."

Production of Cotton Goods in England From 1793 to 1833.

In the article of cottons alone, the exports from England between 1793 and 1815, according to Barnes, amounted in value to £250,000,000. From 1816 to 1833, inclusive, cottons were sent from England to foreign markets to the enormous aggregate value of £570,000,000.

U. S. Import Duty on Cotton Thread, Yarn, Warps, Etc

On cotton thread, yarn, warps or warp yarn, whether single, or advanced beyond the condition of single, by twisting two or more single yarns together, whether on beams or in bundles, skeins or cops, or in any other form, except spool thread, the U. S. import duty is as follows:

	Per lb.	Per lb.
Values not over	25c.	10c.
Values over 25c. not over 40c.		15c.
Values over 40c. not over 50c.		20c.
Values over 50c. not over 60c.		25c.
Values over 60c. not over 70c.		33c.
Values over 70c. not over 80c.		38c.
Values over 80c. not over $1.		48c.

Values over $1. per lb., 50 per cent.

On spool thread of cotton, each spool not to exceed 100 yards of thread, 7c. per dozen spools. On the same, exceeding 100 yards on each spool, for each additional 100 yards of thread, or fractional part thereof in excess of 100 yards, 7c. per dozen spools.

The Largest Cotton Mill in the World.

The largest cotton mill in the world is that of Krahnholm, in Russia. This colossal establishment contains 340,000 spindles and 2,200 looms, disposes of a force of 6,300 horse power, and gives employment to 7,000 hands. The motive power is obtained from a fall on the river Marowa, which actuates eight turbines. Four of these turbines produce a force of 4,000 horse power each, and discharge 16,000 litres of water per second. The shafting of the machinery represents 9,426 running metres. The workpeople are Russians and Esthonians. The week's work is calculated at 79 hours, and the wages vary from 12 to 38 roubles per month.

Hints on Selecting Rope.

A good hemp rope is hard but pliant, yellowish or greenish gray in color, with a certain silvery or pearly lustre. A dark or blackish color indicates that the hemp has suffered from fermentation in the process of curing, and brown spots show that the rope was spun while the fibres were damp, and is consequently weak and soft in those places.

Fastness of Colors.

The term "fast color" generally implies that the color in question resists the fading action of light, but it may also imply that it is affected by washing with soap and water, or by the action of acids and alkalis, etc. In its wide sense it means that the color is not affected by any of those influences to which it is destined to be submitted, but its technical influence is often restricted.

Many colors may be fairly fast to washing with soap and water, and yet be very fugitive towards light; or, they may be fast to light, and yet very sensitive to the action of acids or alkalis.

The term "loose color" generally implies that the color is much impoverished, or even entirely removed, by washing with water or a solution of soap; it may, however, also mean that it is not fast to light.

The word "permanent," as applied to color, generally denotes that it is fast to light and other natural influences.

A "fugitive color" is generally understood to be one which is not fast to light, or which volatises more or less under the influence of heat.

In the absence, then, of any definite meaning being attached to the above terms, it becomes imperative, in speaking of the fastness of a color, to refer specially to the particular influence which it does or does not resist.

The Jacquard Loom.

The Jacquard loom, invented toward the end of the last century, is used for weaving figured goods. In this loom a chain of perforated cards is made to pass over a drum, and the strings by which the threads of the warp are raised pass over an edge with a wire or laden weight of small diameter suspended from each. These weights at each stroke of the loom are presented to each successive card, and some of them are intercepted by the card, while others pass through the holes therein, the latter thus determining which threads of the warp shall be raised. In this way the figure of the card determines the nature of the figure on the fabric.

Chronology of American Cotton Manufactures.

1786—Legislature of Massachusetts made a grant to Robert and Alexander Burr to aid them in building machinery for spinning cotton.

1787—Grant to Thomas Somers, by the Legislature of Massachusetts, to aid him in completing a machine for spinning cotton.

First cotton factory built in the United States at Beverly, Mass.

1788—Some spinning jennies were put in operation in Philadelphia, Pa., and Providence, R. I.

1789—Commencement of the cultivation of Sea Island cotton in Georgia from Pernambuco seed. Sam Slater came to this country, and was employed at New York, where, he said, they had in operation one carding machine and two spinning jennies at the close of the year.

1790—Samuel Slater went to Providence, R. I., and began building a cotton factory.

1791—The Slater factory in Providence, R I., commenced spinning early in the year.

1794—Cotton gin invented by Eli Whitney in 1793, and patented March 14, 1794.

1798—Cotton mill built by Slater at Pawtucket, R. I.

1802—Water mill at Beverly, Mass. had Arkwright machine put in.

1804—First cotton mill in New Hampshire commenced at New Ipswich in 1803, and began operation in 1804.

1805—Second cotton mill built at Pawtucket, R. I.

1806—Cotton mill built at Pomfret, Conn.

1807—Mill built at Smithfield, R. I., by Slater; also a mill built at Watertown, Mass.

1808—Norfolk cotton factory incorporated at Dedham, Mass., and a mill built at New Ipswich, N. H.

1809—First cotton mill in Maine, at Brunswick.

1811—Mill at Dorchester, Mass., incorporated.

1813—Incorporation of Boston Manufacturing Co., known as the Waltham Co.

1814 - Power-looms in operation in Waltham, Mass., being the first in the United States.

1817—William Gilmore migrated to this country in 1815 and put the crank-loom in operation in Rhode Island in 1817.

1822—First cotton manufactory built at Lowell, Mass.

1849—First cotton mill built at Lawrence, Mass.

Index to Selling Agents of Domestic Cottons.

The following is an Index to the Selling Agents of the principal brands of domestic cottons, arranged in such manner as to make it compact, reliable and convenient for quick reference on the part of buyers and dealers generally. The names of agents are represented by figures; e. g., reserving for the letter A figures 1 to 9; B 10 to 19; C 20 to 29; D 30 to 39, and so on all the way through. The various brands of cottons are also arranged in alphabetical order under their general headings, and each brand has attached to it the figure or figures which represent the selling agent.

SELLING AGENTS.

1. ALDRICH, IDDINGS & CO.
2. AMMIDOWN & SMITH.
10. BAILEY & CO., JOSHUA L.
11. BAKER & CO., FRANCIS.
12. BLISS, FABYAN & CO.
13. BREMER & CO., JOHN L.
14. BRINCKERHOFF, TURNER & CO.
15. BUTLER, CLAPP, WENTZ & CO.
16. BERNHEIMER & BROS., JACOB S.
19. BYRD GEORGE H.
20. CATLIN & CO.
21. CHAPMAN, MARTIN & CO.
22. CONWAY & CO., JOHN M.
23. COOKE & CO., CHARLES D.
24. COFFIN, ALTEMUS & CO.
25. CAREY, BAYNE & SMITH.
26. CONVERSE, STANTON & CULLEN.
27. COOKE & CO., JAMES W.
28. CLAFLIN & CO., H. B.
29. CONTINENTAL MILLS.
20a. CARUTH, JOHN G.
30. DALE, REED & COOLEY.
31. DALE & CO., HENRY.
32. DANA, TUCKER & CO.
33. DEERING, MILLIKEN & CO.
34. DENNY, POOR & CO.
35. DUNHAM, BUCKLEY & CO.
36. DAVIS & CO., THOS. J.
51. FARNUM & CO., JOHN (Phila).
52. FAULKNER, PAGE & CO.
53. FISH, JR., & CO., WM.
60. GARVER & CO.
65. GROSVENOR & CARPENTER
66. GRISWOLDVILLE M'F'G. CO.
67. GREER & HERTZEL, (Phila).
70. HARPER, M. ORLANDO.
71. JAFFRAY & CO., E. S.
90. JOY, LANGDON & CO.
100. KNIGHT, B. B. & R.

101. KIBBE, CHAFFER & CO.
110. LANGLEY & CO., W. C.
111. LAWRENCE, TAYLOR & CO.
112. LAWRENCE & CO.
113. LEWIS, H. & W. H.
114. LOW & CO., JOSEPH T.
115. LESHER, WHITMAN & CO.
116. LONG BROTHERS & CO., JAMES (Phila).
120. MINOT, HOOPER & CO
121. MITCHELL, MORRIS & CO.
130. NEVINS & CO.
141. OELBERMANN, DOMMERICH & CO.
150. PARKER, WILDER & CO.
171. ROBINSON, SHACKELTON & COOLEY.
180. SIMPSON, SONS & CO., WM.
181. SMITH, HOGG & GARDNER.
182. STRONG & CO., WM. L.
183. SHERIDAN & CO., G. K.
184. SAMPSON & CO., O. H.
185. SWEETSER, PEMBROOK & CO.
186. STORER, WILLIAM.
190. TOWNSEND & YALE.
191. TEFFT, WELLER & CO.
192. TRAINOR & SONS, D. (Linwood, Pa.).
193. TIBBITS, HARRISON & ROBBINS.
194. TODD, MURPHY & CO.
210. VAN VALKENBURGH & CO, P.
220. WHEELWRIGHT, ELDRIDGE & CO.
221. WHITE, PAYSON & CO.
222. WHITMAN, CREIGHTON & CO.
223. WHITIN, COLLINS & CO.
224. WOODWARD BALDWIN.
225. WEED & BROTHER.
226. WESTBROOK MFG. CO.
227. WILSON & BRADBURY.
228. WOODRUFF, HENRY G.
229. WEST & INGALLS.
230. WILLIS, GRINNEL.

NOTE—This list is made up to December 18, 1889, but as changes of firms and transfers of accounts usually take place about January 1st of each year, some corrections and additions will probably have to be made to it by the insertion of an addenda leaf.

Index to Bleached Sheetings and Shirtings.

A B C, 223; Adriatic, 24; Allendale, 11 and 30; Alpine Rose, 228; Altoona, 11; Alexandria, 13; Alleghany, 70; Amesbury, 90; Amory, 13; Androscoggin, 12; Art Cambric, 223; Atlantic, 20; Aurora, 11; Avondale, 24. Ballardvale, 24; Barker, 33; Bay Mills, 110; Berkley Cambric, 111; Berkley Madapolam, 111; Berkshire, 30; Best Yet, 11; Big Bonanza, 13; Blackstone, 111; Blizzard, 24; Boston, 190, 220; Bric-a-brac, 24; Brentwood, 11; Brighton, 90; Boott, 181; Burleigh Long Cloth, 230; Busy Bee, 11. Cabot, 220; Cascade, 33; Cast Iron, 33; China, 33; Champion, 181; Chapman, 100; Charter Oak, 114; Chicopee Mf'g. Co., 20; Clinton, 100; Cock of the Walk, 223; Clifton Mills, 220; Centreville Mills, 24; Conestoga, 51; Conquest, 114; Columbia 33; Continental, 29; Conway, 120; Cooley Homestead, 30; Copper Fastened, 25; Coral Reef, 24; Cohasset, 13; Crusader, 11; Cumberland, 111. Dauntless, 24; Davol Mill, 24; Defiance, 11; De Soto, 171; Devon, 24; Dial, 181; Diamond Field, 223; Diamond-Hill Cambric, 230; Dunedin, 11; Dwight-Anchor, 120; Dunellen Mills, 30. Easthampton, 70; Edwards, 12; Edward Harris, 23; Eldorado, 13; Elkwood, 228; Ellerton. W. S, 20; Excelsior, 23; Exeter Manufacturing Co, 220. Fairfax, 113; Fairmount, 33; Farmers A., 11; Farmers Choice, 111; Farwell, 220; Fairfield, 24; Family Favorite, 11; Favorite, 223; Fauntleroy, 101; Fearless, 24; Fidelity, 100; First Call, 114; Fitchville, 111; F. P. F. Cambric, 65; Forget-Me-Not, 111; Forrest Mills, 223; Forrestdale, 113; Franklinville, 90; Fruit-of-the Loom, 100; Full Value, 11; First Prize, 11. Garland, 24; Gem-of-the Spindle, 11; Glen Alpine, 11; Glendale, 12; George Washington, 120; Gilded Age, 220; Gilt Edge, 25; Golden Rod, 15; Gold Medal, 223; Great Falls, 120; Golden Wedding, 30; Greene, 111; Green Ticket, 30; Grinnell, 230; Great Republic, 24; Grosvenor Dale, 65; Gypsy Queen, 24; Gibraltar, 33; Globe, 30. Hercules, 33; Harvest, 11; Harvest E., 181; Hillsdale, 229; Homestead, 30; Hope, 111; Hills Semper Idem, 32; Holly Tree Cambric, 193; Hero, 100; Holmesville, 1; Housekeeper, 33; H. G. W., 228; Homespun, 33; Honest Household, 11; H. T. B., 30. Imperial, 13; Indian Head, 32; Iron Pier, 30; Iron Prince, 228; Invincible, 70. Jewitt City, 184; Jacque Rose Cambric, 228; Just Out, 24. King Phillip Cambric, 26; Knight's Cambric, 100; King Bee, 24; K. M. Q., 230. Laconia, 12; Lafayette, 11; Lancaster, 150; Landseer, 100; Langdon, 13; Lexington Mfg. Co., 11; Lily of the Valley, 11; Linwood, 223; Little Chief, 100; Loch Lomond cambric, 31; Lockwood, 33; Lonsdale, 111; Lonsdale cambric, 111; Lowell, 150. Magic, 114; Magnolia, 70; Masonville, 65; Milton Falls, 111; Mohawk Valley Cotton Mills, 111; Shrunk, 23; Monadnock, 150; Mohansett, 24; Monogram, 30. Nantuck, 191; Newmarket, 90; Naumkeag, 13; Nashua, 32; New Bedford, 230; Ne Plus Ultra, 24; New Candidate, 171; No Dicker, 171; New York Mills, 114. Oak Grove, 11; Oak Lawn, 114; Oak View, 90; One of the Finest, 15; Ontario, 11; Our Choice, 11; Our Own, 24; Our Reliance, 24; Oakland, 33. Paragon, 24; Pembroke, 24; Pelham, 20; Peabody, 20; Pennant, 15; Pepperell, 12; Perennial, 13; Plymouth, 11; Pride of the Nation, 30; Pequot, 13; Paragon, 24; Powhattan, 24; Pioneer, 24; Pioneer of the Market, 11; Pennant, 15; Pocahontas, 24; Pride of the West, 24; Prosperity. 24. Quinnebaug, 33; Queen, 70. Reading Dairy, 24; Rutledge, 30; Resolute, 191; Rhode Island, 111; Royal, 24; Rosalind, 181; Rosebud, 100; Rochdale, 24. Scituate, 15; Shamrock, 70; Senate, 114; Second to None, 114; Sea Island, 100; Snow White, 11; Sensation, 24; Security, 24; Sentinel, 24; Signal, 24; Silver Queen, 15; Standard, 100; Star W., 223; Sterling, 24; Sunlight, 24; Social, 23. Tea Rose, 228; Trump Card, 171; Trosseau, 24; The Cooley Homestead, 30; Ten Strike, 223; The Pennant, 15; The Sun Cotton, 120; Tiger Lily, 171; True-as-Steel, 181; Tuscarora, 113; Thistle Mills, 24. Utica Steam Mills, 111; Utica Diamond U., 111. Valley Mills, 171; Victoria long cloth, 230; Vineyard, 220. Wamsutta, 230; Warren Mfg. Co., 12; Washington, 120; Water Witch, 24; Wauregan, 113; Water Lily, 220; Whiting, 24; White Horse, 111; White Rock, 111; Whitinsville, 223; Williamsville, 24; Woodbury, 24; Winchester, 120; Wealth of the Country, 114; Wessacumcon, 90. X, Y, Z, 223.

Index to Brown Sheetings and Shirtings.

Adriatic, 32; Alaska, 11; Allendale, 30; Alligator, 24; Amory Mfg. Co., £, 13; Androscoggin, 12; Anniston, 223; Appleton, 32; Archery bunting, 222; Argyle, 181; Arizona, 24; Ashland, 181; Atlanta, 24; Atlantic, 20; Augusta, 224. Bedford, 181; Bellview, 19; Bennington, 181; Black Crow, 24; Big Bonanza, 13; Blue Ridge, 224; Boott, 181; Boston, 220; Buck's Head, 33; Busy Bee, 11; Burlington 11; Burley, 150. Cabot, 120; Calvert, 33; Cameron, 33; Capitol, 24; Cast Iron, 33; Central Falls, 70; Century, 33; Ceylon bunting, 33; Charleston, 110; Chesterfield, 223; Chieftain of the Glen, 11; Comet, 20; Conestoga, 182; Constitution, 12; Columbia, 33; Crusader, 11; Cresenta, 23; Charter Oak, 23. Darlington, 33; Decatur, 24; Derby, 24; Dwight, 120. Echo Lake, 120; Eldorado, 13; Ellsworth, 191; Enterprise, 224; Ettrick, 19; Exeter, 220; Exposition, 23. Eufaula, 224. Farmer A., 11; Farmer No. 1., 24; Fountain City, 53; Foxhall, 220; Fruit of the Loom, 100; Full Yard Wide, 220. Great Falls, 120; Grafton, 223; Graniteville, 19. Hamilton County, 53; Harvest, 11; Honest Width Yardstick, 181; Housewife, 120; Hill, 32; Huron D., 120. Indian Head, 32; Integrity, 24. Just Right, 120. King Mfg. Co., John P., 53. Laconia, 12; Lancaster, 32 and 150; Langley, 110; Lawrence, 190; Lehigh, 24; Lockwood, 33; Laurel Dale, 24; Log Cabin, 120; Lowell, 150; Lyman, 120. Massachusetts, 181; Mechanics, 24; Milton, 28; Mohawk Valley Cotton Mills, 111; Monadnock, 150; Mystic River, 181. Nabob Royal, 70; Nashua, 32; Natchez, 24; National bunting, 66; Naumkeag, 13; Newberry, 223; Newmarket, 90; New York Mills, 114; Niobe, 90; Norfolk, 90. Oriental, 24; Ozark, 13. Pacific, 20; Pacolet, 33; Park, 24; Pelzer, 110; Plymouth, 11; Pembroke, 24; Pepperell, 12; Pequa, 51; Pequot, 13; Princeton, 183; Piedmont, 224; Pocahontas, 24; Pocasset Canoe, 24; Pioneer, 24; Portsmouth, 2; Prescott, 181; Pride of the Nation, 30; Princess bunting, 66. Riverside, 90, Rockingham, 183; Royal "340," 191; Rosalie, 23; Rose of the Valley, 24. Salisbury, 12; Saracen, 181; Saranac, 32; Scotia, 70; Sea Foam, 33; Sea Shore, 24; Shamrock, 70; Shawmut. 181; Sherman, 70; Springfield, 181; Stark, 13; Statue of Liberty, 191; Sun Tissue, 33; Superior W. E., 220. Tennis, 223. Utica Cotton Co., 111; Utica Steam Mills, 111. Virginia Family, 19. Wachusett, 32; Wamsutta, 113; Washington, 24; Wasuc, 223; Waterville, 33; Whitefield, 33; Williamsville, 24; Winthrop, Continental Mills, World Wide, 220. Yardstick, 181.

Cotton Drills.

Adriatic, 32; Anniston, 224; Appleton, 32; Atlanta, 24; Augusta, 224. Boott, 181. Calvert, 33; Charleston, 110; Clifton, 220; Conestoga, 51; Continental, 51. Darlington, 33. Ettrick, 19; Eufaula, 224. Graniteville, 19. Hamilton, 90; Harper, 70. King Mfg. Co., John P., 220. Laconia, 12; Lanark, 24; Langley, 110; Lyman, 120. Massachusetts, 181. Natchez, 24. Pacolet, 33; Piedmont, 224; Pepperell, 12; Prescott, 181. Rock River, 12; Rosalie, 23. Sheldrake, 23. Royal Standard, 191. Stark, 13; Sibley, 23; Suffolk, 181; Superior, 181. Tennessee, 70.

Denims.

Amoskeag, 13; Artisans, 13. Beaver Creek, 12; Boston Medal, 12. Columbian, 12. Easton, 23; Everett, 181. Hamilton, 90; Haymaker, 12. Jewitt City, 184. Lawrence, 190; Lewiston, 2. Omega, 192; Otis, 12. Palmer, 12; Pearl River, 13; Pemberton, 130. Rosalie, 23. Saco River, 181; Shetucket, 32; Sibley, 23. Thorndike, 12. Uncasville, 170. Wachusett, 181; Warren 12. York, 181.

Ginghams.

Abbotsford, 11; A. F. C., 13; Amoskeag, 13; Arasapha, 10; Arlington 224. Barnaby Mfg. Co., 24; Bates, 12. Calcutta, 20; Cumberland, 22. Everett Classics, 181; Egremont, 224; Empire, 224. Gloucester, 114; Gotham, 67; Greylocks, 224. Imperial Seersucker, 13. Johnson Mfg. Co., 34. Lancaster, 32. Manchester, 23; Manville Co., 141; Marguerite, 224; Massabesic, 13. Normandie, 32. Parkhill Mfg. Co., 34; Park Mills, 170. Renfrew, 210. Saccarappa, 226; Slatersville, 227. Toile du Nord, 34; Tuscany, 224. Wamsutta, 24; Westbrook, 226; White Mfg. Co., 20; Whittenton, 52. York, 181.

Index to Checks and Cheviots.

Amoskeag, 13; Arasapha, 10; Alabama, 1. Bates, 12; Bengalese Cloth, 116. Columbian, 12; Conestoga, 51. Degner, 13; Delhi, 27. Eagle, 12; Everett, 181. Greenville, 12. Easton, 23. Jewitt City, 113. Kenmore, 116. Massabesic, 13. Great Western, 22. Otis, 12. Loch Lomond, 32. Sea Island, 27; Slatersville, 227; Sibley, 23; Slater, 184. Thorndike, 12. Uncasville, 170. York, 181.

Corset Jeans.

Amory, 13; Androscoggin, 12. Biddeford, 12. Conestoga, 182. Edwards, 12; Empire, 2. Kearsage, 220. Laconia, 12; Lexington, 24. Naumkeag, 13; Narragansett, 24. Pepperill, 12. Quinnebaug, 2. Rockport, 12.

Printed Calicoes.

Allen's, 111; American, 12; Anchor; Shirtings, 180; Arnold's. 52. Berlin, 180. Charter Oak, 60; Cocheco, 112. Dresden, 11, Eddystone, 180; Elberon, 11. Garner & Co., 60. Hamilton, 90; Harmony, 60. Imperial, black, 180. Lodi, 34. Manchester, 221; Martha Washington, 24: Merrimack, 220; Mystic Print Works, 184. Pacific Mills, 112; Passaic, 34. Ramapo, 60. Steel River, 60; Stirling, 25; St. Ledger, 60; Sultan, Turkey Red, 180. Victoria, 180. Washington, 24; Windsor, 210.

Silesias and Sateens.

Black Rock, 36. Caledonia, 16; Cambridge, 121; Capitol, 115; Centennial, 136; Conestoga, 182: Crown, 115. English, KK, 16; French, XX, 16. German, AB, 16; Globe, 30. Hopeville, 186. Kearsage, 220. Lonsdale, 111; Lonsdale, colored cambric, 111. Pepperill Sateens, 12. Social, 23. Victory, 20. White Star, 36· Windsor, 36.

Tickings.

Amoskeag, 13. Brandywine Mills, 51. Conestoga, 51; Cordis, 12; Challenge, 20a; Colchester, 27. Everett, 181; Elmwood, 184. Falls Co., 32; Farmers, 184; First Prize, 90. Hamilton, 90; Heifer, 184. Imperial, 90. Jewitt City, 184. Lancaster, 51. Massabesic, 13; Methuen, 130; Monroe, 27. New England, 12. Oakland, 52; Ocean, 113; Omega, 192. Palmer, 12; Pearl River, 13; Pemberton, 130; Poole, 52; Princeton, 184. Rosemont, 51. Slatersville, 227; Shetucket, 32; Swift River, 12. Thorndike, 12; Warren, 12. Yeomans, 113; York, 181.

Cambrics (Flat Fold).

Edwards Mfg. Co., 12. Equity, 2. Fifth Avenue, 2. Lockwood, 33. Slater & Sons, 185. Warren, 12; Washington, 20.

Canton Flannels.

Amoskeag, 13. Chicopee Mfg. Co., 20. Ellerton, 20. Hamilton, 90. Laconia, 12; Lawrence, 190; Lyman, 120. Massabesic, 13; Massachusetts, 181; Methuen, 130. Nashua, 32. Ocean, 12; Otis, 12. Pemberton, 130. Royal Standard, 191. Tremont, 181.

Cottonades.

Aberdeen, 16; Andover, 115; Albany, 15. Bell D. & T., 10; Brunswick 10. Fairhaven, 10; Falls Co., 32. Chicopee, 15. Everett, 181. Golden Rule, 15. Kenmore, 10. Manchester, 15; Merrimack, 181. N. Y. Mills, D. & T., 114; Nova Scotia, 17; Niantic, 16. Our Choice, 15; Oxmead, 16. Park Mills. 170; Pemberton, 130. Southern, 10. Trenton, 186. Unadilla, 186. Wachusett, 181; Wear Well, 10. York, 181.

Stripes.

American, 32; Amoskeag, 13. Bates, 12; Boston, 12. Cordua, 184; Columbian, 12; Conestoga, 51. Eagle, 12; Easton, 23; Everett, 181. Granville, 90; Glasgow, 184. Hamilton, 90. Jewitt City, 184, Massabesic, 13. Omega, 192; Ctiz, 12. Rock River, 23. Sheridan, 184. Thorndike, 12. Volunteer, 184. Uncasville, 170. York, 181.

Analysis of the Widths, Weights, Counts or Picks of Domestic Cottons.

Beginning on page 173, under the respective headings of "Brown Sheetings and Shirtings," "Bleached Sheetings and Shirtings," etc., will be found tables giving the widths, weights, counts of threads or picks of the principal makes of domestic cottons, ginghams, etc. In each instance these have been carefully measured, weighed, and the picks counted by experts, with the aid of the most approved modern appliances used for such purposes. In addition to the ordinary magnifying glass usually employed in counting the threads or picks of cotton cloth, THE DRY GOODS CHRONICLE sent to Switzerland and had specially made to order an improved and graduated thread or pick counter, of which the following is a good illustration :

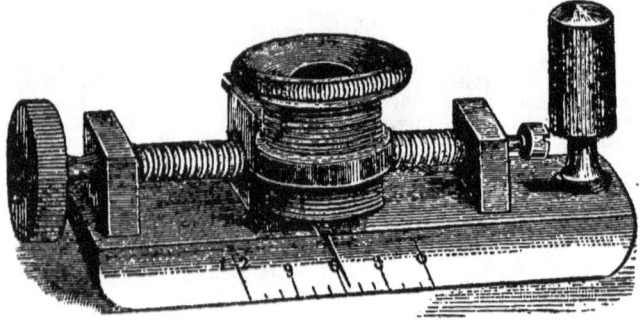

UNIVERSAL THREAD OR PICK COUNTER.

This instrument consists of a highly polished steel plate with beveled sides, upon which the desired scales are engraved. The side containing the scale is placed upon the sample, the threads of which are to be counted running parallel either with the warp or the filling. The lines of the scale are of such a length that the operator, in his counting of the threads, is not confined to certain principal lines, such as one-quarter or one-half inch, but may cease counting at any line he may desire.

Upon the upper face of the steel plate stand two brass uprights with perforations, serving as bearings to a small shaft which is throughout its whole length, from one upright to the other, furnished with a fine screw thread of about one millimeter pitch. When this screw is revolved by means of the small milled head it moves backward or forward a square nut, the lower side of which rests upon the steel plate. Upon the front side of the nut is a magnifier, which can be moved up or down. One-half of it is above the scale on the beveled side of the steel plate, while the other half projects beyond it and includes the weave under examination.

Under the centre of the magnifier, fastened to the lower edge of the square nut, is a fine index needle, reaching to the outer edge of the scale division, so that its point always touches the thread and the scale division at the same place.

When the screw is turned it moves the nut, together with magnifier and index needle, and the operator may at his ease count thread for thread in the steady progress of the needle, it being only necessary to watch the latter and the thread pointed to, until it arrives at a division where it is desired to stop counting. If the operator wishes to continue counting, he may simply jot down the number and proceed after having rested his eye.

The steel plate is beveled upon each side, and corresponding scales are engraved upon each. The needle can be displaced about $1\frac{1}{2}$ inches, and the magnifier can be raised or lowered to suit the eye of the operator.

For these reasons this improved magnifier and thread counter is now the instrument chiefly used in the analysis or inspection of weaves in Switzerland and other European countries. The old magnifier commonly used is set in a piece of metal hinged to an upright, with a foot hinged to the latter. The three pieces, each about one inch square, can be folded together and carried in the vest pocket.

The little square hole in the foot piece of the ordinary magnifier varies in size according to the kind of weave to be examined. On the one hand, a small hole is objectionable, because with the least displacement it causes errors in the counting of the threads. On the other hand, a large hole is equally objectionable, especially if a weave with a close warp is to be counted. Every manufacturer or expert knows how difficult it is to count from thirty to fifty and more threads in a space of one-quarter of one square inch with a magnifier of this kind. The eye tires, and the result is so uncertain that after repeated countings the operator arrives at only approximate results. In order to avoid difficulties of this kind, perhaps nearly every one has recourse to some method of his own invention to assist him in his labor. Most universally used, perhaps, is a fine needle, in order to offer a certain rest to the eye, after having counted a definite number of threads. Even this is not entirely reliable, because, while marking on the paper, the analyzer may forget the number of threads counted, and must recommence counting.

In order to avoid as much as possible the difficulties enumerated, the Universal Thread Counter has been used, in conjunction with ordinary counting glass. The most approved weighing scales and width measures have also been employed, with the results, it is believed, of making generally the most accurate and reliable tables of widths, weights and counts or picks of brown, bleached and colored cottons, ginghams, etc., ever presented to the trade of this country. While the tables in question are not altogether complete in some instances (and possibly some few errors may have unavoidably crept into the analysis of the same), they will in due time be completed, and all errors be corrected in the revised editions of the work, which will appear annually, with added improvements.

BROWN SHEETINGS AND SHIRTINGS.

Name.	Width. Inches.	Yards to Pound.	Picks to Inch.
Aberford Standard	36	2.84	48x48
Acorn	36	4.00	....
Adriatic	36	....	....
Agawan	36	4.00	52x44
Agawan, XX	30	....	....
Alabama	27	12.00	36x36
Albany, LL	36	4.00	56x56
" BB	36	....	64x72
Alaska	36	3.95	72x80
Alexandria	42	....	....
Alpha	36	3.86	64x68
Allendale	54	....	....
"	7-4	2.36	60x64
"	8-4	2.07	60x64
"	9-4	1.84	60x64
"	10-4	1.65	60x64
"	11-4	1.51	60x64
" L	12-4	1.38	60x64
Alligator	27	13.00	36x36
"	26	13.55	40x32
American, XX	36	2.54	52x56
American Mills, C.D.	36	3.98	52x48
Amory Mfg. Co	36	3.84	80x76
"	36	3.68	76x76
" LL	40	3.49	80x72
Anchor, L	36	6.65	44x44
Androscoggin	46	3.36	72x72
"	48	3.10	72x72
"	7-4	2.14	72x72
"	8-4	1.87	72x72
"	9-4	1.66	72x72
"	10-4	1.50	72x72
"	11-4	....	72x72
Antelope, A	36	3.26	44x44
Anniston	36	3.20	48x44
Appleton A	36	2.76	48x52
" A	36	2.80	44x50
" Fine AA	35	4.39	60x60
" Fine AA	35	4.37	60x56
" GG	35½	2.86	....
" Fine GG	35¾	4.53	56x60
" R	36	3.70	64x64
" XX	36	4.17	56x56
Archery Bunting	36	8.20	44x48
Argyle Family cotton	36	3.52	60x64
" "	40	3.25	60x64
Arizona	36	....	....
Arrow	36	....	....
Ascot	36	....	68x76
Ashland	36	....	....
Ashland	36	6.90	44x44
Atlantic AA improved	36	3.00	46x48
" AA	36	3.00	46x48
" BB	30	3.50	48x48
Altantic A	36	2.85	48x48
" H	36	2.95	52x56
" P	36	4.00	56x56
" D	36	3.33	48x48
" V	30	3.61	52x52

Brown Sheetings and Shirtings—Continued.

Name.	Width. Inches.	Yards to Pound.	Picks to Inch.
Atlantic LL	36	5.03	64x64
" LL	36	4.94	64x64
"	5-4	2.69	68x72
"	5-4	2.74	63x68
"	6-4	2.18	68x68
"	7-4	1.82	68x68
"	8-4	1.68	68x68
"	9-4	1.46	64x68
"	10-4	1.32	68x68
"	11-4	....	....
" Comet	36	3.45	64x64
" Comet	40	3.11	64x64
Atlas R	35	3.79	60x60
Augusta A, No. 1	36	3.03	48x48
"	30	3.63	40x40
"	27	4.52	40x40
Aurora LL	36	4.00	56x60
" C	31	5.50	40x44
" R	36	3.50	68x68
" B	36		64x68
Badger State LL	36	4.00	56x56
" RR	36	3.75	64x64
" R	36	3.45	64x64
Bangor J	30	4.13	48x44
" F	36	2.90	48x48
" BB	36	4.05	56x56
" C	30	4.50	56x56
Banner	36	....	....
Baltic HL	33	....	....
Beaver Dam LL	36	4.00	56x56
Bedford R	30	5.96	64x68
Bellview XX	36	....	....
Belfast R	30	....	....
" H	30	....	....
Beacon	36	3.87	56x56
Bennington AL	36	3.15	64x68
" FF	36	2.90	48x48
" M	36	3.54	60x64
" R	30	6.00	64x64
" C	36	....	....
Black Crow	36	3.70	60x64
"	36	3.66	60x64
Black Rock	36	3.61	64x68
Boott FF Standard	36	2.89	48x48
" Sterling	36	3.60	60x64
" 2d *	36	3.81	60x60
" "	36	3.81	62x60
Boott, Warwick	36	....	....
" C	34	4.09	58x60
" Sq. Sterling	36	....	....
" AL	36	3.29	68x68
" PL	40	2.86	68x68
Boston	45	....	....
"	50	2.22	72x72
"	5-4	2.49	68x64
"	6-4	2.29	68x68
"	7-4	1.97	72x72
"	8-4	1.73	72x72
"	9-4	1.52	72x72
"	10-4	1.38	72x72

Brown Sheetings and Shirtings—Continued.

Name.	Width. Inches.	Yards to Pound.	Picks to Inch
Boynton	28	8.38	56x56
Broadway	36	4.50	44x56
Brighton Mills, A	40	3.18	....
" R	36	3.18	....
Busy Bee	36	4.35	64x64
"	33	....	....
"	7-8	....	....
Burlington	4-4	....	....
"	7-8	....	....
Buckshead	36	2.85	48x48
Buck's Head	40	3.17	48x48
Buckingham	36	....	....
Cabot, A (Dwight)	36	2.97	48x48
" No. 10 (M)	36	....	76x80
" W	36	3.45	48x48
Calvert Mfg. Co	36	2.93	48x48
" "	36½	2.86	48x48
Cambria	36	....	....
Calumet, A	36	2.85	48x48
" B	36	2 95	48x52
" C	36	3 30	56x60
" LL	36	4.00	56x56
" X	36	5.45	48x48
Cameron, D	36	..	....
Carlyle	40	....	....
"	28	5.24	64x66
Capitol, A	36	....	....
" B	30	....	....
" C	28	....	....
" XX	36	....	....
Cartwright	36	4.83	48x52
" CW	36	4.64	52x56
Cartwright Mills	36	4.86	52x56
Cary, G. W	36	3.03	48x44
Cast-Iron Brand, C	36	3.13	68x72
" "	36	3.07	68x76
Cedar Falls, AA	36	....	....
Central	36	....	....
"	32	....	....
Central Falls	36	6.22	44x40
Century, A	40	....	....
" B	36	3.69	68x72
" B	36	4.08	68x72
" C	32	....	....
" D	27	....	....
" E	36	....	....
" L	28½	4 82	64x64
Century Cotton B	36	3.69	68x72
" L	28	4.82	64x64
Ceylon Bunting	36	....	....
Charleston O	36	....	....
" RR	30	....	....
" C	27	....	....
" Star	36	....	....
Cherry Mountain	36	....	....
Charter Oak	36	....	....
Champion Mills K	31½	5.92	64x64
Chatham AA Stan'd	36	....	....
Chesterfield Mills A	36	2.75	48x46
Chippewa C	36	....	....

Brown Sheetings and Shirtings—Continued.

Name.	Width, Inches.	Yards to Pound.	Picks to Inch.
Chittenango A	36	4.70	44x44
Clarion LL	36	4.00	....
Clifton CCC	36	3.03	48x44
" CCC	36¼	2.87	48x44
" (World wide) E	36	....	....
" (Arrow)	36	....	....
" CC	31	3.64	48x44
" C	29	....	....
" D	28	....	....
Cohasset A, heavy	36	....	....
"	40	....	....
Comet C	36	3.45	64x64
"	40	3.11	64x64
Common Sense	36	4.02	68x72
Concord	36	....	....
Collingwood	36	....	....
Columbia	36	....	....
Conestoga W	36	3.61	60x60
" S	33	4.18	60x60
" G	30	4.73	60x60
" D	28	5.11	60x60
Conestogo	10-4	1.28	56x52
"	11-4	1.12	56x52
Constitution	36	3.48	64x68
"	9-8	....	....
"	40	3.14	64x68
"	42	2.93	64x68
"	45	2.76	64x68
"	48	2.76	64x64
Continent 1 C	36	3.50	64x68
" D	40	3.27	68x72
" D	40	3.05	64x72
" E	42	2.92	64x78
" W	45	2.75	64x68
" H	48	2.63	64x68
" half bleached	36	....	....
Cotton Valley Mills C	36	3.79	60x62
Crescent D	36	....	....
Crown XXX	36	2.85	48x48
Dan River	36	....	....
Darlington	36	2.85	....
"	40	....	....
Daphne	36	....	....
Dayton C	36	....	....
Decatur	28	8.68	52x52
Derby C	36	....	....
Des Moines	36	4.00	64x72
Diamond B	36	....	....
Dwight	36	3.94	76x84
" Improved X	30	4.65	64x64
" "	27	4.73	60x64
" DMC	36	3.31	72x72
" "	36	3.97	76x80
" Star	36	4.02	80x76
" "	40	3.40	80x76
" Anchor	36	3.25	72x72
" "	40	3.00	72x72
" "	42	....	....
Eagle A	36	....	....
"	36	....	....

Brown Sheetings and Shirtings—Continued.

Name.	Width. Inches.	Yards to Pound.	Picks to Inch.
Echo Lake	36	3.60	72x63
"	40	3.49	64x64
Edgefield A	36	....	....
Eldorado	36	3.20	68x64
Empire AA	36	....	....
"	32	....	....
Enterprise EE	36	3.95	52x52
Ettrick AA	36½	2.81	48x48
" EE	36	2.91	48x48
Eufaula	36	....	....
"	32	....	....
"	27	....	....
Eureka	32	....	....
Exeter A	36	4.08	64x64
" S	33	4.56	64x64
" C	40	....	....
Exposition A	36	4.00	48x48
" B	30	....	....
Fairmount E	28	....	....
" H	36	....	....
Fall Brook	36	....	....
Farwell Mills hf-blc'd	36	....	....
Farmer A	36	4.00	....
" BB	32	4.55	64x64
" extra No. 1	28	6.69	60x60
Fine Sheetings	36½	5.15	44x44
First Call	3-4	....	....
Florida	36	....	....
Forest Mills	36	3.65	68x68
Fountain City	36	4.63	48x52
Foxhall A	27	4.33	36x44
Fruit of the Loom	8-4	1.70	68x68
" "	9-4	1.56	68x68
" "	10-4	1.32	68x68
Georgia A	36	....	....
" B	36	....	....
" —	32	....	....
Germain	36	....	....
Globe BB	34	....	....
Glendale	36	2.96	44x44
"	30	3.40	....
" B	36	4.02	....
Golden Gate	36	....	....
Good as Wheat	36	4.10	76x84
Grafton Extra A	28	6.95	64x68
Granite A	36	....	....
" B	32	4.77	48x52
" C	28	....	....
Graniteville A	36	3.00	48x52
" EE	36	3.00	48x48
" HHH	36	....	....
" C	27	4.67	40x40
" RR	27	3.77	48x48
" RR	29¼	3.42	....
Great Falls Co, E	36	3.00	52x56
" J	36	4.27	64x68
" N	36	5.17	50x48
" XX	36	4.60	56x56
Great Western	36	2.98	48x48
Greystone Steam Mills, R.	26	3.70	64x66

Brown Sheetings and Shirtings—Continued.

Name.	Width. Inches.	Yards to Pound.	Picks to Inch.
Griffin AA	36	....	....
" H	30		
Hamilton Co. Mills	36½	5.15	44x44
H rold M	36	4.17	56x60
Hartford, A	35	5.25	....
Harvest	36	....	....
"	33	....	....
Henderson A	36	....	....
Henrietta EE	36	3.82	....
" FFF	36		
Here You Are	36¾	5.51	52x48
Hildreth A	36⅓	2.86	44x48
Hill Semper Idem	36	4.10	80x64
Hill Semper Idem	36	3.83	....
Holbrook Mills R	36		
Honest Household	36	4.15	72x84
Honest Width	36	3.50	60x60
"	36	3.52	60x60
"	36¾	5.51	52x48
"	40	....	....
"	7-8	....	....
Hoosier LL	36	4.00	....
Housewife Friend LL	36	3.98	
" extra	36	4.05	52x56
Huguenot Mills C	36	3.94	52x56
" A	36	2.73	48x48
" A	36	3.37	48x48
" B	36	2.75	48x48
" H		3.01	52x52
Huron D	35½	4.53	56x56
Hyde Park, AAA	36	....	....
Hyde Park, XXX	36	....	....
Hyde Park, XX	36	....	....
Hyde Park, X	36	....	....
Illinois C	36	....	....
Indiana Standard C	36	3.25	40x48
" LL	36	4.00	
Indian Head A	36	2.83	44x50
" E	48	2.12	46x50
" D	49	2.57	44x50
" B	30	3.42	48x48
Integrity XX	36	....	....
International, C	36	....	....
Invincible	30	5.16	44x44
Ironside A	36	3.02	48x48
Irving Mills XX	36	3.92	...
James River, HH	36	....	....
Jellico Mills, A	36	....	....
" " B	30	3.70	48x48
Jonesville	36	....	....
Jones' long cloth, CC	39¾	3.59	...
Just Right	36	....	....
Juniata, B	36	....	....
King Mfg. Co., AA	36	3.03	48x48
" EX	36	....	....
" EC	32	4.42	56x60
" RR	30	....	....
" EC	32	....	....
" XX	40	....	....
" IXL	40	....	....

Brown Sheetings and Shirtings — Continued.

Name.	Width. Inches.	Yards to Pound.	Picks to Inch.
Laconia	36	....	....
" B	7-4	2.38	64x64
"	8-4	2.12	64x64
"	9-4	1.80	64x64
"	10-4	1.65	64x64
"	11-4	1.48	64x64
Lake George, AA	36	3 15	48x44
" AA	36	4.38	56x60
Lanark, A	36	4 27	44x44
" B	30	5.27	44x48
" C	27	..	44x44
Lancaster	10-4	1-98	60x60
Langdon Fine, '76	36	3.74	72x80
" GB	36	3.50	....
Langley, A	36	3.00	44x44
" A	30	3.90	44x44
"	27	4.60	44x44
Lane	36	....	....
"	30	4.72	....
Laurel Dale	36	....	....
Lawrence, LL	36	3.90	56x56
Lake George, A	36	....	....
" AA	....	....	....
Lenox Mills, H	35⅜	3.91	....
Lehigh, E	36	9.00	36x36
Level Best	36	....	....
Live Oak, C	36	....	....
" S	36	....	....
Lockwood, A	40	3.60	68x76
" B	36	3.88	68x68
" R	36	3.75	68x72
" C	30	4.35	68x76
" D	28	7.20	64x68
" F	30	6.59	64x64
" E	36	....	....
"	42	3.04	64x72
"	5-4	....	....
"	6-4	2.32	68x72
Lockwood	7-4	2.11	64x68
"	8-4	1.75	64x72
"	9-4	1 56	64x72
"	10-4	1 41	64x72
"	11-4	....	68x68
Lonsdale	36	....	76x88
Lowell	10-4	2.13	56x60
Log Cabin	4-4	....	....
Louise	35¾	3.54	....
"	40	....	76x88
Lyman, A	45	2 35	48x48
" B	40	2.56	48x54
" C	36	....	....
Macon, A	36	2.87	48x48
Mathews	36	....	....
Mass. Fine, BB	36	4.00	60x60
" J	29	4.03	48x48
" C	28	4 44	40x40
" Stand'd	36	2 90	48x48
" P	30	....	48x48
Magnet xtra heavy	4-4	....	....
Marlboro	7-4	2 07	72x64

Brown Sheetings and Shirtings—Continued.

Name.	Width. Inches.	Yards to Pound.	Picks to Inch.
Marlboro	9-4	....	68x72
"	9-4	1.45	72x72
Maginnis, EE	36	4.00	...
Master Workman, D	36½	3.38	...
Mechanics, AA	36	12.23	32x28
" C	27	....	....
Milton, R	30	....	....
Middlesex, A	36	....	....
Michigan, LL	36	4.00	..
Mohawk Valley Mills	45		
" "	7-4	2 00	68x68
" "	38	2.14	64x66
" "	8-4	1.98	64x64
" "	9-4	1.70	64x64
" "	10-4	1.53	64x64
" "	11-4	1.36	64x64
" " A	31	....	56x56
Monticello, XXX	29¼	3.92	50x38
Monadnock	8-4	2.55	64x60
"	9-4	1.92	64x60
"	10-4	1.82	64x60
"	11-4	1.70	64x60
" A	36	5.29	48x52
Monhansett Mfg. Co.	36	....	72x64
Mystic River	36	5.59	48x52
Nabob Royal	40	....	....
" C	27	....	....
Nashua, E, Fine	40	3 70	68x68
" R	36	3 53	64x68
" F	42	2.95	68x68
" O	33	3.80	72x72
" P	45	2.74	68x68
" W	48	2.56	68x68
Nantuck Sheeting	10-4	2.19	68x56
Nashville, AA	36	....	....
Natchez, A	36	3.35	48x48
" F	36	4.15	40x44
" 2	35½	2.52	60x60
" 1	30	4.20	48x48
" G	30	5.00	40x44
" H	36	....	....
" S	30	4.40	60x64
Neponset	36	5.50	52x52
New Hartford, AA	36	4 60	44x44
Newburg	36	4.19	56x60
" C	31	....	....
Newberry Mills, A	36	2.87	48x48
Newport, A	36	4.44	....
" D	36	4.47	52x56
Newmarket, B	36½	4.77	48x52
" G	36	3.90	56x60
" N	36	4.00	64x64
" DD	36	4.58	52x60
" X	36	....	....
" K	31	5.86	64x68
" KK	29	....	....
New York Mills	48	2.30	64x64
" "	57	1.83	66x60
" " 9-4	78	1.35	64x68
" " 10-4	86	1.25	64x68

Brown Sheetings and Shirtings — Continued.

Name.	Width. Inches.	Yards to Pound.	Picks to Inch.
New York Mills, 11-4	98	1.13	64x68
" " 12-4	108	1.00	64x68
Niobe, R	36	4.52	52x56
Nonpareil	36	5.38	52x52
Oela, XX	28	....	40x40
Old Dominion, AA	36	....	....
Oriental Bunting, A	36	10.28	36x32
" "	36	10.42	....
Osceola, LL	36	....	....
" B	27	....	....
" Fine	36	....	....
Ostrich	36	....	....
Ozark, AA	36	2.79	48x52
Pacific, Extra	36	2.85	48x48
" H	36	3.13	56x56
"	54	4.33	68x68
"	7-4	1.87	68x72
"	8-4	1.63	64x72
Pacolet Mfg. Co	36	4.07	56x60
Pacolet, LL	36	4.00	....
Palatka Bunting	35½	8.73	56x64
Park, A	33	4.32	44x50
" BB	30	....	44x40
Pedro, B	32	....	....
Pelzer, C	3-4	....	....
" B	4-4	....	....
" A	4-4	2.85	48x48
" Standard	4-4	....	....
Pembroke	45	....	....
"	6-4	....	....
"	7-4	....	60x68
"	8-4	2.15	60x68
"	9-4	1.85	60x68
Pembrooke	10-4	1.63	60x68
"	11-4	1.52	60x68
"	12-4	....	....
Peerless	27	....	....
" K	30	....	....
Pepperell, E	40	3.44	66x68
" R	36	3.70	64x64
" O	33	4.00	64x64
" N	30	4.39	64x64
"	45	2.90	64x64
"	48	....	64x64
" (extra N, 9 twills)	48	....	....
"	7-4	2.36	64x64
"	8-4	2.10	64x64
"	9-4	1.79	64x64
"	10-4	1.63	64x64
"	11-4	1.47	64x64
"	12-4	1.00	64x64
Pequa	10-4	1.51	64x64
Pequot, A	36	3.17	68x64
" B	40	2.80	64x64
"	45	2.59	72x76
" W	48	2.34	68x76
"	6-4	2.18	72x76
"	7-4	2.07	72x76
"	8-4	1.71	72x76
"	9-4	1.45	72x76

Brown Sheetings and Shirtings Continued.

Name.	Width. Inches.	Yards to Pound.	Picks to Inch
Pequot	10-4	1.83	72x76
"	11-4	....	68x76
Pequot E'dorado	36		
Perkins, X	30	4.67	60x60
" Y	33	4.31	64x64
" Z	36	3.90	64x64
Phoenix, AA	39	3.50	64x64
Piedmont	36	3.09	48x48
"	30	....	38x44
"	27	4.62	48x44
Pioneer, XX	28	....	....
Plymouth, H	29½	4.96	
Pocahontas, B	36	3 90	80x72
" E	40	3.65	80x72
" D	30	....	....
Pocasset Canoe, E	40	3.10	64x64
Pocasset, C	36	3.63	64x64
" O	33	....	64x64
Portsmouth, P	28	7.00	64x64
" B	31	9.41	48x48
" C	36	....	....
Prescott, L	36	4.50	64x64
Pride of the Nation	36	3.85	84x84
Preston	36	....	....
Prarie Bunting, A	36	8.63	44x36
Princeton, 401	36	3 93	56x60
Princess	36	....	....
"	40	....	....
Queen	36	....	....
Randolph AA	36	....	....
Rexford Stand'd, AA	36	2.76	48x44
Richmond Co. Mills DB	36	4.69	48x52
Riverside Mills XX	36	5.36	52x48
Rockingham A	36	....	....
Rosalie F	36	2 96	48x48
Royal Standard	36	2.90	52x52
Royal Standard	35	3.60	48x48
Rye Rock A	36	....	....
Salisbury E	39	3.40	64x64
" R	36	3.72	64x64
" O	33	4.05	64x64
" N	30	4.40	64x64
Saracen	36	4.36	54x60
Saranac A	36	4.83	52x52
" E	40	3.08	68x68
" R	36	3.45	64x68
" O	30	....	....
Salisbury R	36	....	....
Scotia Mills O. M	36½	4.74	48x48
Sea Foam	36	....	....
Sea Shore Sheetings	27½	2.73	40x32
Shawmut LL	36	4.00	52x52
" XX	36	3.21	64x64
Shamrock	36	....	....
Sherman	30	5.09	46x40
Sherman, LL	36	....	....
Sibley B	40	2.50	....
" F	40	....	....
Silver Lake	36	....	....
Snow Flake	36	....	....

Brown Sheetings and Shirtings—Continued.

Name	Width. Inches.	Yards to Pound.	Picks to Inch.
Springfield B.	36	....	....
Square.	36	....	....
St. Lawrence.	36	....	....
Statue of Liberty	36	3.96	60x68
Stark AA.	36	2.85	48x48
Sterling AA.	36	....	....
Stanley Mills.	30	4.83	56x56
Superior W. E.	36	4.79	48x54
Superior W. E.	36	4.86	48x52
Superior Sea Island	36	4.76	56x56
Sun Tissues W	37	9.00	....
Swift Creek.	36	....	....
Tallahassee AA.	36	....	....
" A	30	....	....
Tennessee Premium.	36	....	....
Tennis.	36	....	....
Terrace City R.	36	....	....
The Square Shirting.	36	....	....
The Derby.	36	....	....
Tit for Tat AL.	36	4.14	56x60
Trenton Steam Mills.	28	....	....
Tremont O.	36	....	....
" CC.	36	4.00	48x52
Tuckahoe Superior.	36	....	....
Universal.	36	....	....
Utica C.	36	....	48x44
Utica Cotton Co.	36	5.45	48x44
Utica Mfg Co.	36	5.44	48x44
Utica Steam Mills	39¼	3.14	68x84
" " Nonp'l.	40	2.94	92x96
" " "	48	2.23	68x72
" " "	58	1.91	64x64
" " "	9-4	1.37	64x68
" " "	10-4	1.31	68x68
" " "	11-4	1.14	68x68
" " "	12-4	.98	64x68
Veil.	36	....	....
Verona.	36	3.77	88x84
Virginia Family.	36	....	....
Vineland.	36	....	....
Victoria R.	36	3.68	64x64
" AA.	36	3.95	52x52
" E	40	....	64x64
" LL	36	3.92	52x56
Volunteer L.	36	5.42	....
" B.	32	5.98	....
" C.	28¼	8.18	....
" D.	28	6.93	....
Wachusett A.	36	2.85	48x48
" B.	30	3.42	48x48
"	40	2.57	48x52
"	48	2.12	48x52
Warren AA	40	....	....
Wamsutta.	36	....	....
" O, XX.	40	.	....
"	59	1.80	72x76
"	72	1.45	72x76
"	79	1.30	72x76
"	89	1.15	72x76
"	99	1.05	72x76

Brown Sheetings and Shirtings—Continued.

Name.	Width. Inches.	Yards to Pound.	Picks to Inch.
Wamsutta................	108	.96	72x76
Washington, A............	26	3.59	52x60
Wasuc...................	36	....	....
Waterville...............	36½	5.16	64x68
Washaucum, A...........	36	....	....
Wh tfield	36	....	....
" Fine............	40	3.66	56x60
Windsor, H...............	36	5.34	52x48
Winthrop, L..............	36	....	....
"	40	....	....
Williamsville Sea Island...................	36	3.90	80x80
Wolcott, A...............	36	....	....
Yard Stick...............	36	3.52	60x60
Yosemite	40	....	....

BLEACHED SHEETINGS AND SHIRTINGS.

Name.	Width. Inches.	Yards to Pound.	Picks to Inch.
ABC	36	....	....
Alleghany	36	....	....
Allendale	42	....	....
"	45	....	....
"	6-4	2.65	64x60
"	7-4	2.35	64x60
"	8-4	2.08	64x60
"	9-4	1.87	64x60
"	10-4	1.63	64x60
"	11-4	1.50	64x60
Alex	36	....	....
Alexandria	36	3.73	80x80
"	42	....	72x72
"	46	3.23	72x72
Alpine Jacque	36	....	....
Alpine Rose (Batiste)	36	4.50	104x96
" (twilled)	36	3.69	84x96
Alpine Twill	36	....	....
Altoona H	27	....	....
Amesbury C	32	....	....
Amory	36	3.70	88x88
Anchor	32	....	....
Androscoggin AA	36	3.98	88x88
" L	36	4.17	80x76
" L	26	3.65	80x76
"	42	3.64	72x64
"	46	3.37	72x64
"	6-4	2.57	72x64
"	7-4	2.20	72x64
"	8-4	1.92	72x64
"	9-4	1.71	72x64
"	10-4	1.54	72x64
Art Cambric	36	....	100x98
Ashbyrne	36	....	84x88
Atlantic	42	....	....
"	5-4	....	....
"	6-4	....	....
"	7-4	....	....
"	8-4	....	....
"	9-4	....	....
"	10-4	....	....
"	11-4	....	....
Aurora	36	3.80	88x84
" Cambric	36	....	100x100
Ballardvale	36	5.00	64x64
Barker	36	4.25	80x80
Barker	36	4.27	80x76
Bay Mills	36	3.91	88x84
BB fine muslin cambric	36	5.90	100x80
Beaver Falls Mills	26	7.86	64x60
Bell Brand	36	....	....
Berkley cambric	36	5.27	120x108
Berkley cambric	36	5.28	112x112
Berkeley, No. 60	36	5.58	88x84
" No. 150	36	5.27	120x108
" No. 180	36	7.32	120x128
" Madapolam	36	4.40	108x100
Berkshire X	36	4.50	80x80
" RHR	36	....	72x72
" Hiawatha	36	5.38	56x60

Bleached Sheetings and Shirtings—Continued.

Name.	Width. Inches.	Yards to Pound.	Picks to Inch.
Berkshire Lily	33	5.75	72x68
" Peacock	31	6.20	60x60
" Bugle	31	6.20	60x60
" Wire Twist	33	....	....
" AX	36	....	....
" XIX	34	....	64x64
" X	3-4	....	56x60
Best Yet	36	....	....
"	32	....	....
Big Bonanza	30	5.18	64x60
" "	36	....	....
Big Drive	36	....	....
Big Injun	27	....	....
Blackburn AA	36	4.80	68x52
Blackstone Mfg. Co. AA	36	4.45	76x76
" " "	36	4.67	76x76
Boott R	28	5.93	68x60
" E	36	4.34	64x64
Boston	5-4	2.37	76x68
"	42	2.09	76x64
"	45	2.75	72x60
"	50	2.52	76x68
"	6-4	2.33	76x68
"	7-4	1.97	76x68
"	8-4	1.72	76x64
"	9-4	1.52	76x64
"	10-4	1.41	76x72
Bound-to-Win Bunting	26	9.89	60x46
" " Trump Card	28½	5.70	64x48
Branch River	36	....	....
Bric-a-Brac	36	....	....
Broadway	36	....	....
B Shirtmaker's Finish	36	....	....
Burleigh Long Cloth	36	4.63	108x92
" " "	36	4.68	92x88
Cabot	36	4.65	80x76
"	36	4.58	76x76
"	31	5.68	80x76
"	9-8	....	....
"	42	4.25	80x76
"	46	3.92	80x76
Canoe River	27	7.70	60x56
Capitol	36	....	....
Cascade C	36	....	....
Casco	46	3.81	80x76
Cast Iron	36	....	....
Chain Lightning	27	....	....
Champion	36	5.50	60x56
Chapman X	36	4.31	72x64
Chariot	36	....	....
Charter Oak	36	4.80	64x64
Chesterfield	36	....	....
Chestnut Hill	36	5.20	64x60
Clinton A1	24	4.30	84x80
Clover Dell	36	....	....
Cock-of-the-Walk	27	....	....
Commonwealth O	36	....	....
" O	3-4	8.00	56x52
Conestoga Steam Mills	10-4	1.11	60x48
" "	90	....	60x48

Bleached Sheetings and Shirtings—Continued.

Name.	Width. Inches.	Yards to Pound.	Picks to Inch
Congress	36	....	....
Conquest	36	....	....
Continental Mills	36	3.02	70x60
" H	48	2.62	64x68
" LN	36	4.00	88x88
" A	36	4.20	84x84
" half bleached.	36	....	68x72
Conway W	36	....	....
Cooley Homestead	36	....	....
Copper Fastened	35¾	4.38	60x56
Coral Reef A	32	....	....
" B	30	....	....
Cream-of-the-Mill	36	....	....
Crusader	36	....	....
Cumberland	36	....	80x84
Dauntless	36	5.85	60x60
Davol Mill	36	3.75	84x88
Defiance	36	3.90	84x88
"	36	3.90	88x84
De Soto Mills E	36	3.14	52x48
Dexter XX	36	....	....
Diamond Field	36	....	....
Diamond Hill Cambric	36	7.05	88x80
Dorchester	36	....	....
Dunellen Mills	36	....	....
Dunham O C O	36	....	....
Dwight Anchor Co	36	3.48	76x76
" Cambric	36	....	....
"	42	....	....
"	45	....	....
Dyerville A	36	4.00	80x76
East Hampton	36	....	....
Edwards AA	36	....	....
Edward Harris	30	5.85	72x72
Elkwoods	36	....	....
Ellerton WS	36	4.50	72x72
EMC	36	....	....
Excelsior	27	....	....
Exeter	36	4.20	72x68
"	30	5.00	72x68
F-PF Cambric	36	....	88x76
Fairfax	36¼	4.00	88x80
Fairmount Q	36	5.00	64x64
Farmer's Choice	36	5.00	64x64
Farwell Mills	36	4.38	80x80
"	42	3.72	80x80
"	45	3.48	80x80
Favorite	36	....	....
Fearless-of-all-Competit'n	36	4.45	72x72
Fidelity	36	4.30	84x80
Field and factory	4-4	....	....
First Bale	36	5.54	68x64
First Call	36	4.80	68x64
"	32	....	....
"	22	....	....
"	7-8	....	....
"	3-4	....	....
Fitchville	36	4.50	72x72
Flower-of-the-Mill	36	....	....
Forget-me-not	36	....	....

Bleached Sheetings and Shirtings—Continued.

Name.	Width. Inches.	Yards to Pound.	Picks to Inch.
Forrestdale	36	4 25	80x76
Forrest Mills	36	5.00	72x68
"	36	4.77	70x68
"	31	5.80	62x68
"	7-8	4.10	88x84
Fruit of the Loom	36	4 10	68x84
"	31	4 32	88x80
" Night Robe	36	....	.. .
" Cambric	36		
" (100s)	36	3.72	100x100
"	31	4.32	83x80
"	42	3.64	88x80
"	50	2.96	88x72
"	5-4	3.07	88x80
"	6-4	2.78	88x76
"	7-4	1.98	80x60
" (extra)	8-4	1-69	80x64
"	9-4	1.49	80x60
"	10-4	1.12	80x60
"	10-4	1.43	72x64
Full Value	36	....	....
Full Yard Wide	36	.. .	....
Gem of the Spindle	36	....	80x76
George Washington XX	36	3.62	76x72
Gibraltar	36	....	....
Gilded Age	36	....	....
Gilt Edge	36	..·.	....
Gladstone	36	....	....
Glad Tidings	36	....	....
Glen Alpine	36	....	....
Glendale	36	....	....
Globe AAA	36	.. .	.. .
" AA	36	...	....
Glory	36	....	....
Golden Wedding	36	....	....
Gold Medal	36	4 36	76x72
"	32½	5.46	72x64
Great Falls Mfg. Co. J	39¾	4.27	64x68
" S Tiger	31	5.18	72x68
" M. Dog	33	4.72	76x72
Great Republic	36	4.20	80x80
Greene G	36	5.00	64x64
Grinnell fine	9-8	3.47	104x96
"	5-4	3.21	100x100
"	6-4	2.59	104x92
"	7-4	2.58	104x92
"	8-4	2.04	104x92
"	9-4	....	... .
"	10-4		
"	11-4	1.53	104x92
Grosvenor Dale	35	....	....
Gypsy Queen	3-4	....	....
Happy Hit	36	....	....
Hartford	36	....	...
Harvest E	36	....	....
Hercules	36		
Hero	36	4.60	72x72
Highland Mills	36	3.70	76x68
Hillsdale Mfg. Co	36	5.00	68x68
Hill's Semper Idem	36	4.24	80x80

Bleached Sheetings and Shirtings—Continued.

Name.	Width. Inches.	Yards to Pound.	Picks to Inch.
Hill's Semper Idem	36	4.26	84x76
" "	36	4.36	84x80
" "	42	3.76	84x84
" "	7-8	....	....
" " (hf bl'd)	36	....	....
" "	45	3.44	84x84
H E P Fine Cambric	35½	5.75	84x72
H T B	36	....	....
H. W. G. Shrunk Finish	96	....	....
Holly Tree Long Cloth	42	....	....
" Cambric	36	....	....
Holmesville Night Gown	36	....	....
" B	36	5.16	64x64
" H & E	36	4.85	72x68
" H & E	31	6.00	68x64
" W T	33	5.75	68x64
" XXX	36	4.50	72x68
Homespun	36	4.15	76x76
Homestead Mills	36	....	....
" Cooley's	36	....	....
" Cambric	36	....	....
Hope	36	4.80	76x72
Housekeeper	36	....	....
Housewife	36	....	....
Howe	36	4.65	76x72
Hubbard	36	....	....
Ideal Q	36	5.39	60x40
Indian H ad Shrunk	35	....	48x48
" "	45	....	....
Industry	36	....	56x56
Invincible	36	....	....
Iron Pier	86	....	....
Jack Horner	30	5.73	64x64
Jacque Rose Com. Cambric	36	5.40	84x84
Jacque Rose, Cambric	36	5.40	84x84
J. C. Knight, Cambric	33	4.80	....
Jewett City Mills	48	3.65	76x84
John Hancock	36	....	....
Jumping Horse	36	4.75	68x64
Just Out	27	6.15	64x60
Kennebec River XX	36	....	....
" BB	36	....	....
King Bee Cambric	36	....	....
" "	33	....	....
King Philip AP	36	3.80	84x84
" OP	36	3.67	88x84
" Cambric	36	5.75	96x104
" KMQ	36	....	....
King's Shrunk Finest	36	....	....
Knight's Cambric	36	....	....
" "	33	7.00	84x80
Laconia Mills	42	....	....
"	46	2.70	64x64
"	6-4	2.35	64x64
"	7-4	....	64x64
"	8-4	2.09	64x64
"	9-4	1.89	64x64
"	10-4	1.65	64x64
"	11-4	....	....
" Good-Night Cambric	36	2.63	96x80

Bleached Sheetings and Shirtings—Continued.

Name.	Width. Inches.	Yards to Pound.	Picks to Inch.
Lafayette	36	5.00	64x64
Lancaster	10-4	1.90	64x52
Landseer	36	4.10	80x80
Langdon GB	36	3.86	92x84
" "76"	36	3.80	88x84
"	42	....	88x80
"	45	.	....
Langham Cambric	33	...	....
Lexington	36	...	....
Lily of the Valley, h'f bl'd	36	4.25	76x68
Linwood	36	4.30	84x80
Lion	36	...	....
Little Chief Cottons	36	4.71	80x64
Loch Lamond Cambrics	36	5.26	76x68
Lockwood VVV	36	3 75	88x84
" "	42	3.12	72x64
" "	42	3 12	68x64
" "	45	2.99	68x60
" "	45	3.01	68x60
" "	50	2.57	68x64
" "	5-4	....	....
" "	6-4	....	....
" "	7-4	...	...
" "	8-4	1 89	68x64
" "	9-4	1.67	68x64
" "	10-4	1.45	72x64
" "	11-4	...	...
Lonsdale	36	4.31	84x80
"	32	4.70	84x84
" Cambric	36	....	104x96
" Nameless Star	36½	4.37	80x72
Lowell	10-4	....	....
Lucky Hit Cambric	36	...	...
Maconpin Mills	36	....	..
Madapolam Cambrics	36	4.40	108x100
M gic	32	...	....
"	26	8 39	52x40
Magnolia	36	....	....
Masonvill	36	4.02	88x84
"	36	3.98	88x84
Medal	36	...	....
Melrose Mill	36	3 90	84x88
Millview	36	...	....
Milton Falls	36	5.00	64x64
Mohawk	7-8	2.22	72x60
Mohawk Valley Mills	42	....	....
" "	5-4	2.91	64x64
" "	6-4	2.56	64x64
" "	7-4	2.21	72x60
" "	8-4	1.86	72x60
" "	9-4	1.76	68x60
" "	9-4	1.69	68x60
" "	10-4	1.52	72x60
" "	11-4	1.36	64x64
Monadnock	8-4	2.11	68x52
"	9-4	1 88	68x52
"	10-4	1.69	68x52
"	12-4	1.10	68x52
Monohansett h'f b'ld	36	4 46	72x64
" M'f'g Co	36¾	....	72x68

Bleached Sheetings and Shirtings – Continued.

Name	Width. Inches.	Yards to Pound.	Picks to Inch.
Monogram	36	....	....
Mont Clare	36	....	....
Morning Star	36	....	....
Nashua E	36	3.50	76x68
" P	42	3.11	76x68
" W	5-4	3.02	76x68
"	9-4	....	....
"	10-4	....	....
Naumkeag Twill	8-4	1.60	...
"	9-4	1.43	....
"	10-4	1.28	....
Needle Cotton	36	....	....
Netherwood	36	4.30	76x80
New Candidate	35¾	4.72	80x76
New Bedford Sheetings	9-8	....	....
" "	5-4	....	....
" "	48	....	....
" "	50	....	...
" "	6-4	....	....
" "	7-4	....	....
" "	8-4	1.89	92x84
" "	9-4	1.60	88x84
" "	10-4	....	....
" Cambric	11-4	....	....
" Night robe	36	....	....
New Jersey	36	.73	76x68
Newmarket	36	4.55	68x64
New York Mills, Extra	36	4.87	96x96
" " Water Twist	36	....	92x104
" " Twilled Jeans	36	...	...
" "	5-4	2.61	68x56
" "	6-4	2.06	68x56
" "	8-4	1.50	72x56
" "	9-4	1.23	72x60
" "	10-4	1.20	60x48
" "	10-4	1.20	72x68
" " 100	11-4	1.00	68x64
No Dicker	36	....	....
"	31½	4.75	72x68
Nonpareil	36	....	....
Oak Grove	32	5.77	68x60
"	27	....	....
Oakland	36	....	....
Oak Lawn	36	5.17	72x64
"	32	....	....
O Shirtmaker's Finish	36	....	....
Our Choice	36	4.50	76x72
Our Own	30	5.73	64x64
Our Pride	..	....	....
Our Reliance	36	5.60	60x56
Paragon	36	4.40	72x68
Peabody Mills H	36	4.74	60x52
" " Mill View	36	....	...
Pedro	32	....	....
Peerless	27	....	....
Pelham Q	36	4.70	68x60
"	36	4.70	68x64
"	36	4.70	64x64
Pembroke	42	....	..
"	45	.	....

Bleached Sheetings and Shirtings—Continued.

Name.	Width. Inches.	Yards o Pound.	Picks to Inch.
Pembroke................	6-4	2.65	64x64
"	7-4	2.40	64x64
"	7-4	....	60x68
"	8-4	2.15	60x68
"	9-4	1.85	60x68
"	10-4	1.63	60x68
"	11-4	1.52	60x68
"	12-4	....	....
People's Cry. (The).......	36	....	72x56
Pepperell E.................	40	3.44	66x68
" R.................	36	3.70	64x64
" O.................	33	4.00	64x64
" N.................	30	4.39	64x64
"	45	2.90	64x64
"	48	.	64x64
"	7-4	2.36	64x64
"	8-4	2.10	64x64
"	8-4	1.95	68x64
"	9-4	1.79	64x64
"	9-4	1.73	72x60
"	10-4	1.63	64x64
"	11-4	1.47	64x64
"	12-4	1.00	64x64
" Mfg.Co.,Ex-HG I'w'ls	36	3.26	100x60
Pequa....................	10-4	1.51	64x64
Pequot A, Heavy..........	36	3.20	68x64
" B.................	40	2.80	64x64
"	45	2.59	72x76
" W.................	48	2.34	68x76
"	6-4	2.18	72x76
"	6-4	2.29	72x68
"	7-4	2.07	72x76
"	7-4	1.89	72x64
"	8-4	1.71	72x76
"	8-4	1.68	72x72
"	9-4	1.45	72x76
"	9-4	1.49	72x72
"	10-4	1.33	72x76
"	11-4	....	68x76
" Eldorado..........	36	....	....
Perkins Z.................	36	3.90	64x64
" Y.................	33	4.31	64x64
" X.................	30	4.67	60x60
Phœnix AA................	39	3.50	64x64
Piedmont..................	36	3.09	48x48
"	30	....	48x44
"	27	4.62	48x44
Pocahontas R	36	3.90	80x72
" E....	40	3.10	64x64
" D........	30	....	....
Pocasset Canoe E..........	40	3.10	64x64
Pocasset C.....	36	3.63	64x64
" O................	33	....	64x64
Portsmouth C............	36	....	....
" B............	31	9.41	48x48
" P...	28	7.00	64x64
Prescott L................	36	4.50	64x64
Pride-of-the-Nation.......	36	3.85	84x84
Preston...................	36	....	....
Princeton 401.............	36	3.93	56x60

Bleached Sheetings and Shirtings—Continued.

Name.	Width. Inches.	Yards to Pound.	Picks to Inch.
Quinnebaug Co.	36	4.70	80x72
Rochdale (h'f bl'd)	36	4.94	68x68
Rosalind (As You Like It).	36	....	76x76
" "	36	4.32	80x76
Second to None	36	5.32	65x60
"	7-8	....	....
"	27	....	....
Security	30	6.20	60x56
Senate Mills (h'f bl'd)	36	4.18	68x72
Sentinel	27	....	....
Silver Queen	36	....	....
" AA	36	....	....
Shamrock	36	....	....
Sibley	36	....	....
Signal A	32	5.66	64x64
" B	27	6.12	64x64
Snow White	36	....	....
Sonora	36	....	....
Social C	32	....	....
" Q	36	4.75	80x76
" L	36	5.10	72x72
" W	36	5.97	68x64
Standard	36	4.15	88x84
Standish	36	4.35	80x76
Star of the Nation	36	....	....
Star W	36	5.30	64x64
State-of-Maine	36	....	....
Statute	36	....	....
Sterling	32	....	....
Sun	36	3.59	80x68
Sunlight	27	....	56x60
Superior American	36	....	76x80
" Royal Bunting	36	8.97	44x40
Telegraph	30	6 00	60x52
Ten Strike	36	4.50	72x68
The "Cooley Homestead"	36	....	....
The Sun Cotton	36	....	....
The Victor	36	....	....
The Pennant	4-4	....	....
Thorndale Cambric	36	....	....
Top-of-the Heap	36	....	....
"	32	....	....
Trump Card	36	....	....
"	7-8	....	....
"	27	....	....
True-as-Steel	36	....	....
Triumph	36	5.68	68x60
Tuscarora Mills	36	3.28	80x68
"	36	3.28	80x60
" Night Robe	36	....	....
Universal	36	3.55	80x76
Utica Cotton Steam Mills,			
" Ex. Heavy	36	3.00	68x64
" Nonpareil	36	3 30	92x96
" Ex. Heavy	36	3.55	96x80
"	5-4	2.72	68x60
"	6-4	2.17	68x56
"	7-4	....	....
"	8-4	1.31	68x60
"	8-4	1.68	72x72

Bleached Sheetings and Shirtings – Continued.

Name.	Width. Inches.	Yards to Pound.	Picks to Inch.
Utica Cotton Steam Mills.	8-4	1.61	72x60
"	9-4	1 35	68x64
"	10-4	1.31	68x60
"	10-4	1.68	72x60
"	100	1.14	68x60
" Diamond U.	36	3.47	72x72
Valley Mills	27	....	....
" Q	35½	7.89	60x6
" Q	25	6.80	52x44
Victor	36	..	....
Vineyard	36	...	....
Waltham XX (h'f bl'd)	36	3 48	72x60
Wamsutta Mills O-XX	36	3.50	92x92
"	42	....	...
" ST	45	2.33	72x64
"	50	2.28	88x88
"	60	3.36	....
" Cambric	36	....	68x56
" Cambric, fine	36	6.15	100x96
"	9-8	3.47	88x88
"	5-4	3.09	72x72
" ST	6-4	1.98	72x72
"	7-4	2.06	72x64
" Twilled	8-4	1.44	72x68
" "	9-4	1.33	....
"	9-4	1.33	72x72
" Twilled	10-4	1.17	....
" ST	10-4	1.17	72x68
"	11-4	1.03	72x64
"	12-4	....	....
" Ex. Heavy Jean.	36	4 82	68x64
" Gold Medal	36	4.82	68x64
" " NB	36	3.36	63x56
" Night Robes	36	4 82	68x64
" " d'ble warp	35¾	2 82	80x60
Warren Mfg. Co. linen fin.	36	....	....
Washington	36	5.00	64x64
Wessacumcon B	36	....	....
" D	36	4.33	....
Water Witch	36	....	...
" "	30	....	....
Wauregan 100's	36	....	100x100
" No. 1	36	3.90	88x88
" Cambric	36	....	108x94
White Horse	36	5.00	64x64
White Rock	36	4.10	88x80
Whiting	36	....	....
Whitinsville Cotton Mills	36	4 50	80x76
" "	36	4.58	80x76
Williamsville A1	36	3.60	88x64
Winchester	36	...	....
Winona	36	3.60	88x84
Winthrop AA	36	....	....
" E	42	3.62	60x68
"	45	2.75	64x68
Woodbury	36	5 30	64x64
World Wi'e	26	....	....
Worth	36	4.80	72x60

NOTE.—Four ounces to the yard is equal to four yards to the pound avoirdupois; and five ounces to the yard is equal to 3.20 yards to the pound avoirdupois.

Addenda to Bleached Sheetings and Shirtings.

Name.	Width. Inches.	Yards to Pound.	Picks to Inch.
Beaver Falls Mills XXX...	26	7.85	64x60
Edgewood.	37	5.17	60x60
Ideal Q.	36	5.39	60x40
Just Out.	26	6.55	64x60
Monohansett, Hf-Bl'ch'd..	36	4 46	72x64
Nameless Star.	36½	3.37	80x72
Newport Mills.	36	4.92	68x60
Red Star Nameless.	36	4.51	76x72
White Star Nameless.	36	4.94	76x60
Sunbeam Cottons.	36	4.91	72x64

TICKINGS.

Name.	Width. Inches.	Yards to Pound.	Picks to Inch.
Amoskeag Mfg Co	32	1.96	52x80
" "	31¼	2 00	
" " ACA	86	1 85	
" "	31½	1.94	
" "	31½	2.03	
" " A	30¾@31	2.27	
" " B	30¾@31		
" " B	36	2.48	
" " Cimp'd.	30@31	2.60	56x56
" " D	30@31	2 60	
" " E	31	3.07	
" " XXX I'ncy	32		
" " XX "	32	1.86	56x68
" " X "	31@32	2 64	56x60
" " "Awn'g satine	32	1.97	56x80
" " " Garniture	32	2 01	
Belgrade, fancy red 135	30	2.76	76x52
Berwick Mfg Co. BA, fancy colored	30	2.84	84x64
Brandywine Mills, No. 10.	31¾	3.08	44x96
Birmingham			
Conestoga Steam Mills	33	2.04	
" Prem. A	36	1.99	
" FF	33	2 04	
" Extra	36	2 25	
" "	32	2.50	
" Gold Medal	36	2.30	
" CT	36	2.42	
" CCA	31½	2.58	
" AA	29	3.40	
" fancy red RR	33	2.04	32x60
Cordis, ACE	32	2.07	
" No. 1	32	2.07	
" No. 2	32	2 23	
" No. 3	30	2.48	
" WS	29	4.00	60x76
Challenge, fancy	30	3.84	36x84
" "		3.71	36x84
Endurance, fancy	32	2.66	44x96
Everett, plaid PT	30	2.40	
Farmer's		2 88	36x80
Hamilton Mfg Co	30½	2.42	56x56
" BT	30	2 54	52x52
" D	30		68x48
" N	31¼	3.48	64x44
" B "	30½	2.95	64x44
Horse Head	30½	3.45	72x44
Jewitt City	30	2.92	76x40
Lenox, fancy	32	2.16	64x48
"	32	3.84	36x84
"	30	3.71	36x84
First Prize B	30	2 93	
" C	30	2.83	52x88
" D	30	2.68	52x84
" E	30	2.90	48x84
Ocean	27	4.83	64x36
Old Clock Tick O	30	2 83	76x52
" (I) C	30	2.98	72x52

Tickings. - Continued.

Name.	Width. Inches.	Yards to Pound.	Picks to Inch.
Old Clock Tick (Indigo) C..	30	2.54	73x52
" " G..	31¼	2.08	72x56
" " G..	31½	1.97	....
" " K..	28½	4 67	60x40
" " R..	30	3.58	72x42
Omega medal, sup. extra...	36¼	2.38	72x76
" superior....	32	2.37	72x76
" fancy RD...	31	2.16	52x88
Randolph Mills (blue)....	29½	3.51	60x36
Rosemont Mills RLT fancy	31½	3.34	72x36
" " XXX "	32	3.09	104x40
Tiger Mills, No. 1.........	33	2.05	....
" No. 1.........	32½	1.97	76x56
" No. 2.........	31	....	84x60
" No. 3	31	2.60	84x52
" No. 3	31	2.71	72x52
" XXX twills...	33	2 10	56x56
" XXXX	33	1.70	72x76
" fancy........ .	..	2 05	60x68
Swift River.............	30	3.79	76x40
Triumph Man'g Co., No. 3	30	3.01	36x96
York AA....................	32	2 15	....
" T.....................	30	2 40	....

COTTON DRILLS.

Name.	Width. Inches.	Yards to Pound.	Picks to Inch.
Boott A, standard..	30	2.85	....
" 250 boat-sail.........	30	2.50	....
Clifton K ....:	29½	2.87	76x52
Darlington Mills..........	28¾	2.87	72x52
Eureka	29¼	2.77	72x48
John P. King Mfg. Co.....	30	2.93	68x48
London Mills XX..........	30	3.52	64x38
Massachusetts, stan'd...D	30	2.85	....
" DN	26¾-7	2.98	....
" DN	27	3 05	....
" DN	27	3.05	....
" G	29–30	3 80	....
" G	29–30	3 80	....
Normandie, standard......	29.	2.73	70x52
" "	29	2.73	68x52
Pacolet Manufacturing Co.	29½	2.87	....
Pepperell, brown..........	29	2.84	72x52
" bleached.........	27	3 28	80x48
" dragon brand..	27¼	3 36	80x48
Plymouth Standard.......	29½	2 89	....
" 300................	29¼	2.60	....
Prescott, standard blue D.	29–30	3.25	....
Royal, standard brown...	29	2.72	64x68
" 250X	30¼	2.49	68x56
" bleached .	27½-8	3.11	76x48
Stark HD, brown stan'd...	37	2.42	66x52
" A, Imp'd " ..	29½@30	....	....
" A, bleached.........:	28	....	76x52
Suffolk, standard D......:.	30	2.85	....

COTTON CHEVIOTS.

Name.	*Width. Inches.*	*Yards to Pound.*	*Picks to Inch.*
Amoskeag (stripes)	27½	3.32	....
" (stripes)	27½	3.55	....
Alabama (stripes).	26	4.51½	....
Algeron (plaids)	..	4.36	48x33
Bengal (stripes)...........	27½	4.13	....
Crown A (stripes & checks)	26	4.89	....
" (plaids)	27¾	4.16	....
Conestoga (stripes)	28	2.69	....
Falmouth checks, BB.....	27	4 52	....
Forrest Hill..............	28	4.18	36x40
Great Republic	25½	4.26	....
Iadna Mills...............	26⅛	4.84	....
Philadelphia	..	4.51	....
Pioneer Plaids............	28	4.36	40x44
Prodigy (stripes)..........	29½	3.85	....
Rosedale	27	5.42	....
Slater....................	27	3.42	....
Santa Rosa...............	27¼	4.45	....
Real Caledonia, the JCK...	..	4.30	....
Uncasville...............	27	2.37½	....
"	27	2 37	....

DOMESTIC GINGHAMS.

Name.	*Width. Inches.*	*Yards to Pound.*	*Picks to Inch.*
Amoskeag Mfg. Co........	26½	6.28	72x76
" Staples........	26½	5.56	68x76
" Fancy Staples.	26½	5.56	68x76
" Canton	26	6.91	56x60
" " Checks..	26½	6.34	56x60
" Chalon Cloth...	26	7.53	48x72
" Persian........	26½	6.61	48x56
" Zanzibar ...	25⅞	5.58	60x76
Arasapha Mfg. Co	29	6.44	36x40
Bay State................	25½	8.34	36x44
Caledonia................	26¼	6.68	48x56
Elberon, Seersuckers......	25½	6.87½	40x56
Everett Classics..........	26	5.68	52x72
Franklin Suitings.........	26¾	6.89	44x72
Glenarie	25½	6.37	40x48
Gotham..................	25¾	5.91	44x58
Johnson Mfg. Co........	26	6.53	56x68
" Pin Checks.......	26	6.52	56x64
" Plaid Checks.....	26	5.92	64x64
Loraine Knotted..........	29	5 42	76x80
Manchester..............	27	6.04	44x52
Monogram...............	26¾	6.52	48x56
Nevelle Seersuckers.......	26	....	52x68
Parkhill Mfg. Co. (Toile Du Nord)...	25½	6.70	60x72
Pontiac Seersuckers	25	7.58	40x56
Randelman..............	..	...	40x44
Renfrew, Dress...........	26	6.24	60x60
" Novelties........	..	5.86	52x56
Tacoma Cloth............	25⅞	7.27	48x56
Woodboro Mfg. Co........	27	7.08	48x56
York Mfg. Co. Staples.....	26	5.38	52x56

CAMLETS.

Name.	Width. Inches.	Yards to Pound.	Picks to Inch.
York CT	28	2.75	....

COTTON BUNTING.

Name.	Width. Inches.	Yards to Pound.	Picks to Inch.
Archery	36	8.63	38x40
National	..	11.50	34x32

COTTON CHECKS.

Name.	Width. Inches.	Yards to Pound.	Picks to Inch.
Otis, Apron	30	3.21	*

*Difficult to count picks.

FLAT-FOLD CAMBRICS.

Name.	Width. Inches.	Yards to Pound.	Picks to Inch.
Ballou*	25	5.03	68x48

---
*Glove finish.

GLAZED CAMBRICS.

Name.	Width. Inches.	Yards to Pound.	Picks to Inch.
Keystone, black linings	26	7.05	....

NANKEENS.

Name.	Width. Inches.	Yards to Pound.	Picks to Inch.
Wachusetts	..	3.88½	44x52
York Manuf'g Co. XXX	..	3.44	40x56

SUITINGS AND SKIRTINGS.

Name.	Width. Inches.	Yards to Pound.	Picks to Inch.
York Skirting	27	4.84	52x76
Novelty Suitings	26	....	60x60
"	26	....	64x64
Sherwood Suitings	26	7.34	52x68
Fenno Stripes	27	....	60x68

BROWN COTTON FLANNELS.

Name.	Width. Inches.	Yards to Pound.	Picks to Inch.
Ellerton HHH	35⅛	1.44	....
" WH	35	1.78	....
" H	31	1.95	
" WN	35	2.08	
" N	32	2.15	
" O	28½	2.58	
" P	27½	2.84	
" Q	28	2.91	
" R	28	3.10	
" S	28	3.37	..
" T	28	3.56	
" V	27¾	3.98	....
" CL	30¼	4.35	
" CM	28	4.80	
" CN	27	7.10	....
Glendale NN	26	4.88	
Buckskin RR	26	5.00	..
Good Luck 4	27½	4.84	84x48
" 5	..	5.57	....
" 6	28	2.90	....
" 14	28¾	3.49	76x52
" 18	29½	2.57	76x48
" 24	27	2.46	..
" 30	..	3.43	....
Massachusetts R	28	4.00	....
Royal Standard, No. 1	..	...	....
" " 8	28½	4.86	80x56
" " 5	27	4.53	76x52
" " 10	27	3.99	84x56
" " 20	27¼	3.41	84x64
" " 30	27¾	3.34	88x48
" " 40	27	3.57	84x48
" " 45	27½	2.83	84x48
" " 45	27⅞	3.34	84x48
" " 50	28	2.72	84x48
" " 90	35½	1.79	64x44
" " 100	36	1.45	64x44
Tremont M	27½	5.30	....
" DL	28½	5.00	....
" D	28½	4.50	...
" H	28¼	4.00	...
" P	28½	3.60	....
" T	28	3.25	....
" A	28½	3.00	....
" Y	29¾	2.80	....
" Z	28½	2.60	....
" X	31	2.50	....
" XX	30½	2.20	....
" XXX	32½	2.00	....
" XXXX	36	2.00	....
" F	27	5.00	....
" U	26¾	4.50	....

Brown Cotton Flannels—Continued.

Name.	Width. Inches.	Yards to Pound.	Picks to Inch.
Tremont L	26¾	4.00	....
" B	26½	3.75	....
" N	28	3.40	....
" O	28½	3.00	28x48
" E	29	2.75	....
" Z	28½	3.60	....
" W	29	2.35	....
" V	28½	2.20	....
" G	30¾	2.00	....
" RX	31¾	1.75	....
" R	31½	1.60	....
" G—GG	36	1.50	....
Saco, colored plush	..	2.78	52x92
Syracuse, colored plush	28	3.54	24x72

BLEACHED CANTON FLANNELS.

Name.	Width. Inches.	Yards to Pound.	Picks to Inch.
Ellerton HHH	32	1.64	*
" WH	32	2.30	....
" H	..	....	....
" WN	32	2.26	....
" N	29	2.62	....
" O	28½	2.83	....
" P	28	3.10	....
" Q	26	3.10	....
" R	..	....	....
" S	28½	3.62	....
" T	..	....	....
" V	..	....	....
" CL	27	4.67	....
" CM	25	5.29	....
" CN	24	5.49	....
Good Luck "6"	26	4.41	88x48
" "14"	26	3.79	80x48
Royal Standard "50"	28	2.90¼	84x44
" "30"	..	3.48	88x48
" "5"	.	5.57	80x56

*Picks cannot be taken owing to heavy nap.

COTTONADES.

Name	Width. Inches.	Yards to Pound.	Picks to Inch.
New York Mills D and T	37½	2.40	48x60
Wachusett	33½	3.58	48x72
York Mfg. Co. XXX	43	3.75	40x40

DENIMS.

Name	*Width. Inches.*	*Yards to Pound.*	*Picks to Inch.*
Amoskeag Mfg Co. brown D. 9 oz...	27¼@28	1.67	....
" " " "	27¼@28	1.69	....
" " blue D...	27⅜@28	2.20	48x48
" " " 9 oz.	27¾@28	2.24	40x48
Columbian XXX brown....	27¼@28	2.98	48x84
" heavy m'x'd f'cy	27¼@28	2.94	40x72
" XXX blue fancy m'x'd	27¼@28	2.98	....
Everett blue, DD.........	28	2.45	....
" imp'd brown, BD..	28¼@28¾	2.48	28x36
" " " "	28@28¼	2.45	28x36
" slate, SD...... ...	28	2.45	....
" imp'd blue, DDN..	28	2.45	....
" fancy stripes......	28	2.45	....
" " checks......	28	2.45	....
Oakland Mills A brown....	26½	3.78	36x68
Otis DD....................	26¼	3.25	36x64
Palmer Mills, fancy, 418...	27½@28	2 58	48x84
Pearl River BD brown....	28	....	28x44
Sioo River, slate, D.......	28	2.75	....
" blue, DD	28	2.75	....
Shetucket Co., blue........	28	1.84	48x52
Uncasville	28	2.71	40x44
Warren Cotton Mills, 941..	28	2.79	36x72
Whittenton AA...........	27¾	3.25	28x40
York, blue, DD...	28	2.45	....
" brown, DDXX	28	2.45	....
" slate, DDA.........	28	2.45	....
" fancy stripes.......	25	2.45	....
" fancy plaids........	28	2.45	....

SHIRTING CLOTH.

Name.	*Width. Inches.*	*Yards to Pound.*	*Picks to Inch.*
Everett, Tiger Checks JP..	29	2.75	....
" " Plaid JPC..	29	2.75	....
" " Strip's JPS	29	2.75	....

SATTEENS.

Name.	*Width. Inches.*	*Yards to Pound.*	*Picks to Inch.*
Amory Silesia Jean.......	..	4.25	....
Dale River Twills........	..	4.84	64x112
Naumkeag Twills		2.52⅔	....

Widths, Lengths, Reeds, Picks and Weights of British Cottons.

The accompanying table gives the width, yards, reed, pick and weight of British cotton piece goods, such as Madapollams, Shirtings, Jaconets, Mulls, T—cloths, Mexicans, and Long Cloths:

Inches.		Yds.	Reed.	Picks.	Weight Lbs.	Ozs.
32..Madapollams		46	12	10	6	0
32..	"	46	12	12	6	0
32..	"	46	14	14	7	0
39..Shirtings		37½	12	8	5	4
36..	"	37½	12	12	6	0
36..	"	37½	13	11	7	0
39..	"	37½	14	13	7	0
36..	"	37½	16	13	8	8
39..	" (China quality)..	37½	16	15	8	4
39..	"	37½	16	15	8	4
39..	"	37½	17	18	9	12
39..	"	37½	19	19	10	0
45..	"	37½	13	10	7	0
45..	"	37½	14	12	8	0
45..	"	37½	16	15	9	0
50..	"	37½	14	13	9	0
50..	"	37½	16	15	10	0
54..	"	37½	16	15	11	0
60..	"	37½	16	15	12	0
39..Jaconets		20	10	6	1	14
39..	"	20	10	8	2	2
39..	"	20	12	12	2	0
39..	"	20	14	12	2	4
39..	"	20	14	14	2	8
39..	"	20	16	15	2	14
45..	"	20	14	12	2	8
45..	"	20	14	14	2	12
45..	"	20	16	15	3	4
50..	"	20	16	15	3	10
39..Mulls		20	10	8	1	0½
39..	"	20	10	10	1	2
39.	"	20	12	10	1	0¾
39..	"	20	12	12	1	5
39..	"	20	14	12	1	6-7
39..	"	20	14	14	1	8
39..	"	20	16	14	1	9-10
39..	"	20	16	16	1	12
44..	"	20	16	15	2	0
49..	"	20	16	15	2	4
54..	"	20	16	15	2	8
60..	"	20	16	15	2	12
30..T Cloths		24	12	12	4	8
32.	"	24	12	12	5	0
32..	"	24	14	14	6	10
32..	" (Mexican)	24	18	18	7	0
36..Long Cloths		36	12	12	8	0
39..	"	36	12	12	9	0
45.	"	36	12	12	10	0

Early Chronology of Raw Cotton, Cotton Yarn, Cotton Goods, Etc.

The following represents the chronology of Raw Cotton from A. D. 800 to A. D. 1845; Cotton Yarn from A. D. 1530 to A. D. 1837; Cotton Goods from A. D. 1252 to A. D. 1787; and Printing and Dyeing Calico from A. D. 1631 to A. D. 1831:

RAW COTTON.

- 800 Cotton used in Greece as a material for making paper.
- 1298 Cotton used in England for Candle Wick.
- 1560 Cotton imported into England from the Levant.
- 1641 Cotton Wool imported into England exclusively from the Levant
- 1688 450,000 lbs. of cotton wool imported into Marseilles from the Levant.
- 1750 3,831,620 lbs. cotton wool imported into France.
- 1778 Gold medal given by the Royal Society of Arts of England to Mr. Andrew Bennett, of Tobago, for the best specimen of West India cotton
- 1780 The finest grained and cleanest cotton brought to the English market was from Berbice. The prices were per lb.: Berbice, 2s. 1d.; Demerara, 1s. 1d.; Surinam, 2s.; Cayenne, 2s.
- 1781 Brazilian cotton first imported into England from Maranham in a very dirty state.
- 1782 A panic created in Manchester, England, in consequence of 7012 bales of cotton being imported between December and April.
- 1783 Brazilian cotton first brought to Manchester.
- 1785 Premium offered by the Royal Society of Arts of England for the production of oil from cotton seed, and from the remainder of the seed hard cake for cattle.
- 1785 A small quantity of seed sent from the Bahamas is the parent of all the Sea Island cotton of Georgia and South Carolina.
- 1785 Cotton imported into England from America this year: 1 bag per *Diana*, from Charleston; 1 per *Tonyn*, from New York; 3 per *Grange*, from Philadelphia; 9 per *Friendship*, from Philadelphia. Part of these cottons were seized in Liverpool by the Custom House officers, under the impression that cotton was not the product of the United States.
- 1786 6 bags of American cotton imported into England: 2 per *Thomas*, from Charleston, and 4 per *Juno*, from Charleston.
- 1786 A small quantity of cotton of the best quality then known was received in England from the Island of Bourbon, and was sold at from 7s. 6d. to 10s. per lb.
- 1787 109 bales of cotton imported into England from America. Until this year the supply of cotton was principally from the West Indies.
- 1793 Whitney's Saw-gin invented for cleaning cotton.
- 1798 Premium of a gold medal offered by the Royal Society of Arts of England to any person who should import into the port of London during the year 1799 one ton of Bhangulpore cotton, of which cloths were made in imitation of nankeen without dyeing.
- 1823 Long-stapled cotton of excellent quality first imported into England from Egypt.
- 1833 Duty on cotton, the product of, and imported from, any British possession, 4d. per cwt., and of any foreign country, 2s 11d.
- 1844 February 3d, this week 109,000 bales of cotton were sold in Liverpool, England.
- 1845 British duty on cotton wool repealed, 22d March.

COTTON YARN.

- 1530 Spinning wheel invented at Brunswick, Germany, by Jurgen.
- 1641 Cotton yarn imported into England from the Levant.
- 1650 Indian yarn was spun as fine as 29 yards to 1 grain.
- 1688 1,450,000 lbs. of yarn imported into France from the Levant.
- 1738 Machine for spinning with rollers invented in England by John Whyatt, patent taken out by Lewis Paul, a foreigner.

1748	Lewis Paul's second patent taken out in England.
1750	3,381,625 lbs. of yarn imported into France from the Levant.
1753	A cotton reel invented in England by Mr. Earnshaw.
1757	Duty of 4d. per lb. on cotton yarn imported into England from India.
1760	Premium offered by the Royal Society of Arts of England for the best invention of a machine for spinning 6 threads of wool, cotton, flax or silk at one time, and that would only require one person to work and attend it.
1763	First spinning jenny made in England by Highs.
1764	Hargreaves invented a machine in England to spin 11 threads at once.
1767	Spinning by machinery first used in England (the water frame).
1769	Water frame for spinning patented in England by Arkwright.
1770	Spinning jenny patented in England by J. Hargreaves.
1770	Lewis Paul takes out a patent in England for carding.
1771	Messrs. Arkwright's mill built at Cromford, England.
1772	The feeder invented in England by J. Lees.
1773	J. Hargreaves, England, applied a crank, or comb, to take wool off the cards in a continuous fleece.
1775	Mule spinning invented in England by S. Crompton.
1776	Mr. Arkwright took out another patent in England for carding, drawing and roving.
1776	First cotton mill erected in Staleybridge, England.
1777	First " " Preston, England.
1783	Premium given by the Royal Society of Arts of England for improving several machines used in manufacturing, viz.: comb pots, cards for wool and cotton, doubling and spinning wheels, etc.
1783	Arkwright's machinery for spinning and carding cotton by steam first used in Manchester, England.
1784	First machine imported into France (from England) for spinning cotton by M. Mortin, Amiens.
1784	Machinery for spinning thrown open to the trade in England.
1784	A German fined £500 in England for seducing operatives to Germany.
1784	Improved method of carding in England by Arkwright.
1786	A person fined £200 in England for having a quantity of machinery, with a view to export it to Germany.
1787	Forty-one spinning factories in the county of Lancaster, England.
1788	Model of a machine for spinning cotton, etc., presented to the Royal Society of Arts of England by Mr. John Barton.
1788	A gold medal, value £20, was awarded by the Royal Society of Arts of England for the invention of a machine for carding waste silk, cotton, etc.
1789	A mule jenny constructed at Amiens, France, with 280 spindles.
1791	First cotton mill erected in the United States.
1792	A self-acting mule invented by Mr. Kelly, of Lanark Mills, England.
1793	First attempt to spin yarn from 100's and upwards by power in England.
1799	First spinning mule erected in Saxony, Germany.
1802	Subscription of £500 raised in England for Mr. S. Crompton by Mr John Kennedy and others.
1805	Premium given by the Royal Society of Arts of England to Mr. John Beard for a machine for cutting and crooking wires for cards used in cotton and wool.
1806	Cotton manufacturing considered completely established in France.
1812	Number of spindles at work in Great Britain between 4,000,000 and 5,000,000.
1812	Mr. S. Crompton, inventor of the mule, rewarded by the English Government with £5,000.
1812	English Parliament granted Mr. Wright £5,000 for the invention of his double mule.
1815	8 lb. of cotton twist sent out to India on trial.
1816	Yarn trade opened with the continent.

1817	Fly frame introduced from America, patented by Mr. J. C. Dyer in 1825 to 1829.
1821	First notable exportation of cotton twist from England to India.
1825	104 factories in the neighborhood of Manchester, England.
1825	40 " " Preston, "
1825	47 " " Stockport, "
1825	22 " " Staleybridge, "
1825	Mr. Dyer's first patent for cards in England.
1825	Mr. Roberts takes out a patent for a machine for mule spinning in England.
1825	Tube frame patented in England by Mr. J. C. Dyer.
1827	De Jough's self-acting mule invented.
1829	Average price of yarn sent from England to India, 1s. 3¾d.
1832	Capital supposed sunk in cotton mills in England, £10,600,000
1834	Average price of yarn sent from England to India, 1s. 5¾d.
1836	113 cotton spinning mills in Saxony, Germany.
1837	152 cotton spinning mills in Prussia, Germany.

COTTON GOODS.

1252	Cotton goods made in Persia.
1253	Linen first made in England by Flemish weavers.
1328	A quantity of Flemish emigrants came to England, a few settled in Manchester, and made a species of woolen goods called "Manchester cottons."
1330	Manufactures of Flanders introduced into Manchester, England.
1352	Manchester cottons made in England from the fleece in an unprepared state. (These were woolens.)
1368	Cotton manufactured in China.
1390	Cloth first made at Kendal, England (woolen).
1430	Fustians first made in Flanders with a linen warp and cotton weft.
1497	First manufacture of cotton goods in Europe was attempted in Spain or Italy.
1516	The Caffres in Southern Africa wore cotton dresses.
1582	An English mercantile commission sent to Constantinople and other parts of Turkey to learn any secrets in the arts of manufacturing, dyeing, &c.
1590	Cotton cloth brought to London from Benin, on the coast of Guinea.
1634	Linen trade began in Ireland.
1641	At this period in England all warps were made with linen, and wove with cotton imported from Cyprus and Smyrna.
1790	Messrs. Grimshaw, of Gorton, England, erected a factory in Manchester for power looms, under a license from Dr. Cartwright, but the factory was burned down before they commenced work.
1794	A power loom invented by Mr. Bell, of Glasgow, Scotland, but it did not succeed.
1796	Another power loom patented by Mr. Robert Miller, of Glasgow, Scotland.
1801	First application of Dr. Cartwright's power loom.
1801	Power loom adopted in Glasgow, Scotland, by Mr. John Monteith.
1802	A dressing machine invented by Messrs. Ratcliffe and Ross, of Stockport, England.
1803	A patent for a power loom taken out by Mr. Horrocks, of Stockport, England.
1806	A patent for a power loom with a double crank taken out by Mr. P. Marsland, of Stockport, England.
1806	Power looms began to be used to advantage in England.
1806	Machine for dressing warps invented in England by Mr. Johnson.
1809	British Parliament granted Dr. Cartwright £10,000 for his invention of the power loom in 1787.
1817	Persons employed in the cotton trade of Great Britain estimated by Mr. Kennedy at 110,763.
1825	Roberts' British patent for mule spinning.
1825	Persons employed in the cotton trade in Great Britain estimated by Mr. Greg at 160,000.
1825	22,150 cotton looms in Prussia.

1832	The quantity of flour used in the manufacturing of cotton goods in Great Britain this year was 215,824 barrels of 196 lbs., or 176,256 loads of 240 lbs. each; average of each loom being 4 lbs per week.
1841	Number of persons employed in cotton manufactures in England 281,000.
1846	Number of persons employed in cotton manufactures in England 316,000.
1641	Fustians and dimities first introduced into England.
1645	Fustians imported into England from the continent of Europe at a duty of 3d. per piece.
1650	Very fine calicoes and muslins made in India, at Calicut, which were whitened with lemon water.
1670	Muslins first worn in England.
1676	Introduction of the Dutch loom engine in England.
1677	Value of East India calicoes consumed in England £160,000.
1698	First steam engine constructed in England and successfully turned to useful purposes by Savery.
1701	Value of cotton goods exported from England £23,000.
1738	Fly shuttle invented in England by J. Kay.
1739	The manufacture of cotton goods in England, mixed and plain, was supposed to have arrived at great perfection.
1756	Cotton velvets first made in England.
1760	Value of cotton manufactures in Great Britain, £200,000 per annum.
1760	Warping mill invented in England.
1760	Drop shuttle box invented in England by R. Kay.
1760	Previous to this year the machines used in cotton manufacture were nearly as simple in England as in India.
1763	Muslins and cotton quiltings first made in England.
1765	Calicoes (so called from their resemblance to Indian manufactures brought from the province of Calicut) first attempted in England.
1765	Cotton velvets first made in Amiens, France.
1766	British duty on foreign cambrics and lawns per piece of three ells, 3s. (Ell=45 inches.)
1766	Value of cotton goods made in England, £600.000 per annum.
1770	Manufacture of ginghams greatly improved in England by Mr. Meadowcroft.
1772	Messrs. Arkwright & Co. successfully attempted the manufacture of calicoes in England.
1772	First English cotton goods made with cotton warps by Messrs. Strutt, of Derby.
1774	Fabrics made entirely of cotton were declared by Act of British Parliament to have been lately introduced.
1776	Two pieces of calicoes sold in England to Messrs. Peel, Yates & Co. for £5, 9s. 8d.
1780	Muslin trade began to flourish in England.
1783	Act reducing the duty on foreign muslins, calicoes and nankeen cloths to 18 per cent. *ad valorem*, with 10 per cent. drawback on exportation, passed by British Parliament.
1784	Fustian tax imposed in England.
1785	First attempt at the power loom in England by Dr. Cartwright.
1785	Population employed in the cotton trade of England estimated by Mr. Pitt at 80,000.
1785	First steam engine for cotton mills in England made by Watt.
1785	Repeal of the fustian tax, celebrated in Manchester, England, by a grand procession.
1787	Power loom invented in England by Dr. Cartwright.
1787	An immense quantity of muslins and calicoes imported into England from India. Memorial to British Board of Trade, praying that restrictions might be placed on the East India Company's sales, answered, that " the greater part of them had been exported."

PRINTING AND DYEING CALICO.

1631	Painted (printed) calicoes imported into England from India.
1675	Calico printing first introduced into England.
1676	Calico printing commenced in London, in England.
1678	A loud cry raised against the admission of Indian calicoes, muslins and chintzes into England, as it was stated they were ruining the British woolen trade.

1690 A small print works established on the Thames, at Richmond, England.
1700 Act passed forbidding the importation into England of Indian silks and printed calicoes, under a penalty of £200 on buyer and seller.
1712 Duty of 3d. per yard first imposed on printed and dyed calicoes in England. (These were of foreign manufacture.)
1714 Duty on printed calicoes raised in England to 6d. per yard.
1720 Act prohibiting the use or wear of printed calicoes in England, whether printed in England or elsewhere, under a penalty of £5 wearer, and £20 seller.
1736 So much of the act of 1720 repealed in England as forbade the wear or use of mixed printed goods, that is, goods not all cotton.
1763 Bleaching generally introduced in England.
1764 Calico printing first practiced in Lancashire, England.
1765 English printed calicoes exported to Holland.
1774 Duty of 3d. per square yard imposed in England on printed cottons of British manufacture.
1774 Penalties for exporting tools or utensils used in manufacturing from England, of £200 on shipper, and £200 on commander of any vessel.
1774 Chlorine, or oxymuriatic acid, discovered by Scheele.
1777 Green dyes for calicoes introduced into England by Dr. R. Williams.
1782 Act prohibiting the exportation of engraved copper plates and blocks, or enticing any workmen employed in printing calicoes in England to go beyond the sea, £500, and twelve months imprisonment.
1783 Act giving bounties on the export of British printed and dyed cottons, viz.:
Under the value of 5d. per yard before printing, ½d. per yard.
Over the value of 5d. and under 6d. before printing, 1d. per yard.
Over the value of 6d. and under 8d. before printing, 1½d. per yard, besides the drawback of excise duty. This act was repealed shortly afterwards.
1784 Bleachers, printers and dyers compelled to take out licenses in England under an annual tax of £2, by Mr. Pitt.
1784 A tax of 1d. per yard imposed in England upon all bleached cottons. (Repealed May 17th, 1785.)
1785 Cylindrical printing invented in England by Mr. Bell, and greatly improved by Mr. Lockett, of Manchester.
1785 Acid for bleaching introduced by Bartholet, of France.
1786 Bleaching with acid introduced in the bleach works of Mr. McGregor, near Glasgow, Scotland, by James Watt.
1787 First copyright for printers in England.
1787 Excise duty of 3½d. per square yard on printed calicoes imposed in Great Britain, and the same allowed as drawback on exportation, and foreign calicoes charged with a duty of 7d. per yard when printed or dyed in Great Britain. (May 10th.)
1788 Acid first used for bleaching in Manchester, England.
1791 Improved method of bleaching cotton goods in England with acids in five hours,
1798 Chloride of lime for bleaching patented by Mr. Tennant, of Glasgow, Scotland.
1801 Discharge work in printing successfully adapted in England by Messrs. Peel.
1802 New method of block cutting, introducing brass and pin work, in England.
1805 Engraved wooden rollers used, invented in England by Mr. Barton, engraver to Messrs. Peel.
1808 New method of engraving with dies introduced in England by Mr. Lockett.
1810 Turkey red first introduced in calico printing in England by M Koechlin.
1813 Discharging Turkey red with acid in calico printing in England, patented by James Thompson, Esq., F. R. S.
1831 Duty on printed calicoes repealed by Great Britain March 1st.

www.ingramcontent.com/pod-product-compliance
Lightning Source LLC
Chambersburg PA
CBHW020908230426
43666CB00008B/1361